Canoeing
Canada's
Northwest Territories

Monica Kendel - artist

A Paddler's Guide

EDITED BY
Mary McCreadie, NWT Canoeing Association

PUBLISHED BY
Canadian Recreational Canoeing Association

*Cover Photograph: Peter Scott, on one of the famous Peake Brother Expeditions,
crossing Sid Lake between the Dubawnt & the Thelon Rivers.*

Overview Map

MAINLAND NORTHWEST TERRITORIES

Overview of riv
included in this b

Tuktoyaktuk

Aklavik

Inuvik

Fort McPherson

Arctic Red River

to Whitehorse

Paulatuk

HORTON

HORNADAY

ANDERSON

Yukon Territory

Coppermine

Fort Good Hope

Norman Wells

Fort Franklin

GREAT BEAR LAKE

COPPERMINE

MOUNTAIN

Fort Norman

KEELE

NATLA

Snare Lakes

MACKENZIE

Wrigley

SNARE

WECHO

YELLOWKNIFE R.

City of Yellowknife

CAMERON

BEAULIEU

Edzo

Rae

NAHANNI

Nahanni National Park Reserve

Nahanni Butte

Fort Simpson

Jean Marie River

Fort Providence

GREAT SLAVE LAKE

Lut K'e

Fort Liard

LAIRD

to Fort Nelson

Fort Resolution

Hay River

to Peace River

Wood

Buffalo

National

Park

Fort Smith

SLAVE

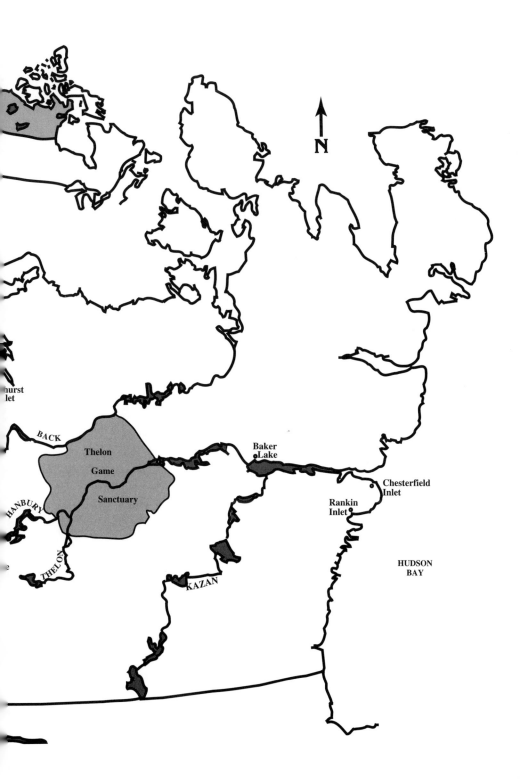

Wilberforce Falls – Hood River

Canoeing
Canada's
Northwest Territories
A Paddler's Guide

Main entry under title:
Canoeing Canada's Northwest Territories: A Paddler's Guide

Includes bibliographical references and index.
ISBN 1-895465-09-5
1. Canoes and canoeing–Northwest Territories–Guidebooks.
2. Rivers–Northwest Territories–Guidebooks.
3. Northwest Territories–Guidebooks.
I. McCreadie, Mary, 1951-.
II. Canadian Recreational Canoeing Association.
GV776.15.N57C36 1994   917.19′2043   C94-9000704-8

Publisher:
CANADIAN RECREATIONAL CANOEING ASSOCIATION
1029 Hyde Park Rd., Suite 5, Hyde Park, Ontario Canada N0M 1Z0
Phone (519) 473-2109 / 641-1261 Fax (519) 473-6560
Sponsored by:

Special thanks to Brent Morton & Susan Thody for their editorial expertise. The Canadian
Recreational Canoeing Association graciously acknowledges the outstanding work of
Mary McCreadie, the Northwest Territories Canoeing Association and the countless volunteer
paddlers who helped to make this book a reality.

Other books published by
the Canadian Recreational Canoeing Association:
Temagami Canoe Routes
Rivière Dumoine
Rivers of the Upper Ottawa Valley
Missinaibi - Journey To The Northern Sky
Nahanni - River of Gold...River of Dreams

ACKNOWLEDGEMENTS

This publication has truly been a cooperative effort. Through its many changes and incarnations, many people have given their time and energy, through a love of paddling and a commitment to have this information made available.

The original manuscript was produced in 1986. It included a series of essays, trip reports and appendices. Special thanks to Barb Cameron who, with capable assistance from Jim Edmondson and Jean-Francois Dumont, coordinated the project. This work was made possible with a Canada Works grant from the Employment Development Branch, Department of Employment and Immigration, Government of Canada and donations from the Yellowknife Inn, Yellowknife Lions Club, Giant Mines, Yellowknife Mens Broomball Association, Ptarmigan Airways and the Legion Ladies Auxiliary. Thanks to many different individuals who wrote essays, did drawings and provided information for the original manuscript. These include Louise Poole, Chris O'Brien, James Darkes, Neil Hartling, Brian Olding, Cathy Ayalik, Susan Fleck, Ed Struzik, Chris Hanks, Barb Winters, Dave Nutter, Kevin Proescholdt, John McGinnins, Tom Andrews, Clayton Klein, Ted Curtis and David Zimmerly. Much of the information for this stage of the project was made available by TravelArctic, GNWT and Parks Canada.

The manuscript was not published and sat in a box for a few years. A group of people, including Mary McCreadie, Jim Edmondson, Chris Hanks, Jane Bishop, Janice Laycock and Miriam Wideman, worked to identify what needed to be done to publish the manuscript and took responsibility to ensure this work was done. We appreciate and recognize in particular the guidance and support of David Pelly, James Raffan and Pat and Rosemary Keough. Much appreciation also goes to Aggie Brockman, Fran Hurcomb and Monica Kendel, who did most of the actual editing, reorganizing, drawing and mapping. Contributions from the NWT Arts Council and the Department of Economic Development and Tourism, GNWT helped make this work possible. We also acknowledge Sport North for their assistance with xerox, phone, fax and general support.

The Canadian Recreational Canoeing Association, in particular their Executive Director, Joseph Agnew, took on the vital role of bringing the renewed, edited manuscript to publication. This project could not have been completed without their hard work and dedication. In particular, we recognize the contributions of Brent Morton, Susan Thody and of Bruce Cockburn for writing the Foreword for the book.

Special thanks goes to the staff of the Water Surveys Branch of Environment Canada for the use of the computer, topographic maps, hydrological data and their constant support, suggestions and encouragement. Thanks also to John Alexander of MultiImaging in Yellowknife, for his computer assistance.

Sincere thanks to the RCMP for their cooperation and assistance with information and with the distribution of blank trip report forms.

Finally and most particularly, we offer very sincere and special appreciation to the many, many paddlers who volunteered journals, trip logs, photographs, slides, stories, information and advice.

Happy Paddling!

Mary McCreadie
NWT Canoeing Association

Virginia Falls – Nahanni River

TABLE OF CONTENTS

TRIP REPORTS

APPENDICES:

FOREWORD

There are still places in the world where the touch of humankind has been so light as to leave virtually no visible damage. Things look and feel as they must have when they were made. One of these areas is Canada's North.

It is a subtle, rolling land of taiga and tundra, of musk-ox and wolverine...a land where the air is so clean that it is sweet to the taste, and where mosquitoes come in clouds too thick to clearly see through. Its stark beauty is profound, unforgiving, and terribly fragile. There is no margin for error.

When you travel in the North you carry your fate in your hands, and you carry as well the fate of the landscape itself. Here – where a footprint can last a hundred years, you need to step very lightly indeed.

The implications of travel in this delicate landscape are several. In a time when we are being conditioned to hand over more and more responsibility for our lives to bureaucracy, an opportunity to feel self-reliant is something to treasure. It is instructive to be reminded of the need for humility in the face of creation's vastness, a perspective which usually goes masked by the trappings of dominance and depredation with which we surround ourselves.

Of course, even if we are not its masters, we affect the system just as the system affects us. Our tiny vessel moving through this huge fluid universe has been affected to the point where we may die in the ultimate loneliness of our works. This makes our North a precious gem, one far more valuable than any amount of diamonds discovered there.

We need to love it and cherish it. We need to know it, not engineered out of existence as a source for minerals or hydro dollars but as a source of spiritual power, of hope that it's not too late, that adventure is not gone from the world.

The information collected for the first time in this book gives us a framework to hang our explorations on, a point of access to our wild northern rivers. Use it. Go prepared. Go in love and respect. May the current be with you, may the bugs be disinterested and may your surprises be ones you can handle!

Bruce Cockburn

Songwriter
Environmentalist
Occasional Wilderness Traveller

PREFACE

Canoeing Canada's Northwest Territories: A Paddler's Guide is the first comprehensive canoeing guide that provides detailed trip reports for nineteen river routes in the NWT and some helpful information for trip planning that is specific to the north. A conscious effort has been made to avoid repeating information about canoe tripping that may be found in other publications, and to focus on the conditions unique to the north that may affect decisions concerning things such as first aid, river rescue, nutrition, equipment needs, and hypothermia.

Canoeing Canada's Northwest Territories: A Paddler's Guide is the result of the contributions of many people, over a period of several years, who share a love of both paddling and the land. The goal of this book is to promote safe, responsible tripping on northern waterways and help other recreational paddlers appreciate this unique part of the world.

This publication is intended as a guide only. Northern river conditions are highly variable, as water levels are capable of changing by the day and from year to year. The trip reports cannot replace detailed maps, scouting rapids, and using appropriate judgement and skills. The Northwest Territories Canoeing Association and the Canadian Recreational Canoeing Association do not accept any responsibility for misinterpretation of information or the failure of paddlers to accurately assess their situation or capabilities.

Every attempt has been made to present accurate and complete information. Canoeists are invited to comment and provide updates, corrections, reports, and information that may be useful for any future edition.

Monica Kendel - artist

"Rivers must have been the guides which conducted the footsteps of the first travellers. They are the constant lure, when they flow by our doors, to distant enterprise and adventure, and, by a natural impulse, the dwellers on their banks will at length accompany their currents to the lowlands of the globe, or explore at their invitation the interior of continents. They are the natural highways of all nations, not only levelling the ground, and removing obstacles from the path of the traveller, quenching his thirst, and bearing him on their bosoms, but conducting him through the most interesting scenery, the most populous portions of the globe, and where the animal and vegetable kingdoms attain their greatest perfection."

– Henry David Thoreau

The Northwest Territories is a paddler's dream – a boundless mosaic of vast, uninhabited land and clean, pure lakes and rivers. One tenth of the world's fresh water laps the shores of this immense, awe-inspiring and diverse land.

The waterways of the NWT are passage for travel. Every community can be reached by water, although with the rise of modern technology, most have also become accessible by other means such as highways, winter roads, bush planes and jumbo jets. Today, the canoe is as ideal a way to travel this magnificent land as thousands of years ago when it was assembled of bark or animal hides.

No one knows when the first watercraft appeared in the north, but the tradition of plying the waters of the NWT in small boats dates back thousands of years. The canoes and kayaks of the modern tripper owe their origins to the technology of the early residents of the north. It is assumed that the ancient ancestors of the Indians who moved into the western Arctic following the retreat of the last glacial age, approximately 10,000 years ago, had some form of boat. The early European explorers who entered the northern forests of the NWT in the late 18th century found the Dene using small canoes made of spruce bark, birch bark or untanned moose hides, depending upon what materials were available. During the late 19th century, the Mountain Dene combined the technology of the moose hide canoe with the design of the Hudson's Bay Company's york boat, creating a thirty to forty foot boat, propelled by oars, used to travel downriver from the mountains to the fur trade posts – along the Mackenzie River.

Along the Arctic coast, the earliest evidence of boats among Inuit ancestors dates from the Dorset culture prior to AD 800. During the subsequent migration of the Thule people from Alaska to the Canadian Arctic around 1000 years ago, skin kayaks and large umiaks were evident. The Thule ancestors of the modern Inuit used their boats for hunting Bowhead whales and other large sea mammals in ice leads.

These indigenous, aboriginal people view the natural world "like a mother", providing all that one needs, and they travel on the land not so much as a vacation, but as a continuation of a lifestyle centred on the harvest of meat, fish and fur for subsistence. There is perhaps less than one would expect in the way of artifacts, ruins, or garbage to reflect the thousands of years of aboriginal travel and land use. The Dene and Inuit consider the land their home and their languages have no word for "wilderness"; the concept is foreign. Recreational paddlers often embrace these attitudes of being part of nature and finding spiritual connections and renewal in the northern landscape.

A northern paddling trip brings people close to the natural world, to animals in their natural habitat, where evidence of industry and many other human activities are absent. It offers time to live in harmony with nature and the opportunity for inner discovery and peace. The everyday stresses of life are replaced by the rhythms of travel and the simple pleasures and pain of physical activity, eating, sleeping, and sharing with nature.

Monica Kendel - artist

Human impact on the land and water has never been very great in the NWT and there are more uncultivated and uninhabited places here than virtually any other part of the planet. The current population of 55,000 occupies a land that is one third the total area of Canada – over 3.3 million square kilometres (approximately 1.3 million square miles). "Wilderness" is still the norm and not limited to parks, preserves or sanctuaries. From the boreal forest and mountain peaks to the vast expanses of tundra, the emotional appeal of feeling that you could have been the first person to step on a piece of the earth defies your better judgment. It is remarkably easy to imagine that this is how the world looked to the first European travelling this vast land.

Written information about the north first became available through explorers, adventurers, surveyors and fur traders, as the Dene and Inuit had no written languages until relatively recently. Mackenzie, Back, Hanbury, Franklin, Hearne and Hood are just some of the names etched onto northern maps in memory of those whose journeys first informed the outside world of the magic and beauty of the north. The oral culture of the aboriginal people provides important information about their perspectives of this land, its history and its people.

The waters of the Northwest Territories are often described in superlatives, such as Canada's longest river, the Mackenzie; its second largest lake, Great Bear; and its deepest lake, Great Slave. There are many other superlatives and the potential for paddling adventure and inspiration is endless.

A REGIONAL OVERVIEW

THE MACKENZIE MOUNTAINS

Mountain rivers offer exciting whitewater and scenery that compels one to seek a totally new vocabulary. The Mackenzie Mountains, west of the Mackenzie River, are a northern extension of the Rockies. Although not as high as their southerly relatives, these mountains are full of heady grandeur and wonderful secret places. The Natla, Keele, Mountain, and South Nahanni are the most popular canoeing routes in this region and they all flow into the Mackenzie River.

Mountain vegetation includes both the boreal forest and alpine tundra, providing a varied habitat for wildlife. White spruce fringe the rivers and extend up mountain slopes to the edge of the alpine. Black spruce intermingle with the white, primarily on northern and eastern slopes, and groves of pine trees are found on higher and drier benchlands of sandy soil. Tamarack and occasional birch and balsam poplar are also seen along river and stream banks. High water flows that undercut the river banks frequently turn these trees into sweepers.

Where the current is slower and the valleys wider, beaver dams entrap side channels and streams, forming quiet retreats for ducks and trumpeter swans. Alder and willow thickets along the shoreline are good areas for moose. A paddler may spot a mouse or a small bird that has been impaled on a willow bush – the food cache of a shrike, a handsome grey and white bird of prey. When the valleys narrow and rapids roar, canoeists are often too busy paddling to look up at the cliffs. If they do they might see patches of bright orange lichen and whitewash that signal the nest sites and perches of raptors. Golden eagles, rough-legged and red-tailed hawks, and ravens usually build large stick nests, while the more exotic peregrine and gyrfalcon deposit their eggs on a bare rock ledge.

The flight patterns of cliff swallows, who nest in colonies along cliff faces, echo a natural barometer. They are mere specks in the sky when air pressure is high and the sun shining, and when they forage for insects down near the river's surface, the weather is due to change to clouds and rain.

Boulder-strewn streams tumbling out of side valleys are favoured spots for small birds bobbing up and down and in and out of the water. Dippers or water ouzels are small, black, year-round residents of the river, who build their nests under small waterfalls. The light grey and white spotted sandpipers are summer visitors to the mountains. More uncommon are the wandering tattler and Harlequin duck who fly up and down the small streams searching for aquatic insects.

The main rivers in the mountains are often laden with silt. Drinking water may have to sit overnight to allow sediments to settle. Fishing is usually most successful at the mouth of a small side stream as it enters the silt-laden main river. Fresh dolly varden, lake trout, whitefish and grayling are a welcome addition to the menu.

Hiking up the side valleys provides a pleasant change of pace, an opportunity to observe wildlife not found along the river, and a different perspective on the mountain landscape. Ptarmigan, surrounded by their chicks, strut among the willow bushes and the elusive wheatear is known to nest in these remote valleys. Male mountain bluebirds flash a streak of blue through the bush, while a yellow flash is likely a warbler. Male ruffed grouse drum with their wings and the explosive flight of spruce grouse can startle a hiker. Holes in tree trunks provide homes for woodpeckers, ant-eating flickers, and sparrow hawks or kestrels, whereas hollowed-out trees near ponds may contain golden-eye ducks or buffleheads.

Climbing higher, the unmistakable scent and sight of sprawling alpine fir signal the top is near. Above the tree line, alpine flowers such as dark blue lupines, rare pink parrya, and star-shaped white mountain aven peek out from behind rocks. Yellow arnicas nod in the sun and blue-backed anemones lurk near receding snowbanks.

In this high country, Dall's sheep graze quietly on cliff faces – rams in their own little groups separate from the ewes and lambs. Natural caves provide shelter during inclement weather and black swifts sometimes build nests in the roof of those caves. Mountain caribou range in the high country during the summer and unlike other members of the deer family, both male and female have antlers that are shed every year. Grizzlies and black bears roam the entire region. Near scree slopes, rocks emit shrill whistles – the sound of the rock pika, a rodent related to the rabbit.

Nahanni National Park, in the southwest corner of the NWT, is recognized for its natural beauty and unspoiled ecosystems by UNESCO (United Nations Educational, Scientific and Cultural Organization) as a World Heritage Site. The South Nahanni River, with hotsprings and a canyon almost as deep as the Grand Canyon, is the source of tales about sometimes tragic searches for gold. Place names like Deadman's Valley and Hell's Gate perpetuate the mystery of this land and lure present travellers, as gold did in years gone by. Spectacular Virginia Falls, twice the height of Niagara Falls, is the most-photographed landmark in the north. A Nahanni orientation exhibit and film theatre is open year-round at the park headquarters in Fort Simpson.

The Nahanni area is part of the land of the Dene people who speak the South Slavey language, and who presently live in the communities of Fort Simpson, Fort Liard, Wrigley, Kakisa, Hay River, Jean Marie River, Trout Lake, Fort Providence, and Nahanni Butte. The people who speak the North Slavey language, the Hare and Mountain Dene, presently live in the communities of Fort Norman, Norman Wells, Colville Lake and Fort Good Hope. The Mountain Dene travelled down the Keele and Mountain Rivers each spring in mooseskin boats to trade at posts along the Mackenzie. Further north are the lands occupied by the Gwich'in, who presently live in the NWT communities of Inuvik, Fort McPherson, Aklavik and Arctic Red River, as well as the northern Yukon and Alaska. Late summer draws many people to their fish camps where dry fish, a tasty traditional northern food, is produced in abundance.

The Mackenzie, into which the mountain rivers flow, remains an important transportation route for communities along the Mackenzie River and Arctic coast. Barges provide a welcome and cheaper alternative to air freight for those centres not accessible by road. Mountain river trips begin in and travel through a remote land, and generally end in one of the communities along the Mackenzie River.

THE BOREAL FOREST

From Arctic Red River to Churchill runs an unusual border made of trees. North and east of that border lies the tundra – a treeless domain. South and west of that border and east of the Mackenzie Mountains, lies the boreal forest. Over long periods of geological time, this border moved south and north as the glaciers advanced and receded. Much of the ancient granite and gneiss rock of the Precambrian Shield has been exposed by glaciers and the low relief and glacial melt have filled the many pockets in the bedrock with water. This land of endless water, rock, and trees has a quiet dignified beauty.

The most popular canoe routes within this region are the Yellowknife, Beaulieu, Cameron, Wecho, Snare and Slave rivers. Some routes on the tundra, such as the Anderson River, begin in the forest, where trees provide shelter from cold winds, fuel for cooking and warmth for both the body and spirit. Rivers here are characterized by ledges, cascades and rapids that connect the various lakes on their systems. "Railroad tracks" is a common euphemism derived from the repetitious symbol found on topo maps, marking the rapids in this region. Portaging and lining can be a regular activity.

The boreal forest alternates between open parkland covered in a deep carpet of lichens and dense bush and muskeg with wet, mosquito-plagued swamps. The trees are similar to those of the Mackenzie mountains – white spruce and birch groves; black spruce, tamarack and pine; willow and alder thickets. Glaciers have removed much of the soil, and trees appear to grow out of bare rock. Forest fires, climate and poor soil conditions contribute to the small size of most trees.

Shrubs bearing blueberries, gooseberries, Saskatoon berries, currants and less often, raspberries, are found throughout. Bog cranberries and cloudberries carpet the forest floor in places. Flowering shrubs such as white-blossomed labrador tea, yellow cinquefoil and pink, sweet-smelling wild roses colour the shorelines. Smaller flowers such as the pink and yellow rock harlequin hug the rocks and in the mid-summer heat, purple fireweed waves in the breezes.

These lakes and rivers are filled with fish – lake trout, whitefish, Arctic grayling, inconnu, pike and pickerel – abundant food for humans and fishing birds such as red-breasted and common mergansers, grebes, osprey, and bald eagles. Small islands in lakes are frequently home to colonies of Arctic terns, mew gulls and black-headed gulls whose dive-bombing behaviour is intended to drive away paddlers who venture too close to nests. These quiet lakes evoke memories of the antics and laughing calls of the loon. Occasionally rivers pass beside clay banks riddled with holes, the homes of belted kingfishers or swallows. A loud humming sound in the evening sky may be a nighthawk diving in its hunt for small insects, and great horned owls and boreal owls may be heard hooting in the distance.

The boreal forest is home to large numbers of fur-bearing animals – otter, mink, muskrat, beaver, marten, wolverine and lynx. Moose forage in the shallows of lakes, while the seldom-seen woodland caribou wander in groups of two or three. During the summer, wolves are at their den sites which are most common where sandy eskers occur near the tree line. Black bears roam the entire region and, although more common in the mountains and the tundra, grizzlies occasionally wander into northern areas of the boreal forest.

Four kayakers in the Eastern Arctic

Straddling the Alberta border in the southern NWT is Canada's largest national park, Wood Buffalo. Established in 1922 to protect the world's largest free-roaming herd of wood bison, this UNESCO World Heritage Site has the only natural nesting colony of whooping cranes and the only salt plains in the country. The Slave River borders the park; this river was an important waterway during the fur trade, despite the rigours of a 25 kilometre (15 mile) portage from Fort Fitzgerald, Alberta to Fort Smith, NWT. The first trading post within the present NWT was established in 1787 at Fort Resolution on Great Slave Lake near the mouth of the Slave River.

Fort Resolution and Fort Smith have large Cree and Chipewyan populations. Snowdrift, at the east end of Great Slave Lake is a Chipewyan community. North of Great Slave Lake are the lands of the Dogrib people. The Dogrib communities of Wah Ti, Rae Lakes, Snare Lake, and Rae-Edzo are on river systems.

Within the boreal forest, aboriginal people traditionally travelled by canoes made of bark – either spruce or the more durable birchbark. Spruce bark canoes were light, rapidly made, and sturdy – designed to traverse lakes and rivers to gain access to remote hunting areas. They were easily portaged and could carry one or two people and some gear. Although often made for immediate use and then abandoned at the end of a season or in favour of overland travel, a well-made and cared for spruce bark canoe could last up to five years. Spruce bark canoes are easier to make than birchbark canoes. Birchbark must be pieced together to form the hull, while spruce bark canoes are made from a single sheet taking less time and work.

"In 1983 I watched Mr. Johnny Klondike of Fort Liard build a spruce bark canoe. It took him four days, but he insisted that as a young man, he could make one in two days. The first day he would have collected the materials, and the second would have been spent assembling the canoe. The first day we found and limbed four small black spruce trees used to make the gunwales. The second day Johnny trimmed and fitted the gunwales, collected the willow sticks he used for the ribs and the spruce gum we used to pitch the canoe. The third day Johnny found a large spruce tree that did not have any limbs on the lower section of the trunk, felled the tree, and peeled its bark. Later that day we found spruce roots used to sew the bow and stern. The last day Johnny showed me how the canoe was assembled. First he took the inwales, which had been tied at each end and spread in the middle to form a pointed ellipse, and placed it on the rough side of the bark. He folded the bark up to form the hull, making four tucks that raised the bow and stern keel sections slightly. This rocker made the canoe much more manoeuvrable. He propped the bark up, securing it in the hull form with stakes. Then he tied the gunwales to the hull with babiche, sandwiching them around the bark. Next he trimmed and fitted the ribs and secured the thwarts. Turning the canoe over, he closed and pitched the bow and stern. Finally he pitched the small holes in the hull... Johnny told me how he used to cover his canoes. In the spring he would cut and peel large pieces of fresh spruce bark. He would put them on the canoe, inner bark to inner bark layers."

– *Barb Winters*

Today, sections of boreal forest river systems continue to be used for traditional hunting and trapping activities and subsistence fishing. Sport fishing occurs on many lakes. Commercial fishing is limited to Great Slave Lake.

THE TUNDRA

Often referred to as the barrenlands, the tundra is anything but barren to eyes attuned to its unique contours and life, and the special attractions of a three hundred and sixty degree view unencumbered by trees or mountains. Like the boreal forest, the tundra is a land marbled with water. The most popular tundra rivers are the Horton, Burnside, Mara, Back, Hood, Hornaday and Coppermine, which drain into the Arctic Ocean, and the Kazan, Hanbury and Thelon, which drain into Hudson Bay through Baker Lake and Chesterfield Inlet.

North of the tree line, the ground is patterned by the annual cycle of freezing and thawing of the top layer of permafrost. Other frost features, such as hummocks and boils are noticed when wandering the tundra. Jumping up and down on a frost boil will eventually cause the water particles trapped within the soil to flow, transforming seemingly solid ground into a jello-like terrain. Permafrost makes the tundra particularly sensitive to the impact of humans and it takes many years for plant growth to resume once it has been disturbed.

Throughout July the barrens are carpeted with a variety of wildflowers. Large-blossomed pink willowherb blooms among the rocks, and Arctic lupines, the colour of lapis lazuli, and yellow Arctic poppies hide among pink louseworts and yellow arnicas. White anemones, star-shaped white avens, and fuchsia rhododendron hug the higher ground and the tops of hummocks. Cushion plants such as bright pink moss campion occur in the sandy, drier areas, while in wetter areas fields of fluffy white cottongrass wave in the wind. Occasionally a paddler is startled by a moose sticking its head out of willow thickets that line the shores of most rivers. Most of the shrubs are too small for forest dwellers, and cooking fires. Many varieties of lichen colour the ground and Barren-ground caribou are particularly fond of several species.

The caribou wander the tundra in the summer and winter in the boreal forest. They number more than one million animals and form four distinct herds, each named after the tundra area where its calves are born – Bathurst, Beverly, Kaminuriak, and Bluenose. During July after calving they move south toward their winter range. Long lines of snorting bodies with clicking heels flow into the rivers to swim across. For those not fortunate enough to witness a crossing, evidence of their passing remains as a "bathtub ring" of hair that floats along the edges of rivers and lakes and becomes part of the high water mark.

Wolves follow in the footsteps of the caribou herds from late August to May, but during the summer months denning activity restricts the movement of the wolves somewhat. Barren-ground grizzly bears and wolverines also wander the tundra. The distribution of wolverines is so sparse, that few paddlers see more than their tracks. Muskox, Arctic hares, Arctic fox, ptarmigan and gyrfalcons are among the few animals to live all year round on the barrens. Traces of qiviuq, the warm wool undercoat of the muskox, can often be found among willow bushes.

The tundra hosts a wide variety of bird life. Cliffs along the river banks provide nesting sites for golden eagles, peregrine falcons, gyrfalcons, rough-legged hawks, and ravens. Near the Arctic coast, loon populations include yellow-billed and red-throated loons. Whistling swans, several species of geese, and various dabbling and diving ducks are common. Along the shores of the rivers, many different sandpipers or "peeps" run along the sand and mud searching for insects. The clear whistle and handsome black belly, white sides and golden back of the American golden plover distinguish it immediately. The northern phalarope is a small bird that swims in circles, causing a vortex which brings insects up from the bottom of shallow ponds. The common snipe is not often seen, but during courtship it flies high in the sky and the wind passing through the feathers makes a whistling sound that can be heard from a great distance. Over the tundra, horned larks flutter in the wind and give their tinkling call. Lapland longspurs and redpolls hop in the grasses and bushes searching for seeds. Huge, gangly, sandhill cranes nest on the ground and hop with outstretched wings in mating and greeting dances. Predatory long-tailed jaegars can be seen hovering over the ground searching for lemmings which are also the favoured food of the white-rumped marsh hawk and the short-eared owl. Near the Arctic coast and on the Arctic islands, snowy owls nest on the ground.

The king of northern fish, the Arctic char, is found in some barrenland rivers flowing into the Arctic Ocean. Lake trout, whitefish and Arctic grayling are also found in tundra waters. An occasional seal ventures upstream of the river mouth near the Arctic Ocean.

The Thelon River flows through the Thelon Game Sanctuary, where paddlers are often treated to spectacular sightings of large and small game. Established in 1927 to protect a dwindling muskox population, the Thelon Game Sanctuary is under consideration for designation as a national park.

Trips on the Kazan and Hanbury-Thelon Rivers end at Baker Lake, the geographic centre of Canada. Baker Lake is the only inland Inuit community in the territories. The communities of Tuktoyaktuk, Paulatuk, Holman, Coppermine, Bathurst Inlet, Gjoa Haven, Taloyoak (formerly Spence Bay), Pelly Bay, Igloolik, Hall Beach, Repulse Bay and Coral Harbour dot the Arctic coastline, where the Inuit continue to depend on sea mammals. Such is also the case for the communities of Rankin Inlet, Chesterfield Inlet, Whale Cove and Arviat along the Hudson Bay coast and the Baffin Island communities of Pond Inlet, Clyde River, Pangnirtung, Iqaluit, Cape Dorset and Lake Harbour.

The original quinnat or kayaks were designed for hunting caribou as well as whales, walrus and seals. The designs of these boats varied among the different Inuit groups.

Today, the tundra remains the homeland of the Inuit, although the Dene continue to travel through and use parts of this region. Isolation and long distances to communities characterize any canoe trip here.

TRIP PLANNING

Many people return north year after year, drawn repeatedly to the adventure, tranquillity and challenge of the water and land. For others, paddling in the NWT will be a once in a lifetime experience. Poring over maps, reading about the north, and making arrangements fill the months leading up to a trip with joyful anticipation.

SELECTING A PADDLING ROUTE : With tens of thousands of lakes and hundreds of rivers, selecting a paddling route in the Northwest Territories can be challenging and exciting. Some paddlers know exactly what they are looking for or perhaps have a life-long dream centred on a specific route – to paddle the Mackenzie to the Arctic Ocean, or see the remains of John Hornby's cabin on the Thelon. For other paddlers, the choice involves poring over maps, gathering information, and dreaming of the endless possibilities. Traditional travel routes of the Dene or Inuit, and the paths of early European explorers and fur-traders can be retraced on many rivers such as the Wecho, the Coppermine, the Back, and the Slave. The Mackenzie River offers an opportunity to visit many communities. On many routes, paddlers can be virtually guaranteed weeks of solitude. Some routes are more likely to provide opportunities to see a wolf, a grizzly, a herd of caribou, or particular forms of bird life. There are numerous variations in geology, fishing opportunities, geography, climate, wildlife, plant life, and the water itself.

Perhaps the most important considerations in choosing a route are paddling expertise and wilderness experience. Some routes offer continuous whitewater, demanding a high level of technical river paddling skills. Crossing watersheds and entering different river systems is a great adventure, requiring advanced navigational and wilderness tripping skills. Some routes have enormous lakes, others more frequent or longer portages.

There are also important considerations of time and money. Trips for a day or an entire season are possible. Many paddlers desire to allow extra time to accommodate birdwatching, hiking, fishing, poor weather or just lazing around. The major expense of any paddling trip in the NWT is transportation. Charter flights are required to the headwaters of most rivers. Some routes end in isolated areas and a charter flight is also needed to return. Some trips end or begin in a community with scheduled air service, making charter flights unnecessary for that portion of the trip.

An alternative to organizing your own trip is to participate in a guided trip. Several outfitters offer trips on a variety of river routes within the NWT (See Appendix E). These people make all the arrangements and experienced guides are usually well-informed about the area you travel through.

GETTING HERE: Driving is an economical although time-consuming way to reach the north, especially if paddlers want to transport and use their own canoes. Yellowknife, Inuvik, Fort Simpson, Fort Liard, Fort Smith, Hay River, Rae-Edzo and Fort Providence are on NWT highway systems. Some mountain rivers are accessible from Ross River, Watson Lake or Mayo, which are all on highway systems in the

Yukon Territory. Depending on where you live or where your trip begins, paddling routes in the eastern NWT may be more easily and cheaply reached from Saskatchewan or Manitoba.

The Mackenzie, Liard and Dempster highways are characterized by long stretches of gravel road, few services, and basic camping facilities in territorial campgrounds. A well-maintained vehicle is recommended and it is necessary to carry a good spare tire and some basic tools. It is advisable to slow down when passing an approaching vehicle to minimize the impact of restricted visibility, due to the ubiquitous dust and flying rocks. Foreign driver's licenses are valid in Canada; however, non-resident insurance coverage should be obtained before leaving home.

Canadian Airlines and Northwest Territorial Airways, an Air Canada connector, fly into the NWT with daily flights to Yellowknife from Edmonton. There are also frequent flights to Inuvik, Hay River and Fort Smith from Edmonton; to Rankin Inlet and Baker Lake from Winnipeg and Churchill; and to Iqaluit on Baffin Island from Ottawa and Yellowknife. Most other communities can be reached with scheduled service from one or more of the NWT regional centres.

Transporting canoes in scheduled aircraft means checking air cargo costs. Some airlines only carry canoes when space is available. It may be necessary to ship canoes well ahead of the travelling date to be guaranteed their arrival in time for the scheduled paddling adventure.

CHARTER FLIGHTS: There are few northern river trips which do not require a charter flight at either the beginning or end of the journey, and sometimes both. A flight in a float plane is usually a welcome feature of a northern paddling trip.

Charter aircraft companies are accustomed to a variety of requests. Communication by facsimile is a boon to arranging charter flights, giving paddlers quick written confirmation of options and arrangements. Organizing charter flights after reaching the north is possible, but during the busy summer season it may mean waiting.

It is not practical to list here all the different types of aircraft used in the NWT and their various load capacities. There are many factors that affect the load carried by different aircraft, or even by the same type of airplane under varying conditions. For example, a longer flight with a greater quantity of fuel carried may mean reduced cargo capacity. Insurance can affect the number of passengers allowed on board the aircraft. There is often an extra charge for carrying a canoe on the floats. It may be cheaper to charter a couple of smaller planes, such as Cessna 185s, than a larger but more expensive aircraft, such as a Twin Otter.

Rates can vary from company to company and it is wise to shop around. Appendix D lists charter aircraft companies. What the aircraft company needs to know is the number of people in the party, the weight of the gear, the number and length of the canoes, and the destination. Other details such as whether or not the canoes nest inside each other with the thwarts and seats removed may be important.

Aircraft companies in the north are regulated and monitored by the Canadian government. Allow extra time in the schedule for the unexpected. High winds or poor visibility can delay a drop-off or pick-up by a small aircraft. The sun may be shining on calm waters where the plane is located, but the weather at the destination could be an entirely different matter. Emergency medical evacuations or forest fires can occasionally take precedence over a booked charter flight. This is all part of northern travel and a good sense of humour and patience can go a long way under such circumstances. If nothing else, the recounting of a northern river journey during the coming winter will have additional interesting details.

> *"A few years ago we were mistakenly dropped off by a charter aircraft on a land-locked lake 11 kilometres east of our intended destination, a lake on the Yellowknife River. We tried unsuccessfully for three days to attract the attention of several aircraft flying overhead, before a low-flying Single Otter pilot noticed our signal fires and waving life jackets."*
>
> *– Aggie Brockman and Terry Wolf*

RENTING A CANOE AND OTHER EQUIPMENT DECISIONS: The days are gone of renting a canoe from a Hudson's Bay store and dropping it off at another company post at the end of the trip. More canoe rental options are now available in the Northwest Territories than ever before. A canoe rental must be arranged well ahead of a trip to ensure a boat is available, but will alleviate the hassle, expense, and risk of transporting your own boat. A listing of rental businesses can be found in Appendix F.

The potential of purchasing camping equipment and tripping supplies is limited in smaller communities. Yellowknife has the largest selection of equipment and food supplies and paddlers can be assured of finding most of the things they want. The cost of living in Yellowknife is approximately 20% higher than in Edmonton, although this does not mean that all food or equipment will necessarily cost more than in southern Canada.

> *"Our stores consisted of two barrels of gunpowder, one hundred and forty pounds of ball and shot, four fowling pieces, a few old trading guns, eight pistols, twenty-four Indian daggers, some packages of knives, chisels, axes, nails, and fastenings for a boat; a few yards of cloth, some blankets, needles, looking-glasses, and beads; together with nine fishing nets, having meshes of different sizes."*
>
> *– John Franklin, 1820*

Most stores are closed on statutory holidays and Sundays. During the summer months, holidays include Canada Day, July 1; the Civic Holiday, the first Monday in August; and Labour Day, the first Monday in September. Grocery stores in Yellowknife are open on Sundays.

> *"Our provision was two casks of flour, two hundred dried reindeer tongues, some dried moose meat, portable soup and arrowroot, sufficient in the whole for ten days consumption besides two cases of chocolate, and two canisters of tea... We remained to pack our stores in bales of eighty pounds each..."*
>
> *– John Franklin, 1820*

Whitewater on the Natla/Keele River

PREPARING FOR
NORTHERN CONDITIONS

Isolation, wild waters and the unique northern landscape are just some of the elements which contribute to outstanding paddling experiences in the NWT. These same conditions demand special consideration when planning a northern paddling expedition.

ISOLATION: The remoteness of most northern river systems can be a significant hazard as well as a major attraction. Few canoeing parties are equipped with radios and paddlers usually depend on their own skills and knowledge of wilderness travel and survival. All risks must be carefully calculated, as caution and safe practices take on new importance when there may be no second chances. It is possible, even probable, to never encounter other people on a six-week canoe trip in the Northwest Territories. Scouting is advised for all whitewater and when in doubt, portage – nobody ever drowned on a portage. Good judgement demands an awareness of the hazards of the river and the abilities of the paddlers. Maps are required for any canoe trip and a combination of 1:50,000 and 1:250,000 topographical maps provide important details plus an overall perspective of the trip, although many maps of the NWT contain errors and omissions. The key ingredients of good judgement are foresight, prudence and the ability to know when not to take risks.

Maps are available through the Canada Map Office, 615 Booth St., Ottawa, Ontario K1A 0E9. Phone: 613-952-7000. Fax: 613-957-8861. Map numbers for 1:250,000 topo maps are given for each of the trip reports included in this book. For other routes, map numbers are provided in an index map available from the Canada Map Office. The office staff will research the numbers, but it is important to be specific and accurate in a request. Unless the mistake is theirs, the office will not refund money. The Canada Map Office takes VISA and Mastercard credit cards. Maps can be sent C.O.D. within Canada, but advance payment is required for orders outside of Canada.

Maps are also available in Yellowknife at Tgit Geomatics Ltd., #204-5110 50th Ave., Box 244, Yellowknife, NWT X1A 2N2. Phone: 403-873-8438, fax: 403-873-8439. It's a good idea to order maps well in advance of a trip.

CHANGING WATER LEVELS: The water levels of northern rivers, especially mountain rivers, can change dramatically in an unbelievably short length of time. Some fluctuations are predictable, some are capricious. More than one canoeing party has had an experience similar to a group on the Nahanni in 1983, who woke one morning to a flooded campsite, with all the food packs missing. After rising two metres overnight, the river had washed the packs away. Fortunately, the canoes were tied higher up on the bank and the packs were retrieved 13 kilometres downstream.

Water levels may also vary drastically from year to year for the same river. The river reports in this book include hydrographs for each river to illustrate monthly mean discharges. The hydrographs represent conditions found in a specific place at a specific time. There is no substitute for being there.

ICE CONDITIONS: Break-up is a special time of year in the north, as migratory birds and paddlers flock to the first sections of open water. Many communities have contests which involve guessing the day and time the ice on the local river will break-up and move downstream. A few rivers break-up by mid-May and the canoeing season usually begins around mid-June and goes into September. Ice-free conditions can vary considerably year to year and from one location to another. For example, the large lakes east of Great Slave Lake are often frozen until mid-July, whereas similarly-sized lakes to the west are open in early July. Even if a river is clear, it is not uncommon to encounter ice-covered lakes or ice floes on the larger lakes of a river system. Pilots and aircraft companies are among the best sources to consult to confirm break-up. Travelling on ice is not recommended. It is much safer to wait for a strong wind to open a clear passage, and also to be prepared for a change in wind direction to close those leads without warning. This is one of many northern paddling predicaments where progress can be delayed and extra food a godsend.

WEATHER: Northern summers generally bring clear, sunny weather with little precipitation. Summer temperatures usually range between 10 and 22 degrees Celsius, although they have been known to plummet to freezing in July or reach in excess of 30 degrees Celsius. During August strong winds, cooler temperatures and rain become more frequent. Snowstorms are possible at any time of the year. Clothing and tents should be water and windproof, and suitable for extreme weather conditions. High winds are not uncommon, although they usually subside in the evening and the long hours of summer twilight are delightful for paddling.

During the long hours of summer light, the usual sense of time is skewed, a liberty not often afforded people in today's world. North of the Arctic Circle, the sun never sets in July. Despite long hours of sunshine, most northern lakes and rivers seldom get warmer than 10 degrees Celsius between break-up and freeze-up. Canoeists who capsize run a serious risk of immersion hypothermia and paddlers should be familiar with the symptoms and treatment of this condition. Life jackets provide some thermal protection and should be worn at all times.

> *"In September, 1955, Arthur Moffat swamped his canoe in a rapid on the Dubawnt River, 250 miles from Baker Lake. His companions picked up all the packs first, then the swimmers. Although Moffat was conscious when his friends pulled him out of the water, he was in a serious hypothermic condition. He insisted that he was "okay", however, and was placed in a sleeping bag inside his tent. No attempt was made to warm him or give him hot drinks. Sometime later he was found dead."*
>
> *– Author Unknown*

WILDERNESS TRIP REGISTRATION PROGRAM: The Royal Canadian Mounted Police have a Wilderness Trip Registration Program. All paddlers are strongly advised to file a trip plan with the RCMP, indicating the route of travel, names of party members, and the expected completion date. This will aid in a search and rescue operation should a party not complete their trip in the time planned. RCMP search and rescue operations are expensive and often risky, and paddlers have a responsibility not to make such rescues necessary if they can be avoided. Paddlers are also responsible to cover the costs of search and rescue, should this occur. Most communities have an RCMP detachment.

BITING INSECTS:

The stunning beauty of the northern landscape and the quality of northern paddling opportunities are adequate compensation for the inconvenience of mosquitoes and black flies for many people. For others, biting insects are considered a physical and psychological danger. One veteran of several northern canoe trips has concluded that mosquitoes and blackflies are the true guardians of the north.

Mosquito and blackfly populations peak in most areas in June and July. Insect attacks are most severe in the early morning, after sunset and before storms. The best defence against bugs is a good offence. Select breezy, exposed points of land for campsites and lunch stops. Reduce the amount of exposed skin by wearing long-sleeved shirts, pants, socks and a hat. Light-coloured clothing is somewhat less attractive to insects than dark colours.

Most bug dope contains solvents that damage synthetic fibres and plastics. Bug jackets and/or pants, which reduce the need to apply repellent directly on the skin, are gaining well-deserved popularity in the north. One style is made of lightweight mesh material that is saturated with repellent. Another style is made of tightly woven mesh which does not require repellent.

A dilute solution of baking soda and water applied to a bite can alleviate the itch and swelling. If a person is highly sensitive to insect bites, antihistamines and anaesthetics can also soothe a bite. Skin infections can result from scratching – so don't. Happily, there are no poisonous snakes or spiders in the Northwest Territories.

Arctic bugs – be prepared

GETTING ALONG ONCE YOU ARE HERE

RESPECTING THE LAND AND THE ANIMALS

One of the joys of paddling in the Northwest Territories is the chance to see a landscape in the same state it has been in for thousands of years, and to view wildlife in its natural habitat. Each paddler shares the responsibility of making sure these opportunities remain available for future generations. The guiding principle of wilderness travel should be to leave both the land and water as you found them – take only photos and leave only footprints.

In all wilderness areas there are occasional conflicts between the animals who live there and human visitors. This is the only home the animals have and paddlers are visitors on their turf. All wild animals are just that – wild. Although they are generally afraid of humans, wild animals should be considered unpredictable.

For most wilderness travellers, bears are the only animals which come to mind when they think of negative animal-human encounters. However, muskox have been known to charge for no reason and most wild animals with their offspring become aggressive towards people if disturbed. A protective cow moose weighing three to four hundred kilograms is definitely a force to be reckoned with.

Danger to paddlers is not the only problem that can arise between humans and animals. Disturb all animals as little as possible. Birds such as the snowy owl will permit humans to approach their nests closely, but the Arctic fox has been known to follow the scent of a human and raid every nest that a person has approached.

Fish mortalities can be reduced by filing or pinching down the barbs on hooks. In many areas fish are tagged to assist with fishery management studies. Tags and information on the location and time of the catch, the size of the fish and lure used can be sent to the Department of Fisheries and Oceans, Box 2310, Yellowknife, NWT X1A 2P7.

YOU ARE IN BEAR COUNTRY: The black bear range includes most of the forested areas of the western Territories. Grizzlies are found in the mountains, foothills and the tundra west of Hudson Bay. In summertime polar bears are most commonly found near the Arctic and Hudson Bay shorelines.

All bears should be considered dangerous. Some kind of deterrent device is recommended, although the choice will depend on the philosophical convictions and the skills and comfort of paddlers in using the device. Shotgun slugs which will kill or injure a bear can be replaced with cracker shells or plastic 12-gauge shells. Noise deterrents include pistol and pencil flare guns and boat horns. At close range a Capsicum spray can be used; this is an industrial-strength mace for bears made from a derivative of red pepper.

Everyone in the canoe party should be familiar with the proper use of the bear deterrent chosen. The wildlife officer nearest to the chosen route can be an excellent source of local information about bears, and any bear problems should be reported at the earliest opportunity to the nearest Renewable Resources office.

IT'S THE LAW: Wildlife and heritage laws are meant to protect and preserve the natural and human history of the Northwest Territories for the future.

PARKS, PRESERVES AND SANCTUARIES: Canoeists paddling on the South Nahanni and Slave rivers must obtain a special permit to fish within Nahanni or Wood Buffalo National Parks. For more information, contact Nahanni National Park, Box 300, Fort Simpson, NWT X0E 0N0 or Wood Buffalo National Park, Box 750, Fort Smith, NWT X0E 0P0.

There are 16 Migratory Bird Sanctuaries within the Northwest Territories. Virtually any outdoor activity which does not disturb the birds or damage their habitat is acceptable in a sanctuary, although the Canadian Wildlife Service may at times impose conditions or restrict the timing, location and intensity of canoeing and camping activities. It is recommended that paddlers apply for an entry permit. This enables the Canadian Wildlife Service to monitor human impact, and helps justify the existence of sanctuaries in light of their tourist appeal. Allow 45 days for processing. Information about bird sanctuaries and permits is available from the Enforcement Officer, Canadian Wildlife Service, Box 637, Yellowknife, NWT X1A 2N5. Phone: 403-920-8530.

FISHING AND HUNTING: Most paddling trips offer only a limited amount of time to hunt and fish, and there are legal restrictions on these activities.

A fishing license is required to fish by any method in the NWT for anyone 16 years of age and over. An Inuvialuit Settlement Region Stamp is required to fish within the Inuvialuit Claim area (see below, Aboriginal Lands). A special stamp is also required to sport fish on Great Bear Lake. Licences and stamps are available from most sporting goods and hardware stores, as well as RCMP detachments and area offices of the Department of Renewable Resources. Information on catch limits and other restrictions can be obtained when buying a licence. Canoeists are often able to supplement their diet with fresh fish, but it is not advisable to rely exclusively on this for food.

A license must be obtained to hunt small game, and hunting is restricted in wildlife sanctuaries or preserves. The open season for hunting migratory birds begins September 1. Non-residents of the Northwest Territories must be accompanied by a licensed guide to hunt big game, which includes caribou, wolf, wolverine, bears, moose, mountain goat, muskox and Dall's sheep. It is legal to shoot a bear in self-defense when life or property is threatened but a person may not keep any part of that bear and must report the kill to the nearest Renewable Resources Officer as soon as possible. For more information on restrictions and permitted hunting methods and equipment contact: Canadian Wildlife Service, Box 637, Yellowknife, NWT X1A 2N5 or the Department of Renewable Resources, Box 1320, Yellowknife, NWT X1A 2L9.

EXPORTING ANIMAL PARTS: Permits are required to export any wildlife or wildlife parts, other than a manufactured product, to a place outside the Northwest Territories. A manufactured product means wildlife that is prepared for use through a tanning or taxidermy process, a carving, processed food or a garment. Certification is also required for Dall sheep horns, wood bison horns, caribou antlers, birds of prey, grizzly bear, polar bear, narwhal and muskox.

MIGRATORY BIRD SANCTUARIES:

Activities within these areas require a permit from the Canadian Wildlife Service, Environment Canada. For more information contact:
Canadian Wildlife Service
Northern Conservation Branch
Western and Northern Region
Box 637, Yellowknife, NWT X1A 2N5
Phone: (403) 920-8531 Fax: (403) 873-8185

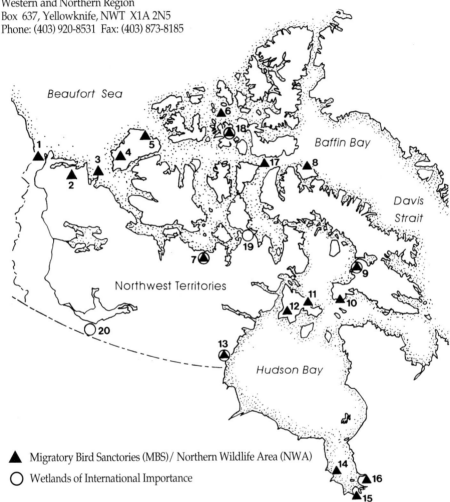

▲ Migratory Bird Sanctories (MBS)/ Northern Wildlife Area (NWA)

○ Wetlands of International Importance

1 - Kendall Island MBS	11 -East Bay MBS
2 - Anderson River MBS	12 -Harry Gibbons MBS
3 - Cape Parry MBS	13 -McConnell River MBS
4 - Banks Island #1 MBS	14 -Akimiski Island MBS
5 - Banks Island #2 MBS	15 -Hannah Bay MBS
6 - Seymour Island MBS	16 -Boatswain Bay MBS
7 - Queen Maud Gulf MBS	17 -Prince Leopold Island MBS
8 - Bylot Island MBS	18 -Polar Bear Pass NWA
9 - Dewey Soper MBS	19 -Rasmussen Lowlands
10 -Cape Dorset MBS	20 -Wood Buffalo National Park

The Convention on International Trade in Endangered Species of Fauna and Flora (C.I.T.E.S.) controls the import and export of rare or endangered species between countries. The Department of Renewable Resources can be contacted to determine if a C.I.T.E.S. import permit is required, as well as an NWT export permit for animal parts which paddlers may want to remove from the Northwest Territories. It is the responsibility of the individual concerned to be aware of the import laws of any country into which a person is considering taking wildlife parts. No export permit is required for fish.

ARCHAEOLOGICAL SITES AND ARTIFACTS: All historic sites are protected from any disturbance by law. Removing artifacts or altering structures destroys unique information from the past. Leave all human-made items where found. More information on archaeological sites can be obtained by contacting the Senior Archaeologist, Prince of Wales Northern Heritage Centre, Government of the NWT, Box 1320, Yellowknife, NWT X1A 2L9.

ABORIGINAL LANDS: The Northwest Territories is the only jurisdiction in Canada where aboriginal people make up a majority of the population. The Dene, Inuit and Inuvialuit are the original peoples. There is also a significant Métis population. Numbering less than 200 at the turn of the century, increasing numbers of non-aboriginal people are making the NWT their permanent home.

Generally, casual recreational travel is unrestricted on aboriginal lands, as long as no significant damage occurs and aboriginal use and enjoyment of the land is not interfered with. Paddlers are invited to contact the appropriate aboriginal group, particularly when planning non-recreational use of the land or when travelling with a large group (see map following).

The Inuvialuit signed their land claim agreement in 1984. For information about travelling on lands in the Inuvialuit Settlement Region, contact the Inuvialuit Regional Corporation, Inuvik, NWT X0E 0T0. Phone: 403-979-2737 or fax: 403-979-2135.

The Gwich'in Dene signed a regional land claim in 1992. Information about travelling on Gwich'in lands may be obtained by contacting the Gwich'in Tribal Council, Box 97, Fort McPherson, NWT X0E 0J0. Phone: 403-952-2330, fax: 403-952-2212

The Nun Agreement was signed in 1993. The NWT will separate into two political jurisdictions, Nunavut and a western Territory, in 1999. It may be wise for paddlers to contact Nunavut Tunngavik Inc., 130 Albert St., Ottawa, Ontario. Phone: 613-238-1096 fax: 613-238-4131, to get information about any potential restrictions for use of Inuit lands.

The Sahtu land claim was signed in 1994. For information on travelling these lands, contact the Shihta Tribal Council, Box 297, Norman Wells, NWT, X0E 0V0. Phone: 403-587-2654, fax: 403-587-2805.

Other Dene and Métis groups and Treaty 8 and 11 peoples are in the process of negotiating with the federal government concerning aboriginal self-government mechanisms and regional land claims agreements. Paddlers can contact the Department of Aboriginal and Intergovernmental Affairs, Box 1320, Yellowknife, NWT X1A 2P2 to get information about the status of these claims. Phone: 403-873-7143, fax: 403-873-0233.

Land Claims Area

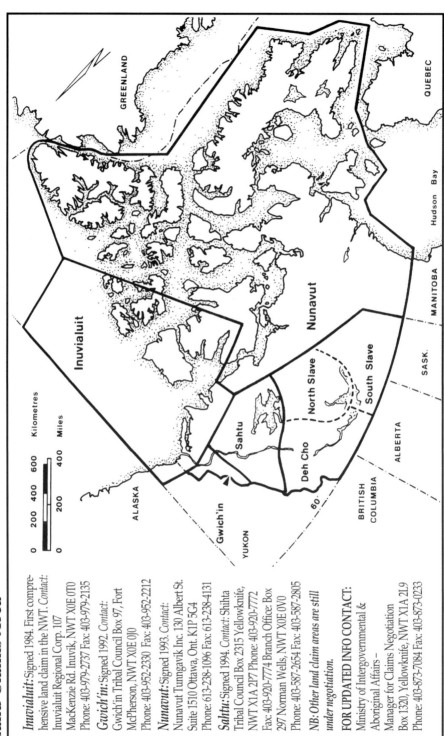

Inuvialuit: Signed 1984. First comprehensive land claim in the NWT. *Contact:* Inuvialuit Regional Corp. 107 MacKenzie Rd. Inuvik, NWT X0E 0T0 Phone: 403-979-2737 Fax: 403-979-2135

Gwich'in: Signed 1992. *Contact:* Gwich'in Tribal Council Box 97, Fort McPherson, NWT X0E 0J0 Phone: 403-952-2330 Fax: 403-952-2212

Nunavut: Signed 1993. *Contact:* Nunavut Tunngavik Inc. 130 Albert St. Suite 1510 Ottawa, Ont. K1P 5G4 Phone: 613-238-1096 Fax: 613-238-4131

Sahtu: Signed 1994. *Contact:* Shihta Tribal Council Box 2215 Yellowknife, NWT X1A 2P7 Phone: 403-920-7772 Fax: 403-920-7774 Branch Office: Box 297 Norman Wells, NWT X0E 0V0 Phone: 403-587-2654 Fax: 403-587-2805

NB: Other land claim areas are still under negotiation.

FOR UPDATED INFO CONTACT:
Ministry of Intergovernmental & Aboriginal Affairs –
Manager for Claims Negotiation Box 1320, Yellowknife, NWT X1A 2L9 Phone: 403-873-7084 Fax: 403-873-0233

THERE'S MORE THAN TO LIFE THAN PADDLING

During a paddling trip in the Northwest Territories, most of the time will be spent away from communities and other people, except travelling companions. At the beginning or end of a river journey, paddlers may choose to join northern residents at one of the many special events or festivals held each summer.

An experience of northern social life could be as unforgettable as a canoe trip – especially if a person is game enough to enter the goose plucking contest at the Ikhalukpik Jamboree in Paulatuk or take part in a Dene drum dance. Annual summer games are held in each region and feature both traditional and modern sports. Music festivals are held in Yellowknife, Midway Lake (near Fort McPherson), Arviat, Iqaluit, and Fort Smith. People from across the Territories and beyond participate in an annual Festival of the Arts in Inuvik. Every year during the August long weekend, canoes and kayaks ply the waters of the Slave River rapids in competition and fun, and in September a mountain bike race is held on the portage route from Fort Fitzgerald to Fort Smith. Northerners celebrate their short summers with vigour and visitors are always welcome.

FOR MORE INFORMATION: There are 19 river routes detailed in this book. While one shouldn't be discouraged from pursuing the many other paddling possibilities, accurate information on other routes is not easily accessible. Information on other routes is best obtained from someone who has travelled there. It is important to determine and compare water levels of the year of a potential trip and the year of the trip of the informant. More than one source should be checked whenever possible, as river conditions can vary dramatically year to year and within one season.

A few years ago a party of four seasoned northern paddlers attempted to cross a watershed by travelling up the Sloan River from Great Bear Lake to the Coppermine River. They had allowed two weeks for the fifty-mile upstream stretch, including a 14-mile portage. As it turned out, the portage was along huge boulders, with no viable alternate routes. The steep embankment was covered in scree while the top of the hill was a mass of impenetrable willows and swamp. Careful preparation had preceded the trip, but the contour lines of maps and the information gathered provided no forewarning of the scree or willows which would eventually force the party to turn back. The happy ending is that once back at a fishing lodge on Great Bear Lake, the party managed to charter an aircraft to the Coppermine River and complete their journey to the Arctic coast.

Water conditions change each year – plan ahead to have
current information and expect the unexpected

HOW TO USE THE RIVER REPORTS

B efore using the river reports, paddlers are advised to read this section to understand the definitions and meanings used here.

Each report has been confirmed by a minimum of three different paddlers who have travelled the route. Some reports have received more attention than that. All information is offered as a guide only. Every attempt has been made to provide accurate information to ensure both safety and enjoyment for paddlers. Canoeists should keep in mind the factors of time, subtle changes in topography, and changing water levels that affect virtually all the information about the river routes discussed in this book.

TOTAL DISTANCE: Distance was measured with a computer and digitizer using National Topographic Series 1:250,000 and 1:50,000 scale maps. The Water Surveys Branch of Environment Canada provided access to a computer for this process. This method provides the opportunity to travel the course of the river as would a canoeist, following the shorelines of larger lakers and portages. Distances are expressed in both kilometres and miles.

DURATION OF TRIP: This is a conservative estimate of the duration of the trip expressed in days.

START AND FINISH: These sections describe the most popular access and egress points for each river route based on information from journals and personal communication. Paddlers can use other places to begin and end their trip depending on the length of time they have available to paddle and whether or not there are good locations for aircraft to land or other access.

ACCESSIBILITY: This section provides up-to-date information on how to get to and return from the various rivers. This could be affected by new road construction and other changes in transportation.

RIVER NOTES: This section provides information about geography, climate, flora, fauna, and human history.

RIVER PROFILE: This section gives a detailed description of the river itself, including rapids, falls, portages, points of interest and, sometimes, good campsites.

MAPS REQUIRED: The required National Topographic Series maps for each river route are listed here. Most of the routes list the 1:250,000 scale maps (one inch to 4 miles). It is recommended that paddlers purchase one set of maps for each canoe. Although there are some discrepancies between the maps and reality, they are generally accurate and provide vital information on the location of rapids and other landforms.

AVERAGE GRADIENT: This is the average drop of the river over its length expressed in metres per kilometre and feet per mile. Usually a river becomes more difficult to paddle as the gradient increases. A river with a gradient less than 1 metre per kilometre (5 feet per mile) would generally be slow moving with few rapids. A river dropping 1 to 4 metres per kilometre (5 to 20 feet per mile) would probably have Class 1 rapids. A river gradient of 6 metres per kilometre (32 feet per mile) is usually the limit for loaded open canoes. Gradients greater than this are usually only suitable for decked boats and the upper limit of navigability is about 12 metres per kilometre (62 feet per mile).

This information may, however, be misleading, especially where rapids and falls occur in concentrations along the river route. For example, the average gradient of the Slave River from Lake Athabasca to Fort Resolution is 0.11 metres per kilometre (0.6 feet per mile). One could interpret this to mean that the river is wide and slow moving, but between Fort Smith and Fort Fitzgerald there are several extremely dangerous rapids that are not navigable in open or closed boats. Most mountain rivers typically drop over steep gradients near their source and level off in lower country near their mouth. Canoeists would therefore expect more difficult sections of whitewater on the upper stretches of a mountain river. Thus, the average gradient only indicates what conditions may be expected overall. Careful scouting and map reading are still required for all rapids.

HYDROGRAPH: This graph illustrates rate of discharge, expressed in cubic metres of water flowing past a particular point in one second. The graph is divided into months, with the top line representing highest discharge, the bottom line representing lowest discharge and the middle line the mean discharge for the day. Paddlers should note the scale when reading these hydrographs as they vary from river to river.

SOURCE INFORMATION: The river reports have been based on information from historical and contemporary journals, personal interviews, and surveys. The NWT Canoeing Association encourages paddlers to continue to provide information about these and other routes. A suggested outline for a trip report is found in Appendix B. It is impossible to include everything that might be of interest to every reader and a bibliography of relevant reading material has been included in Appendix G.

CUMULATIVE DISTANCE: Represents distance accumulated from the start, to various significant points along the route, and to the finish, and is expressed in kilometres and miles, using the same computer and digitizer as explained in the Total Distance section (p 27).

ANDERSON RIVER

TOTAL DISTANCE: Colville Lake to Nicholson Point – 679 kilometres (424 miles). This includes a 41 km (25 mile) paddle along the coastline of Wood Bay and an open ocean crossing of 3 km (1.5 miles) to reach Nicholson Point.

DURATION OF TRIP: 3 to 4 weeks.

START: Most trips start at the community of Colville Lake, located on the lake of the same name, about 130 km (80 miles) northwest of Great Bear Lake. Paddlers having less time can start further downstream, as float planes can land almost anywhere along the river.

FINISH: A common finishing point for this trip is at the airstrip on Nicholson Point, a DEW Line station in Wood Bay. Nicholson Point is actually an island, not a point, and a short ocean crossing is needed to get to it. Care should be given to this crossing as pack ice can jam the opening and wind and waves from the Beaufort Sea can add to the hazard. It is recommended that paddlers arrange to be picked up at the Canadian Wildlife Service cabin at Krekovick Landing or at one of the beaches on the east side of Wood Bay. Some groups choose to paddle back to Inuvik, along the coast through Liverpool Bay and Eskimo Lakes. Another 2 weeks should be added to the trip to complete this 360 km (225 mile) leg. Travel in this area can be hampered by high winds and dangerous waves.

ACCESSIBILITY: This route is accessible only by air. Colville Lake can be reached from either Norman Wells or Inuvik. Trips starting further downstream are probably best to charter from Inuvik. Pickup can be arranged from Inuvik.

Both Norman Wells and Inuvik have regular scheduled air service to Yellowknife and Edmonton. Canoes can be barged to or from either Norman Wells or Inuvik from Hay River via Northern Transportation Company Limited (NTCL) or trucked to Inuvik on the Dempster Highway. This is a less expensive way to transport canoes than flying them, but requires more organization and time. Canoes can also be rented in Inuvik.

RIVER NOTES: The Anderson River is a very remote route offering an incredible variety of scenery and wildlife. This is not a river for paddlers seeking a wild whitewater experience, although there are major rapids along the way. By allowing more than 3 weeks to complete the trip, paddlers will have ample opportunity to hike, take photos, fish and view wildlife.

Although the trip begins in a semi-forested area at Colville Lake, the land beyond the river's edge for the last part of the route is tundra. A short hike to virtually any vantage point along the river provides paddlers with a spectacular panorama. Wildlife, especially caribou, are plentiful and can be seen right along the river's edge.

Paddlers should be prepared for some poor weather, especially near the Arctic coast. High winds and cold temperatures can impede progress. This is a very remote river, so canoeists must be well versed in wilderness camping skills and river paddling. The Anderson River offers an excellent all-round wilderness experience.

Anderson River

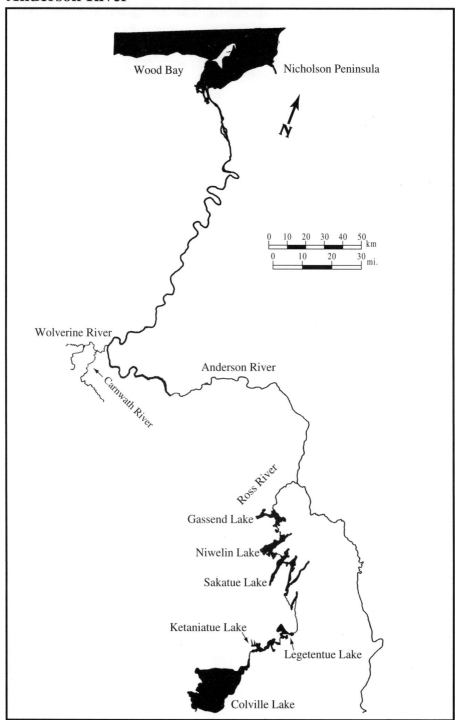

Wood Bay

Nicholson Peninsula

N

0 10 20 30 40 50 km

0   10   20   30 mi.

Wolverine River

Carnwath River

Anderson River

Ross River

Gassend Lake

Niwelin Lake

Sakatue Lake

Ketaniatue Lake

Legetentue Lake

Colville Lake

GEOGRAPHY: Most of the route of the Anderson River passes through a geological structure called the Anderson Plain. This is part of the larger Interior Platform which extends northward from the Prairie Provinces. It is generally low, hilly topography marked by numerous lakes and streams. Along the upper portions of the river limestone layers and ledges form rapids and canyons. Pleistocene glaciers covered the entire route at one time, leaving behind moraines, eskers and other glacial deposits.

The final 50 km (31 miles) of the river passes through the Arctic Coastal Plains or Arctic Continental Shelf. This permafrost landscape is characterized by ice-wedge polygons and pingos. The ground is generally stone-free clay loam and much of the surface is covered with one to three metres of peat.

CLIMATE: The Anderson River passes through two distinct regional climatic zones, the Continental Subarctic zone and the Arctic Coastal zone. The Subarctic region, which covers the first two thirds of the trip, is characterized by long, cold winters followed by fairly warm, sunny summers. The mean temperature in July is about 15°C (59°F) with little variation throughout the day because of the 24 hours of sunlight.

The Arctic Coastal Plain climate, experienced near the end of the trip, is much colder, with the mean July temperature ranging from 7°C to 10°C (45°F to 50°F). Cloud, rain, snow and high winds are not uncommon, especially near the coast. Good rain gear, parkas, tents and warm sleeping bags are a must.

FLORA: The Anderson River begins in the transitional vegetation zone called the taiga, between the true boreal forest and the open tundra. The taiga is characterized by scattered spruce forest with many open patches. Travelling northward, the trees thin out until most of the land beyond the river valley is tundra. Cranberries, blueberries, labrador tea, dwarf birch, moss and lichen are plentiful. Driftwood for campfires is usually available along the shores right to the Arctic coast.

FAUNA: The variety and abundance of wildlife is perhaps the best reason for canoeing the Anderson. Caribou from the Bluenose herd migrate through the area in August and hundreds or even thousands of the animals can often be seen along the river or crossing it.

The Anderson is also prime grizzly bear habitat. Grizzlies are the one species of wildlife that most campers and paddlers would just as soon not see. Some groups paddling the river have seen anywhere from 4 to 10 bears on a three week trip. Particular care should be taken to keep camps clean. The vegetation along the riverbank seems to be ideal for grizzlies and travellers should be constantly alert, especially when hiking through willows or other treed areas. An excellent publication called "Safety in Bear Country" is offered free of charge by the Dept. of Renewable Resources, Government of the NWT.

Birds also abound along the river. Often-sighted species include peregrine and gyrfalcons, eagles, geese, swans, ducks, shorebirds, loons and songbirds. Make sure to bring your field guide to North American birds on this trip.

Wolves are common along the river, generally in association with caribou herds. Muskoxen are plentiful east of the river and marten and fox are frequently seen.

As you approach the coast, seals are occasionally encountered. One party reported seeing a seal two days upstream from the mouth of the river. They are very curious and will approach a boat if given the chance.

Fishing is good along the entire route. Lake trout are the dominant species at the beginning of the trip. Grayling and "connies" or inconnu can be caught further down the river. Inconnu are very rich, silver fish which can grow to over 15 kg (33 pounds) in weight.

HUMAN HISTORY: The Anderson River has been used historically by both the Inuit and Dene. A number of Inuit archaeological sites have been discovered along the Arctic Coastal Plain near the Anderson River. The earliest known sites date back to around 1350 A.D. Inuit habitation is actually likely to have come much earlier with the Paleo-Eskimo migration from Alaska and Siberia around 2500 B.C. Most of the Anderson River Inuit sites were left by the Thule cultures which migrated to the Canadian Arctic from Alaska from around 1100 A.D. to 1400 A.D. These people were very advanced in dealing with the harsh Arctic conditions and used skin boats like the kayak for summer travel and dog teams in the winter.

Mary McCreadie

The Anderson River

Little is known about the very early North American Indian history of the area. Among the first to inhabit the upper reaches of the Anderson were the Hareskin Dene, whose descendants live today at Colville Lake. When the first Europeans arrived in the area, there were approximately 1000 Hareskins living there.

Naturalist-explorer Roderick MacFarlane was one of the first Europeans to explore the Anderson River Valley. In 1857, while manager of the Hudson's Bay Company post at Fort Good Hope on the Mackenzie River, he travelled to the Anderson, known then as the Begh-ula, by way of the Iroquois and Carnwath rivers. He encountered a group of

Inuit hunters who forced him and his crew to abandon their canoes and return on foot to the "Forks", where the Carnwath and Anderson Rivers meet. From there, MacFarlane and his party made their way to Colville Lake in a makeshift canoe.

In 1861, the Hudson's Bay Company established a post about 50 km (31 miles) downstream from the Forks on the east side of the river. It was named Fort Anderson after James Anderson who was a District Supervisor at the time. Roderick MacFarland was in charge of Fort Anderson from 1861 to 1865. The post was closed in that year because of a scarlet fever epidemic which wiped out a good part of the population of the area. Only a few charred axe-hewn timbers remain today to mark the site.

Catholic missionary Father Emile Petitot visited many of the Inuit and Dene camps in the area between 1864 and 1878. He was very interested in the cultures of the aboriginal people and from his observations produced a monograph documenting the customs and lifestyle of the Hareskin.

Well-known explorer Vilhjamur Stefansson also made a number of trips in the area between 1908 and 1912, and the next year wrote a book describing the lifestyle of the people he encountered.

About 20 white trappers lived and worked in the region during the first part of the century, but the last of them moved to Aklavik in 1956. A whaler started building a cabin at Krekovick Landing in the 1960's to establish a trading post there, but unfortunately he drowned before completing it. Today, the cabin is occupied in the summer by a biologist for the Canadian Wildlife Service.

There are few people living between Colville Lake and Nicholson Point now, although there are still cabins which are obviously in use for part of the year.

RIVER PROFILE: Paddlers beginning their trip at the community of Colville Lake must paddle approximately 42 km (26 miles), heading east and then north, to reach the outlet of the lake. Caution must be used on the lake because of the possibility of sudden, heavy winds. At the outlet, Colville Lake Lodge maintains two cabins and facilities where overnight accommodations are available. A tall, bare ridge called Bidzi Aui, "Place Where the Bull Caribou Go", dominates the horizon to the west of the lake.

From the outlet, paddlers follow a fast stream with a number of runnable rapids (if water levels are high enough). Within 5 km (3 miles), the stream enters a small lake called Ketaniatue, meaning "The Narrows Lake". The lake is constricted in the middle by a narrow channel.

After Ketaniatue, a 4 km (2 mile) stream of rocky, but runnable, rapids drops into Lake Lugetentue or "Frozen Fish Lake". The Dene often camped near the outlet of this lake near a small cemetery site. From here, the stream runs north through fast riffles before entering a series of small lakes – Sokatue, Niwelin and Gassend Lakes. Cabins from the old Dene village of Soka can be seen just north of the river between Sokatue and Niwelin Lakes. The rapids/falls between Niwelin and Gassend should be portaged. Both of these lakes have sandy beach campsites.

From Gassend Lake, paddlers follow the Ross River for about 25 km (15 miles) to reach the Anderson River. The rapids along this river are runnable, depending on water levels.

The water level at this point on the Anderson will determine the pace for the remainder of the trip. At high water, the river is fast-moving with high standing waves and rapids which may require frequent portaging. At low water, portaging might also be necessary to negotiate shallows, exposed rocks and ledges.

The following sections of the river are notable either because they should be paddled with care or because they are obvious landmarks.

FALCON CANYON – Starts at 68° 18′ latitude and 126° longitude. This is a very scenic canyon about 8 km (5 miles) long.

AIR WEAVE CANYON – Starts at 68° 30′ latitude and 126° longitude. A smaller canyon about 3 km (2 miles) long.

LIMESTONE STEPS – Starts at 68° 32′ latitude and 127° longitude. A series of ledges, rapids and waterfalls that MUST BE PORTAGED. This is the longest portage of the trip. It is located on river left and stretches for just less than one kilometre.

FLATROCK RAPIDS – Begins just downstream from the Limestone Steps. This section is very fast and needs scouting. It can either be paddled or easily portaged.

JUNIPER RAPIDS – Starts at 68° 21′ latitude and 127° 50′ longitude. These are actually several sets of rapids formed from limestone ledges. These rapids are the last whitewater on the trip. Look for abundant fossils near the rapids.

CARNWATH RIVER – This is the first large river to enter the Anderson. From this point, the Anderson swings abruptly to the north. The water downstream from the Carnwath tends to be more silty. During high water, the discharge from the Carnwath makes it difficult to find good campsites for quite a distance downstream. Old Fort Anderson is located about a day's paddle from the mouth of the Carnwath.

There are many areas of interest between the Carnwath River and Nicholson Point. Any of the valleys dropping into the Anderson offer good hiking opportunities. High points along the river provide an excellent overview of the Anderson Valley. This is particularly true as the river passes through the Anderson Delta. As the river nears the ocean, strong headwinds can severely impede paddling. Canoeists may find that they have to paddle in the evening to avoid them.

NICHOLSON POINT – The map shows that Nicholson Point is connected to the mainland. This is not the case except perhaps when the sea is extremely low. Crossing to Nicholson Point can be very dangerous because of the high winds that are common in the area. Paddlers are well advised to be picked up at Krekovick Landing or elsewhere along the east shore of Wood Bay.

MAPS REQUIRED:
(1:250,000) Aubrey Lake 96 M
             Lac Maunoir 96 N
             Simpson Lake 97 B
             Crossley Lakes 107 A
             Stanton 107 D
For those who plan to paddle to Inuvik, these additional maps are necessary.
             Mackenzie Delta 107 C
             Aklavik 107 B

AVERAGE GRADIENT: The average gradient from Colville Lake to the Arctic Ocean is 0.41 metres per kilometre (2.2 feet per mile).

HYDROGRAPH: Anderson River below Carnwath River, 1969 – 1988

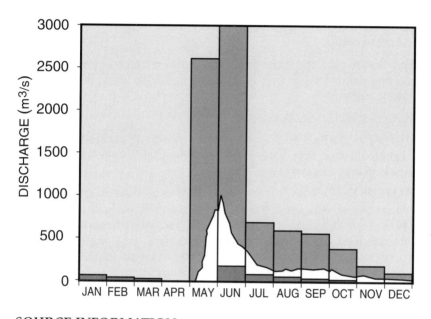

SOURCE INFORMATION:
1. Proescholdt, Kevin: The Anderson River.
2. Northwest Territories River Profiles: The Anderson River.
3. Wideman, Miriam: Personal Communication.

CUMULATIVE DISTANCE:

Location	Kilometres	Miles
Community of Colville Lake	0	0
Colville Lake Outlet	42	26
Niwelin Lake Inlet	146	91
Gassend Lake Outlet	177	111
Ross and Anderson Rivers Confluence	202	126
Carnwath and Anderson Rivers Confluence	407	254
Mouth of Anderson River	638	399
Nicholson Point Air Strip	679	424

BACK RIVER

TOTAL DISTANCE: Aylmer Lake to Chantrey Inlet: 1077 km (673 miles).

DURATION OF TRIP: Approximately 6 weeks from Aylmer Lake to Chantrey Inlet on the Arctic coast.

START: Both Sussex Lake, the actual headwaters of the river, and Aylmer Lake are common starting points for this trip. Numerous other lakes along the Back offer alternate starting points.

FINISH: Chantrey Inlet on the Arctic coast.

ACCESSIBILITY: The Back River can only be reached by air charter. Sandhill Bay on Aylmer Lake is approximately 368 km (230 miles) from Yellowknife. Paddlers must arrange for pick up from Chantrey Inlet.

RIVER NOTES: The Back River flows swiftly from its headwaters at Sussex Lake to Chantrey Inlet on the Arctic coast. It is the longest river in Canada situated entirely within the Barrenlands. Although it begins as a small and not particularly impressive stream, by the time it leaves Muskox Lake it swells considerably. During its course, the Back drops over numerous falls and more than 80 sets of rapids. In addition to this, there are enormous lakes to be navigated and several long portages.

The landscape varies from rugged and forbidding rock to gentle, rolling hills and long, undulating sand eskers. Caribou from the Beverley-Kaminuriak herd are usually numerous along the river and there is a good possibility that paddlers will see groups numbering in the thousands.

Because of the length and isolation of the river, and the amount of demanding whitewater, some of it unmarked on maps, many experienced paddlers consider the Back to be the most challenging river in the NWT. Canoeists attempting the Back should be very experienced whitewater paddlers and wilderness campers. The Back River is no place to learn the ropes. Lots of time should be added onto a pickup schedule to account for days spent windbound. Spray decks are recommended for whitewater sections. Gas stoves are essential for cooking.

GEOGRAPHY: From its source at Sussex Lake, the Back River flows entirely through Barrenland topography. It is surrounded mainly by low, rolling hills and rocky knolls covered with tundra vegetation. The river banks alternate between sandy beaches and rugged, boulder strewn shores. Eskers, created from glacial deposits, frequently rise along the river. Impressive rapids are found where the river cuts through the hard granitic rock.

A series of large lakes is located in the lower reaches of the river. These lakes are frequently very windy and may also be plugged with ice, even in July. Aylmer and Muskox Lakes, nearer the headwaters, also share these characteristics.

CLIMATE: The weather along the Back River is extremely variable. High winds can create hazardous conditions very quickly, especially on the big lakes. Delays due to wind must be taken into consideration when scheduling pickup.

Summer temperatures in this region can be extreme. Daytime temperatures average around 10°C (50°F) in July and may drop to near freezing at night. Snow squalls are common at any time and by the end of July signs of fall are obvious. Rain is common, although not usually in huge quantities. Warm clothing, a parka, and a good sleeping bag are essential, as are good rain gear and a wind proof tent.

On the bright side, because of the Back's northerly position, paddlers will experience long summer days, even in August.

Break-up on the lakes usually happens in mid-July. It's a good idea to check with air charter companies before being dropped off to ensure that progress downstream is possible. Spring ice can be very dangerous and can cause long delays for paddlers.

FLORA: The tundra surrounding the Back River is generally covered with lichens, grasses and sedges. Although stunted spruce trees grow along the river valleys of this drainage basin there are few along the Back itself.

Because of the short growing season, most arctic wildflowers are perennials. Species such as fireweed, Arctic poppy and Lapland rhododendron add spectacular colour to the land during their brief growing season in July.

FAUNA: The Back River Valley is home to a variety of Barrenland animals. Caribou from the Beverly-Kaminuriak herd are common and groups of several thousand are regularly seen. Muskoxen are also common along the river, in groups or individually. Wolves, fox, wolverine and grizzly bears are frequently spotted.

Falcons and eagles nest in the high rocky outcrops and the rare yellow-billed loon nests along the shores. A wide variety of waterfowl, shorebirds and songbirds also thrive along the river. Fish are abundant, especially at the base of rapids, and paddlers can expect to supplement their diet with lake trout, whitefish, grayling and Arctic char.

HUMAN HISTORY: The Barrenlands of the Back River area were originally inhabited by two groups of Inuit, the Caribou and the Netsilik. While the Caribou Inuit travelled across the southern half of the Keewatin district hunting caribou for survival, the Netsilik originally camped along the Arctic Coast near the mouth of the Back. During the winter they hunted seals on the sea ice, moving inland during late summer along the Back to harvest Arctic Char. In the nineteenth and early twentieth centuries descendants of the Netsilik settled in three distinct groups. Near Pelly, Garry and Macdougall Lakes lived the Ualiarlit, or "the westerly ones". Farther downstream lived the Haningajormiut and nearer the river mouth at Lake Franklin lived the Utkuhigjalingmiut, or "dwellers of the soapstone place". Inuksuit and tent rings are all that remain today as evidence of their occupation. Paddlers are reminded not to disturb these sites and to leave all objects and artifacts where they are.

The Chipewyan Dene of Great Slave Lake, who travelled to this area, called the river Thlew-ee-choh-dezeth, or "Great Fish River". After George Back descended the river in 1834 it was known as "Back's Great Fish River". This was later shortened to the Back River.

In 1834, Back, with a crew of 10 men, set out to explore this little-known waterway in a two-ton wooden row boat. The original purpose of his journey was to find a lost British expedition. When the lost men turned up safely, Back decided to go ahead down

Back River

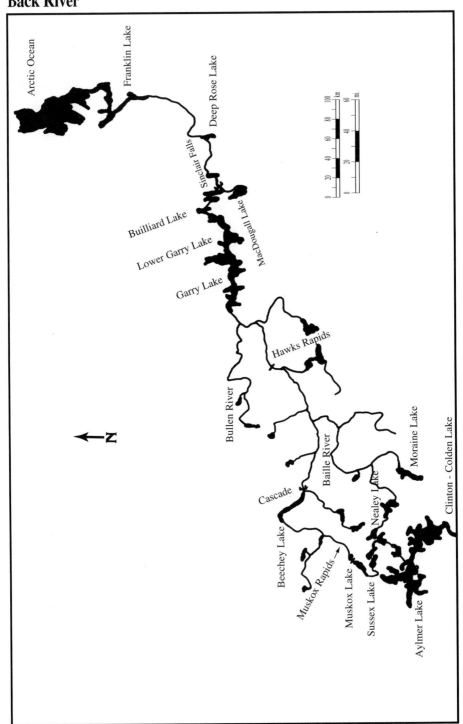

the river anyway and "map as much unknown territory as the season would allow." Akaitcho, the Dene chief who had guided Franklin to the Arctic Ocean in 1821, warned Back about the dangers of the river "which none of the present race of Indians had the least knowledge of." He openly voiced his fear that he would never see Back again. Akaitcho's fears were groundless. Back and his crew successfully navigated the river to its mouth in 31 days. After reaching the Arctic Ocean he mapped sections of the coastline before travelling the full length of the river again – this time upstream.

A second Back River expedition was organized in 1855 to search for clues to the fate of Sir John Franklin and his crew. James Anderson, chief factor of the Hudson's Bay Company, led this trip. No survivors of the Franklin expedition were found, although Anderson and his crew were told by some Inuit that they had seen some weak travellers a few years earlier. The expedition found some debris from Franklin's vessels and 5 shallow grave sites. The fate of Franklin's party remains a mystery.

Between 1948 and 1955, a Catholic mission was established on an island in Upper Garry Lake. Father Buliard O.M.I. and several nomadic Inuit families settled here in the only settlement ever established on the Back River. Father Buliard died mysteriously in 1956 and the mission was abandoned. The Inuit were relocated by the Government of Canada to the community of Baker Lake. The mission hut is still standing and in fairly good condition. It can be used as an emergency shelter. Today, the Back River has no permanent residents and is travelled only by canoeists and geological survey crews.

RIVER PROFILE: Sandhill Bay on Aylmer Lake and Sussex Lake, the actual headwaters of the river, are two common starting points for a Back River trip. Starting on Aylmer Lake requires a short portage over the height of land to the Back drainage system. An esker of coarse gravel-like sand separates Aylmer and Sussex Lakes. Even in July, these lakes may be choked with ice.

The headwaters of the river are rocky and shallow. Low water levels may make some wading and portaging necessary. After Lake 1105 paddlers encounter a long stretch of flat water paddling as far as Muskox Rapids at the outlet of Muskox Lake, another popular starting point for this trip. Ice can also be a problem on Muskox Lake. The surrounding countryside is rocky, with many cliffs and precipices. Muskox Lake forms the northern boundary of the Heywood Range which rises to heights of approximately 396 metres (1300 feet) on the left bank. Muskox Rapids can be portaged on river left.

Downstream from Muskox Rapids the river widens as it flows north and east. There are several sections of fast water and rapids in the stretch upstream from Malley Rapids. Many of these are unmarked on the maps, so paddlers should scout any water that looks questionable. It is 116 km (73 miles) from Aylmer Lake to Malley Rapids. Back describes these rapids as "a long and appalling rapids, full of rocks and large boulders; the sides hemmed in by a wall of ice and the current flying with the velocity and force of a torrent..." More recent paddlers have implied that his description may be a bit exaggerated. A short portage can be made along river left. A series of marked rapids follows about 6 km (4 miles) downstream. Care should be taken through all these rapids.

A set of rapids marks the inlet to Beechey Lake, 53 km (33 miles) downstream from Malley Rapids. A horseshoe bend sends the river in a southerly direction, forming the 50 km (31 mile) long Beechey Lake. When Back arrived here he was disappointed at the

Dave Nutter

The Back River

dramatic change in direction. He feared that the river led not to the Arctic Ocean, as expected, but to Hudson Bay. The 18 metre (60 foot) falls at the outlet of the lake can be avoided by a 3 km (1.5 mile) portage on river right.

The next 100 km (62 miles) from Beechey Lake to the confluence of the Back and Baillie Rivers has many rapids, some unmarked on topographic maps. Back described the river in this area as "a long line of rapids, which now appeared breaking their furious way through mounds and ranges of precipitous sand-hills of the most fantastic outline." Large caribou herds numbering thousands of animals are sometimes spotted along this stretch of river.

Sand bars, strong currents and rapids characterize the next 100 km (62 miles) to the Hawk Rapids. These rapids rush through a canyon of red granite cliffs. While they can usually be run close to shore, these rapids require very careful scouting. Back named them for three screaming hawks who "frightened from their aerie, were hovering high above the middle of the pass, gazing fixedly upon the first intruders on their solitude." Inuit campsites, marked by tent rings and inuksuit dot the tundra along this stretch of the river.

As the river approaches Pelly Lake the terrain becomes less sandy. Pelly is the first of several enormous lakes on the lower third of the river. These lakes mark a change in the character of the Back River. Until this point, the river has been relatively small and intimate. After the lakes, however, it swells into a much bigger river.

Pelly Lake, Upper Garry Lake, Garry Lake and Lower Garry Lake are "most embarrassing to the navigator", according to George Back. Huge bays, numerous islands, and a lack of definite landmarks make careful map reading a necessity. Add frequent high winds to the equation and paddling these lakes is, for many, the low point of the trip. These lakes represent 220 km (138 miles) of flatwater paddling. Father Buliard's cabin can be found on an island in Upper Garry Lake high above a sandy beach.

Rapids are found in the short river stretches between all of the lakes. The stretch between Buliard and Upper Macdougall Lakes is especially challenging and several of the rapids are not marked on the maps.

Rock Rapids at the outlet of Lower MacDougall Lake marks the beginning of an extensive section of major rapids and falls. While some of the rapids can be run, many must be portaged. Sinclair Falls, just downstream from Rock Rapids, must be portaged. Several sets of unshootable rapids between Rock Rapids and Sinclair Falls can be avoided by making a fairly long portage. It begins at the end of a long, skinny bay on river left, downstream from Rock Rapids, and upstream from a large island surrounded by yet more whitewater.

The river continues to grow in size and power. Escape Rapids, Sandhill Rapids and Wolf Rapids all present obstacles to the paddler and must be portaged, either in part or completely. Back's description of this part of the river sets the tone: "The current, always swift, now rushed on still faster and soon became a line of heavy rapids, which more than once made me tremble for our poor boat; for in many parts, not being able to land, we were compelled to pull hard to keep her under command, and thus flew past rocks and other dangers with a velocity that seemed to forebode some desperate termination." Downstream from these rapids the Back heads north, widens and passes through several more rapids and fast sections. The surrounding terrain becomes more rugged and mountainous. The Meadowbank River and Mount Meadowbank, both on river right, are two of the more obvious landmarks. A cabin, maintained by the Water Survey of Canada is located on river left downstream from Mount Meadowbank. High hills and rocky outcrops surround the river as it continues to widen.

There is little whitewater now, except for Whirlpool Rapids, which mark the inlet to Franklin Lake. From Franklin Lake there are only a few more sets of rapids before Cockburn Bay on the Arctic coast. Paddlers should arrange to be picked up here rather than venturing any further into Chantrey Inlet.

MAPS REQUIRED: (read maps from left to right)

(1:250,000)		
	Aylmer Lake 76-C	Healey Lake 76-B
	Beechey Lake 76-G	Duggan Lake 76-H
	Jervoise Lake 66-E	Pelly Lake 66-F
	Deep Rose Lake 66-G	Joe Lake 66-J
	Amer Lake 66-H	Montresor River 66-I
	Mistake River 56-L	Sherman Basin 66-P
	Lower Hayes River 56-M	

AVERAGE GRADIENT: The average gradient from Sussex Lake to Chantrey Inlet is 0.4 metres per kilometre (2 feet per mile).

HYDROGRAPH: Back River below Beechy Lake, 1965-1988

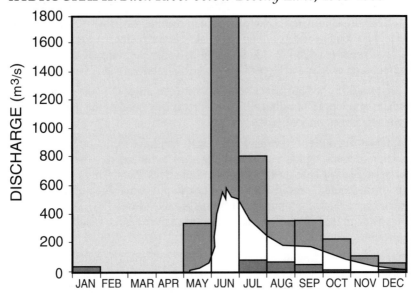

SOURCE INFORMATION:

1. Oleson, Kristen: Personal communication.
2. Perkins, Robert: Personal communication.
3. Back, Captain George: *Narrative of the Arctic Land Expedition to the Mouth of the Great Fish River and Along the Shores of the Arctic Ocean in the Years 1833, 1834 and 1835.* M.G. Hurtig Ltd., Edmonton, 1970.
4. Perkins, Robert: *Into the Great Solitude. An Arctic Journey.* Henry Holt and Company, New York, 1991.
5. Pelly, David F.: *Expedition, An Arctic Journey Through History on George Back's River.* Betelgeuse Books, Toronto, 1981.
6. Perkins, Robert: Video, *Into the Great Solitude.*

CUMULATIVE DISTANCE:

Location	Kilometres	Miles
Sussex Lake	0	0
Outlet Muskox Lake	42	26
Malley Rapids	109	68
Outlet Beechey Lake	220	138
Hawk Rapids	420	263
Outlet Pelly Lake	565	353
Outlet Lower Garry Lake	663	414
Rock Rapids (Outlet Lower Macdougall Lake)	730	456
Escape Rapids	774	484
Confluence Meadowbank River	830	519
Whirlpool Rapids	964	603
NW entrance to Cockburn Bay	1077	673

BEAULIEU RIVER

TOTAL DISTANCE:

A. Spencer Lake to Reid Lake campground: 180 km (113 miles).

B. Spencer Lake to Great Slave Lake: 197 km (122 miles).

DURATION OF TRIP: 10 to 14 days for either trip.

START: There are dozens of possible starting points for the Beaulieu River. This report starts at Spencer Lake.

FINISH:

A. Reid Lake campground on the Cameron River at km 64 (mile 40) of the Ingraham Trail.

B. Great Slave Lake at Beaulieu Bay on the Hearne Channel.

ACCESSIBILITY: Spencer Lake is 128 kilometres (80 air miles) from Yellowknife by air charter. Reid Lake is 64 km (40 miles) from Yellowknife along the Ingraham Trail (Highway 4).

Beaulieu Bay is 77 air kilometres (48 miles) from Yellowknife by air charter. Pickup can also be arranged from Yellowknife by motor boat. If you're really keen, it's only about a 100 km (66 mile) paddle to Yellowknife on Great Slave Lake.

RIVER NOTES: The Beaulieu River is a challenging white water route, requiring considerable paddling skill and wilderness camping experience. Although not a large river, it offers variety – rapids, falls, scenic lakes, good fishing and easy accessibility. Lots of portaging is required but most of the trails are easy to find and not too difficult.

The large lakes on the route can present difficulties because of the ever-present threat of high winds. Stick close to shore when possible. Campsites are most readily found along the fast flowing sections of the river. The shorelines along the slow moving sections are boggy, making campsites harder to find.

Although the actual headwaters of the river are just above the tree line, the trip described in this report takes place entirely in the boreal forest.

GEOGRAPHY: The Beaulieu runs through the rocky outcrops and countless lakes of the Canadian Shield. The large lakes are deep and clear and the river itself is relatively sediment-free. The rugged beauty of the area makes the Beaulieu a rewarding trip.

CLIMATE: Spring breakup on the Beaulieu River generally happens in May, however most of the larger lakes don't break up until June. Summers in the area are usually warm and dry. Daytime temperatures average around 20°C (70°F), cooling off at night. In June and July, there is never complete darkness, just twilight stretching out for around 4 hours before becoming bright again. This allows for lots of midnight activity!

Although not a rainy region, rain gear is still a must as is warm clothing, and a good sleeping bag and tent. Don't forget the bug dope!

FLORA: The forests in the area are dominated by spruce and birch, which get larger as the river moves south. A wide variety of boreal plant life can be found, including many species of berries and edible plants. A good guide to northern boreal plant life would be an asset.

FAUNA: Although the Bathurst caribou herd winters in the forest, they are found on the tundra in the summer. Moose, beaver, muskrat, black bear, and otter are quite common, and shy species like wolf and lynx are sometimes spotted by careful observers. Eagles, loons, waterfowl and dozens of species of songbirds are plentiful.

Fishing is good, with lake trout being common in the large, deep lakes. Grayling and whitefish can be caught on the river, and pike are common in shallow water.

HUMAN HISTORY: The Beaulieu River is one of the traditional routes inland from Great Slave Lake that has been used by the Dene for thousands of years. Chipewyan, Dogrib, and Yellowknife Dene all used this route on their way to the rich caribou hunting grounds on the barrenlands.

It is possible that the Beaulieu River is the route that Samuel Hearne followed to Great Slave Lake in the winter of 1771. He and his Chipewyan guide Matonabee were on their way back to Hudson Bay from the Coppermine River.

The river is named after Francois King Beaulieu, a Métis trader and chieftain from Fort Resolution. Beaulieu was one of Franklin's guides on his inland trip to Great Bear Lake. Today, the area is used in the winter by trappers from the Yellowknife area.

RIVER PROFILE: The Beaulieu River leaves Spencer Lake at the southeast corner. The first of two sets of rapids is encountered almost immediately. Downstream of the next lake, the river turns east and enters rapids which are followed by a small falls that can be portaged on river left. From here to the 1200 ft contour line, a series of rapids and ledges are encountered, many of which are not marked on the map. The lake below the contour line is reached after a long portage over the rocks. At the outlet of this lake, there is a ledge marked as a rapid which can be portaged on river left. The river valley widens at this point and the next 22 km (14 miles) to Sunset Lake flows through a series of small lakes and rapids. The river exits Sunset Lake from the southeast arm and immediately swings west. The next 12 km (8 miles) to Lake 957 contain many sets of rapids, especially in the last kilometre. Each set has at least one ledge and some of them must be portaged.

The outlet of Lake 957 is at its southwest corner. At first the river is low and marshy, however rapids soon appear. The first portage is on river right around a rapid and falls. The second is across an island to get around a ledge. The next portage is a well-marked trail on river right around a long chute.

The outlet from Turnback Lake is located on its southern shore. There is a waterfall here which must be portaged. The river from Turnback to Tumpline Lake is generally flat and slow moving. About halfway along this stretch, there is a short section of class 2 or 3 rapids which can usually be run on river left without much difficulty.

The upper and lower thirds of the run from Tumpline to Cleft Lake are similar to the calm stretches upstream of Tumpline. However, the middle 4 km (2.5 miles) is

Beaulieu River

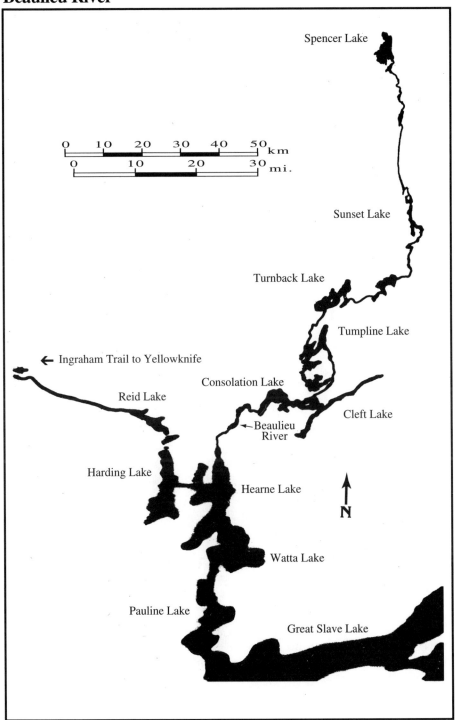

Spencer Lake

Sunset Lake

Turnback Lake

Tumpline Lake

← Ingraham Trail to Yellowknife

Consolation Lake

Reid Lake

Cleft Lake

← Beaulieu River

Harding Lake

Hearne Lake

N

Watta Lake

Pauline Lake

Great Slave Lake

0   10   20   30   40   50 km

0   10   20   30 mi.

characterized by three stretches of almost continuous class 2 and 3 rapids, broken up by two small pools. The rapids after the second pool can be scouted from a lookout on river left. There is an excellent campsite on the left shore just upstream of the island where the rapids end.

The next 4 km (2.5 miles) to Cleft Lake are slow-moving, however the river tumbles into Cleft Lake over a 1.5 metre (5 foot) high ledge. There is an excellent campsite on the portage on river left. The next 22 km (14 miles) traverse Cleft Lake and the narrow channel between it and Consolation Lake. There are several cabins on Consolation and one on Cleft, and lots of good campsites.

From the outlet of Consolation Lake, the next 3 km (2 miles) are broken by 4 major drops. The first is a long, cascading falls of 25 metres (82 feet). There is a good portage trail on river left. The next 3 rapids/falls can be portaged in a group on a trail on river right. The beginning of this 1 km trail is often submerged during high water levels.

After another short, calm stretch there is a dangerous chute and falls combination which can be portaged on river left. Following a quiet paddle of perhaps 4 km (2.5 miles), there is a 500 metre portage on river right around 3 ledges.

The Beaulieu River – Turnback Lake

The next 3.5 km (2 mile) stretch of calm water ends in class 4 rapids, which can be portaged on river left. A further 300 metres downstream is another major rapid which drops 3 metres (10 feet). This can be portaged on river right. This entire section can be avoided by taking a good 1.5 km (1 mile) trail which cuts inland on river right just above the first rapids.

Following another 500 metres of quiet water, there is a 20 metre (66 foot) falls which is bypassed on a good trail on river right. From here to Hearne Lake is an easy paddle. The river is flat and slow-moving with a shortage of good campsites.

Hearne Lake is a large lake prone to strong winds which can make progress difficult. Paddlers heading to Reid Lake should follow the west shore of Hearne Lake, looking for a large bay with a narrow opening situated about 8 km (5 miles) down the lake. From this bay, follow a small creek that heads north into a tiny lake. From here, the trail, an old "cat train" road, should be easy to find. It takes several hours of portaging and paddling through swamp and muskeg to arrive at the long, narrow east arm of Harding Lake.

Harding is another big lake on which north winds can severely hamper progress. The portage route to Reid Lake is located at the north end of the lake, beside a fishing lodge. This portage is a continuation of the winter road from Hearne Lake and again runs through a series of small lakes. The Territorial Government campground on Reid Lake is located on the north shore. From here, paddlers can drive to Yellowknife.

Paddlers who are continuing down the Beaulieu to Great Slave Lake will find it is better to stay to the east or left-hand shore of Hearne Lake. It is a 12 km (7 mile) paddle to the bay leading to Watta Lake. Strong south winds can make this a long paddle.

Between Hearne and Watta Lakes is a 10 metre (33 foot) waterfall. This is quickly followed by a split in the river. The left channel is navigable in low water. At this point, there is a fishing lodge on river left. This entire stretch can be bypassed by an excellent trail on river right. Watta is another big, deep lake, known for its excellent lake trout. It is a 12 km (7 mile) paddle across Watta Lake to the outlet of the river.

The 19 km (12 mile) stretch from Watta to Pauline Lake is characterized by flat stretches of water broken by occasional rapids and ledges. Depending on water levels, many of these rapids can be run. Where needed, portages are well marked. This section of the river is more lush than upstream, with much larger trees. Pauline Lake is a smaller lake, with several good campsites. The best is at the outlet of the lake beside an unnavigable waterfall. The portage and campsite are on river right.

Downstream from Pauline Lake are several sets of rapids and a long, cascading falls which drops about 15 metres (50 feet) over a distance of 50 metres (164 feet). Again, in this section of the river the portages are easy to find and follow.

At its mouth, the Beaulieu empties into a large, shallow bay, protected from the main part of Great Slave Lake. It is probably too shallow for a float plane, so pickup is best arranged at the narrow channel leading into the main lake or on one of the islands in front of the bay. A trapper's cabin can be found on the right shore at the narrows.

MAPS REQUIRED:
(1:250,000)   Upper Carp Lake 85 P
              Hearne Lake 85 I
              Yellowknife 85 J

AVERAGE GRADIENT: Between Spencer Lake and Hearne Lake, the average gradient is 1.3 metres per kilometre (7 feet per mile).

HYDROGRAPH: According to the Water Survey Office of Canada in Yellowknife, no hydrographs have been recorded on the Beaulieu River.

SOURCE INFORMATION:
1. Bayly, John: Trip Report, 1974.
2. Nutter, Dave: Trip Report, 1985.
3. Hans, Brenda: Trip Report, 1986.

CUMULATIVE DISTANCES:

Location	Kilometres	Miles
Spencer Lake Outlet	0	0
Sunset Lake Outlet	42	27
Turnback Lake Outlet	77	48
Hearne Lake Inlet	142	88
Watta Lake Outlet	170	106
Great Slave Lake	197	122
Reid Lake Campground	180	113

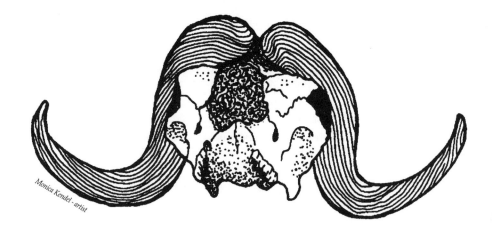

Monica Kendel - artist

BURNSIDE and MARA RIVERS

TOTAL DISTANCE:
A: Burnside River: Contwoyto Lake to Bathurst Inlet – 258 kilometres (161 miles)
B: Mara and Burnside Rivers: Nose Lake to Bathurst Inlet – 266 kilometres (166 miles)

DURATION OF TRIP:
A: 10 to 14 days
B: 8 to 10 days

START:
A: Contwoyto or Kathawachaga Lake
B: Nose Lake

FINISH: Bathurst Inlet

ACCESSIBILITY: Accessible by float plane from Yellowknife. Contwoyto Lake is 430 km (269 miles) from Yellowknife. Yellowknife can be reached by the Mackenzie Highway or by flights from Edmonton and Winnipeg. Return from Bathurst Inlet by air charter is 575 km. Canoe rental and charter packages are available through Bathurst Inlet Lodge (see Appendix E).

RIVER NOTES: Both the Burnside and Mara Rivers are classic tundra rivers flowing into the Arctic Ocean. Isolated and rugged, they both offer challenging whitewater, dramatic scenery and abundant wildlife. Canoeists travelling either river should have advanced paddling skills and lots of wilderness camping experience. This is no place to learn the ropes. Spray covers for open canoes are recommended.

As with most northern rivers, variable water levels greatly affect the character of both rivers and the location and size of rapids. The Mara in particular is very difficult to paddle once water levels drop in the late summer. Paddlers should be aware that many rapids are not marked on the maps and scouting is imperative.

Hazards aside, both rivers offer many rewards. The landscape is dramatic with rolling tundra punctuated by narrow canyons, waterfalls and sandy beaches. There are lots of good hiking opportunities and wildlife is plentiful. Caribou and muskoxen in particular are abundant.

The Burnside enters the ocean near the tiny community of Bathurst Inlet. Groups can arrange to stay at Bathurst Inlet Lodge or can be picked up by chartered float plane anywhere in the vicinity.

GEOGRAPHY: The Burnside originates at Contwoyto Lake and the Mara at Nose Lake. Both rivers flow across the Contwoyto Plateau which rises out of the Precambrian Shield. This plateau has an average elevation of 460 metres and is characterized by granite boulder till mixed with sand. Eskers are very common features on this rolling landscape. The hills above the river valleys provide impressive views of the surrounding countryside.

Near the Arctic Ocean the Burnside enters the Wilberforce Hills region, characterized by deep river valleys, spectacular cliffs and canyons. This is especially evident along the final few kilometres of the river.

Mara/Burnside

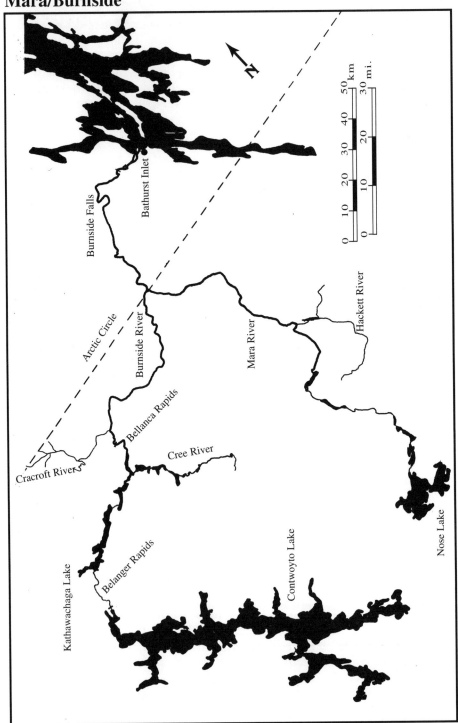

CLIMATE: One of the most important factors influencing any canoe trip is the weather. Nowhere is this more true than on the barrenlands. There the weather can change very quickly and high winds whipping across hundreds of miles of flat landscape can create extremely dangerous paddling conditions in a very short time. This is especially true on large lakes like Contwoyto and Kathawachaga. Winds are also funnelled along the river valley causing poor travelling conditions. Because of this, it's always a good idea to add a few extra days onto your trip schedule.

Summer weather in the area may vary from intense, round-the-clock hot sun to foggy, windy, cool days, made even better by rain and sleet and even snow. July temperatures average about 10°C (50°F) and often drop to near freezing at night. Rainfall over the summer months averages a mere 12 cm. The ice on Contwoyto Lake usually breaks up around mid-July although this varies from year to year.

Canoeists are well advised to bring good rain gear, wind resistant tents and a 3 season sleeping bag. Warm clothing and a parka are also a good idea.

FLORA: Both rivers flow entirely through the tundra. Because this area is in a zone of continuous permafrost the tallest plants, dwarf willow and alder, are rarely more than a metre high. Several varieties of lichen and moss carpet the ground along with species of wildflowers and berries. Because of the scarcity of wood, canoeists are advised to bring along a gas stove for cooking.

FAUNA: Muskoxen and caribou are the two animals most commonly seen along both the Burnside and the Mara. The Bathurst caribou herd, which numbers over 300,000 animals, crosses the river on its way to and from its calving grounds. Huge numbers of caribou often cross between Contwoyto and Kathawachaga Lakes in July and early August. Wolves, which follow the herd, may be seen along the river and there are many good denning sites in the area.

Muskoxen can be seen along the length of both rivers, appearing individually or in groups of up to 30. Photographers can get quite close, but should keep in mind that muskoxen will sometimes charge and can cause serious injury.

Grizzly bears are also seen along the river, so caution is advised when hiking and camping. The Department of Renewable Resources in Yellowknife has excellent pamphlets on camping in bear country which it gives out free of charge.

Foxes, Arctic hare, Arctic ground squirrels (sik sik) and several other small mammals are also common.

In the Wilberforce Hills region, there are many birds of prey, notably gyr and peregrine falcons. These magnificent birds make their nests on rocky cliffs.

Arctic char, lake trout, Arctic grayling and whitefish are found both in the rivers and in the big lakes.

HUMAN HISTORY: The Burnside River area has been well used by the Inuit for a long time. Their passage through the area is marked by the numerous archaeological sites along the river. Tent rings and graves can be seen at several locations. The most important known site is on the tiny island of Nadlak, located just downstream from Kathawachaga Lake. The name in Inuktitut means, "place where the deer cross". Here, in the summers of 1985 and 1986, the National Museum of Civilization unearthed more than 40,000 segments of caribou antlers that formed the framework for several winter homes used by a semi-permanent group of Copper Inuit. These people were driven south from the Arctic Ocean during the mini ice age that took place between the early 1500's and the 1800's. Needles and tools more common to the Dene people who lived south of the tree line were also found at the site, leading archaeologists to conclude that the Inuit and Dene had some sort of trading system in place. After the cold spell, it is believed that the Inuit returned to Bathurst Inlet. Today there are only about 25 people living in the community of Bathurst Inlet and another 60 at Bay Chimo, 100 kilometres to the north.

Sir John Franklin explored the area in 1821-22. With a party of 20 men, he travelled along the river, naming the Bellanca and Belanger rapids after two men in his crew. It wasn't until 1920 that a permanent settlement was established at Bathurst Inlet. In that year, the explorer Charles Klengenburg wintered his crew and schooner at the Inlet. Fourteen years later the Hudson's Bay Company established a trading post there. However, the community actually grew around a mineral exploration site established in 1929. In 1964, the HBC pulled out of Bathurst Inlet and today the old trading post is the site of Bathurst Inlet Lodge.

The Inuit families living in Bathurst Inlet today have chosen an isolated and traditional way of life. However, in the summer, the community in conjunction with a family from Yellowknife operates Bathurst Inlet Lodge. This lodge is well known world wide as a naturalist's retreat and offers lodgings and guided exploration of the surrounding area, including outfitting packages on the Burnside River.

RIVER PROFILE: **A. CONTWOYTO LAKE TO BATHURST INLET:** The headwaters of the Burnside River are at Contwoyto Lake. By beginning a trip at the north end of the lake near the river outlet, paddlers can avoid a long and often hazardous paddle across the frequently windswept lake.

The scenery around Contwoyto is typically barren with rolling hills and eskers. From Contwoyto to Kathawachaga Lake, 22.5 km (14 miles) downstream, the river is a continuous series of rapids. The current is swift in this stretch, with an average gradient of 2.2 metres per kilometre (11.5 ft. per mile). Marked rapids are mostly class 2, interspersed with sections of class 3 water and connected by swiftly-flowing class 1. The Belanger Rapids, named after a member of Franklin's crew who nearly perished in the cold water, are located about 4.8 km (3 miles) downstream of Contwoyto and require careful scouting.

Although usually runnable, all rapids in this stretch require careful scouting and there are several unmarked sets. Particularly worth watching for is an unmarked set just beyond the islands at 66° 10' N, 111° 12' W, with two nasty holes at the bottom. The last marked set is about a mile upstream of Kathawachaga Lake.

Kathawachaga Lake is 395 metres (1297 feet) above sea level in the middle of a gently rolling plain spotted with rocky hills. There is an excellent camp site on a sandy beach near the inlet to the lake. A nearby archaeological site contains traces of an ancient Inuit camp. There are also many superb fishing holes in the area.

Kathawachaga is another popular starting point for the Burnside River trip. Although it is smaller than Contwoyto and protected by surrounding hills, wind can still be a problem. A few kilometres downstream from the lake is a small island called Nadlak, which is an important archaeological site. Downstream from Nadlak, the river

Dave Nutter

The Burnside River

George Drought

Muskox on the Mara River

constricts and the current increases, forming challenging rapids, including some that may be class 3 or 4. The Bellanca Rapids is considered to be one of the most difficult on the river. It consists of a series of ledges as the river sweeps to the right. The water is deep and very swift with big holes and standing waves. The rapids can be run at certain water levels or can be lined and portaged on river left. There are plenty of superb campsites downstream from these rapids.

After the Bellanca Rapids, the river moves swiftly, offering class 2 whitewater as far as the boulder island which marks the confluence of the Cracoft and Burnside Rivers. Downstream from the island there is a major rapid which, depending on water levels, can either be run or lined on river right or portaged on river left.

At the 90 degree bend in the river, the landscape changes temporarily as the river valley deepens. Red rock cliffs ranging in height from 10 to 70 metres come right to the water's edge. Downstream the river widens and braids into many small, shallow channels, some of which are navigable. Paddlers will be aided by the swiftness of the current, which drops at a rate of 3 metres per km (15 feet per mile).

An archaeological site of Inuit tent rings is located where a small unnamed river flowing from the south (109° 27' N) joins the Burnside. From here to its confluence with the Mara, the Burnside slows down.

The landscape changes again at the confluence of the Mara and the Burnside. The rolling hills of glacial till remain but the river valley itself becomes much more pronounced. At this point the Burnside begins to drop sharply again and continues to have a steep gradient for the rest of the trip. About 16 km (10 miles) downstream from the Mara-Burnside confluence there is a Federal Water Survey recording station. Downstream from the station rough water begins again with many navigable but unmarked rapids, generally of class 2 or 3. Frequent high standing waves characterize this portion of the river. (*See note at end of River Profile p. 55.)

There is a proposed hydro-electric dam site at 66° N, 108° 34'W. From here to the portage at the falls, the river presents exciting and dangerous sections of whitewater. Many rapids are unmarked on the maps and scouting is recommended.

A 6 km (4 mile) portage is necessary around the red and white quartzite canyon housing the spectacular Burnside Falls. Don't miss the exit! It is on river left and was marked in 1985 by a huge inukshuk. Paddlers are advised to walk over the large hill staying on the high eskers and rock outcroppings rather than near the edge of the canyon. This is a long, difficult portage taking about 90 minutes to walk one way. The reward is a beautiful white sand beach at the end with a great view of two waterfalls. The current is extremely strong here and a canoe can easily be pulled into the pool below the falls.

From here it is a short paddle to Bathurst Inlet where paddlers can visit the lodge or be picked up by charter aircraft.

B: MARA RIVER – NOSE LAKE TO MARA/BURNSIDE CONFLU-
ENCE: This 266 km (166 mile) trip begins at Nose Lake and follows the Mara River to its junction with the Burnside. From there, it follows the Burnside to Bathurst Inlet. It is characterized by marked variations in landscape, ranging from barrenlands to

canyons. The Mara is considered more difficult than the Burnside and, because it is shallow, can only be paddled early in the season.

Nose Lake is situated high on the Contwoyto Plateau, 420 metres (1377 ft.) above sea level. The first 24 km (15 miles) of the river flow through flat, nearly uninterrupted barrenlands. The river is quite shallow in the narrow sections making the rapids hard to run because of submerged boulders.

The river is often over 1 km wide and is punctuated by rapids and narrows every few kilometres. The flatness of the countryside provides little protection from the wind. The first significant rapid occurs about 11.8 km (7.4 miles) downstream from Nose Lake. It has a small ledge and is best portaged on river right. Beyond this ledge there are two more rapids and a shoal requiring paddling through shallow water.

Roughly 25 km (16 miles) downstream from Nose Lake the river narrows and becomes a continuous rapid for several kilometres. The river valley becomes more pronounced, with steep walls coming to the water's edge. The first difficult rapid in this section occurs at kilometre 39 (mile 24.6) where the river suddenly drops over a two metre (6 ft) ledge. This ledge must be approached with great care as it is not marked on the map. There is a short portage on river left. A kilometre further downstream, another rapid is encountered with very fast, shallow water and many rocks. Paddlers should be wary as most of the rapid is concealed by a bend at its outset. This rapid is best lined or portaged.

The river volume increases at the confluence of a river, not named on the map, flowing in from the southwest at kilometre 43 (mile 27). The current here, if combined with strong headwinds, can make progress difficult. Because of poor drainage the land is quite marshy with lush vegetation.

After roughly 16 km (10 miles) of flatland, the river valley deepens again. The 40 km (25 miles) downstream from the junction of the Mara and Hackett Rivers offer some very challenging paddling. Many rapids are encountered and the current is swift as another unnamed river joins the Mara.

A small ledge is encountered at the bottom of the rapid at kilometre 123 (mile 77). While runnable, it requires care. At kilometre 146 (mile 91.4), a class 2 or 3 rapid occurs in a small canyon. The portage, if needed, is located on river left. The last significant rapid on the Mara occurs at the junction of the Mara and Burnside Rivers. From this point, the Burnside is followed to Bathurst Inlet. (See * previous page for River Profile from confluence of Mara and Burnside.)

MAPS REQUIRED:
(1:250,000)   **Mara River:**
Nose Lake 76 F
Mara River 76 K

Burnside River:
Contwoyto Lake 76 E
Kathawachaga Lake 76 L
Mara River 76 K

AVERAGE GRADIENT:
A: 1.7 metres per kilometre (9 feet per mile)

B: 1.6 metres per kilometre (8.3 feet per mile)

HYDROGRAPH: Burnside River near its mouth, 1976-1988

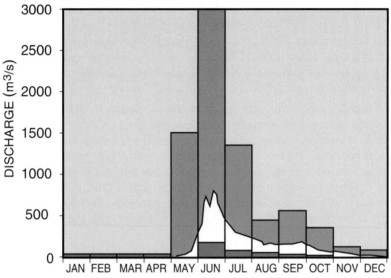

SOURCE INFORMATION:
1. Raffan, James and Gail Simmons: *A Narrative of a Journey by Canoe to Bathurst Inlet and Overland to Wilberforce Falls.* Downward Bound Expeditions. A report prepared for Parks Canada, 1981.

2. *The Burnside River:* Northwest Territories River Profile.

3. Poole, Kim and Louise: Personal communication.

4. Bathurst Inlet Lodge: Personal communication.

BURNSIDE RIVER CUMULATIVE DISTANCES:

Location	Kilometres	Miles
Contwoyto Lake outlet	0	0
Kathawachanga Lake outlet	27	17
Bellanca Rapids	90	56
Burnside and Mara River confluence	175	109
Burnside Falls	242	151
Bathurst Inlet	258	161

MARA/BURNSIDE RIVERS CUMULATIVE DISTANCES:

Location	Kilometres	Miles
Nose Lake outlet	0	0
Hackett and Mara River confluence	105	67
Mara and Burnside River confluence	182	114
Burnside Falls	249	156
Bathurst Inlet	266	166

CAMERON RIVER SYSTEM

TOTAL DISTANCE:
A: Gordon Lake to Prelude Lake – 110 km (69 miles)
B: Gordon Lake to Yellowknife – 157 km (98 miles)

DURATION OF TRIP:
A: Gordon Lake to Prelude Lake – 10 days
B: Gordon Lake to Yellowknife – 12 days

START: Gordon Lake

FINISH: This report finishes at the Yellowknife River Bridge on the Ingraham Trail just outside Yellowknife. Note: Canoeists can paddle shorter sections of the system beginning or ending at any of the lakes accessible from the Ingraham Trail.
Trips can range from two to twelve days in length.

ACCESSIBILITY: Gordon Lake can be reached only by air charter and the south end of the lake is 75 km (47 miles) from Yellowknife. Shorter trips along sections of the river can be accessed by vehicle from the Ingraham Trail (Hwy 4). This road runs northwest from Yellowknife and parallels the Cameron River as far as Tibbitt Lake.

Yellowknife, located at the end of the Mackenzie Highway, is served by daily flights from both Edmonton and Winnipeg.

RIVER NOTES: The Cameron River is a relatively small river, starting near the edge of the barrenlands, northeast of Yellowknife. Paddlers wishing a longer wilderness trip favour starting at Gordon Lake near the river's headwaters. Parties looking for a shorter and less challenging river trip have a choice of several good starting points which are accessible by vehicle from the Ingraham Trail.

The route is relatively easy but paddlers should still have a basic knowledge of white water paddling. The upper section of the system is very isolated and good wilderness camping skills are necessary.

Three major drops, one at the outlet of Reed Lake, followed in the next several kilometres by the Little Cameron and Cameron Falls, present serious hazards to canoeists. In addition there are numerous rapids, several of which are unmarked on the maps. Low water levels may necessitate frequent lining or additional portaging, and lining ropes are essential. Because of the many portages and lakes on the system, canoeists should have a basic knowledge of map reading and compass use.

GEOGRAPHY: The Cameron River system is located entirely in the Canadian Shield physiographic region. The route is characterized by rugged rock outcrops, many lakes, some muskeg and dense spruce forests.

CLIMATE: Summer weather in the region is generally warm and dry, with average daytime temperatures of 21°C (68°F) and 10°C (50°F) at night. Although rainfall is usually light, paddlers should be equipped with rain gear and a waterproof tent. During the month of June and early July, there are 20 hours of daylight, allowing paddlers to keep moving well into the evening. Spring breakup generally occurs in early May on the river and the lakes are generally ice free by the second week of June.

FLORA: The route is located within the transitional zone between open woodland tundra and the boreal forest, and the vegetation is common to both. Mosses, lichens, blueberry and crowberry may be found along the upper reaches of the system. The small lakes and muskeg that dot the surrounding countryside are home to a variety of sedges, willows, and bog birch. Black spruce and jack pine dominate the dense forests, although secondary tree growth includes aspen and birch. The trees are stunted because of the discontinuous permafrost and short growing season. Many varieties of wildflowers and berries can be found along the route throughout the summer and early fall. A guide to the plant life of the northern boreal forest and open woodland tundra is recommended (see Appendix G).

FAUNA: Although Gordon Lake is within the limits of the wintering range of the Bathurst Caribou herd, the animals won't be seen during the summer months when they are near their calving grounds hundreds of kilometres to the north. Moose, black bears, beaver, muskrat, otters and wolves occupy the area. Dense bush may limit sightings. Hawks, eagles, loons and a variety of waterfowl and song birds summer in the area.

Fishing is best on the upper reaches of the system where lake trout and grayling are found in abundance early in the season. As the waters warm throughout the summer anglers must fish the deeper, colder waters. Northern pike, grayling and whitefish are abundant along the entire system.

Monica Kendel - artist

HUMAN HISTORY: The Cameron River system is one of the Yellowknife Dene routes to the edge of the barrenlands. The entire area was once home to the Yellowknife Dene who controlled a large area stretching from Yellowknife Bay to the Barrenlands. John Franklin gave them their name because of their copper bladed knives. Akaitcho, who led Franklin on his overland journey in the 1820's, was a chief of the Yellowknives. The tribe was decimated by influenza and wars with neighbouring tribes. Their numbers had dwindled by the early 20th century. Today, the area is the hunting and trapping ground of the descendants of the historic Yellowknife and Dogrib Dene from the Yellowknife area.

The Cameron River system has been steadily explored by prospectors over the past 50 years and several small abandoned gold mines can be found near the route. Today there are still a handful of independent gold mining operations active during the summer months in the Gordon Lake area.

The Ingraham Trail, named after early Yellowknife resident Vic Ingraham, is "cottage country" and a popular recreation area for Yellowknife residents.

RIVER PROFILE: Gordon Lake is the largest lake on the Cameron River system. Technically it is not on the Cameron River at all but is located several kilometres to the west. Paddlers can begin their trip at the south end of Gordon Lake to avoid the often strong winds. From Gordon Lake, canoeists can either follow a small river to Lee Lake, a trip which will include several portages, or they can follow the winter road portage. This portage is marked on maps and starts in a bay to the west of where the small river leaves Gordon Lake.

After crossing Lee Lake, paddlers will encounter a set of rapids at the outlet. The portage is located on river left. One km downstream, where the river narrows, there are two sets of falls. A 250 metre portage is found on river right.

The confluence with the Cameron River is another 6 km (4 miles) downstream, with a couple of rapids and a beaver dam in between. Many rapids are not marked on the maps and portaging may be necessary. If water levels are high enough experienced canoeists may find some of the rapids runnable.

The remains of an old mine are located on the south shore of Dome Lake. Between Dome and Pensive Lake there are 2 sets of rapids which must be bypassed. The first portage of 150 metres is on river left, while the second, shorter trail is located on river right.

There are two alternate routes from Pensive Lake to Tibbitt Lake. One route continues to follow the Cameron River through Lower Pensive Lake. In low water this may be almost impossible. Even under normal water conditions it will require lots of portaging and lining.

The alternative is to portage to Ross Lake and follow the Ross River to Saunders Lake. The first portage on this route begins on the south shore of Pensive Lake (UTM grid 827N548E on Hearne Lake topo map 85 I) and follows a winter road for about 400 metres to a small slough. A second portage of 250 metres follows the winter road to a bay at the northwest corner of Ross Lake. Following the north shore of Ross Lake is the safest way to reach the outlet on the island-dotted east side of the lake. The 1:250,000 scale map doesn't show this outlet very clearly. Paddlers should refer to the 1:50,000 scale map.

The 8 km (5 mile) stretch of river to Saunders Lake is spotted with rapids. Some can be paddled, others lined, and during low water longer portages may be necessary. Again, paddlers should refer to the 1:50,000 scale map to find the connection south of Saunders Lake.

To reach Upper Terry Lake from Saunders Lake there are once again two options. Canoeists can follow the Ross River on a U-shaped route through Trough Lake and Terry Lake. This option involves 4 portages which are difficult to find, but the countryside is very beautiful. The first portage is located on river right at the outlet from Saunders Lake. The second is on river left, just past a small creek running into the Ross

Cameron River

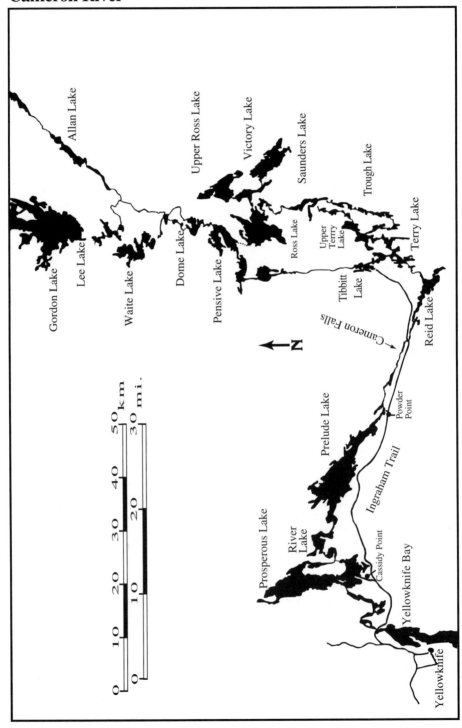

River from the south. A very high beaver dam built on a ledge across the river marks the third portage. The trail is on the left bank and angles southwest going into an unnamed lake just south of the river. The final portage is located on river left where the Ross River flows into Upper Terry Lake.

The second and shorter alternative involves only two portages. This route begins with a portage located on the west shore of the unnamed lake between Saunders Lake and Trough Lake (UTM grid 872N404E on Hearne Lake map 85 I). This 200 metre trail to a small lake is in very good condition. The second portage begins in the southwest corner of the lake on the left side of a small creek. The first 200 metres of this trail are good but it then disappears into a swamp. This trail should be scouted first. If water levels are high, paddlers may be able to pole through this section. There is one marked rapid between Upper Terry Lake and Terry Lake.

From Terry Lake paddlers have the option of a short upstream paddle to Tibbitt Lake, where they may end their trip. Tibbitt Lake is the end of the Ingraham Trail. There is one marked rapid between Terry and Tibbitt Lakes.

For those who continue on, or those who begin their trip at Tibbitt, the paddling is easy until the outlet of Terry Lake which splits around a large island. The left channel is the best route. Near the end of this island there are two rapids which can be portaged on river right along a well used, 300 metre trail. There are two sets of double rapids and one single set before Reid Lake. The first two sets are portaged on the river left, while the third can be lined or portaged on river right.

To reach the Reid Lake Territorial campground follow the right shore. There are both camping and picnic sites with firewood and drinking water. Once again, this site has road access to the Ingraham Trail and is only a 40 minute drive from Yellowknife.

There is a falls at the outlet of Reid Lake followed by 2 chutes before the river reaches a small bridge over the Ingraham Trail. The river cascades under the bridge and there is an easy portage here. Just downstream is a larger falls about 6 metres (20 feet) high. The 300 metre portage is on river left and ends at the foot of the cascade.

The next major hazard is Cameron Falls, located only 10 km (6 miles) downstream. Paddlers must be very careful on their approach to the falls. The take-out is at the flat, rocky bank on river right where the river narrows and makes a sharp left turn. Missing this take-out will likely have fatal results. The portage is 300 metres in length down a steep, well used trail. There is another short portage on river right where the river drops into Prelude Lake. The Powder Point Boat launch is located directly across the lake and may be used as a take-out point.

Prelude Lake is a popular fishing, camping and cottage area for Yellowknife residents. Because it is a large lake, paddlers must watch for sudden strong winds. A territorial park on the south shore offers campsites, firewood and a radio-telephone. This campsite is a 30 minute drive from Yellowknife.

River Lake is a small lake downstream from Prelude. There are 2 short portages between here and Prosperous Lake. The first 20 metre portage is on river right above some falls and the second, longer portage begins on river left at a break in the willows and ends in a small lake below the falls. From here, the river winds around a long peninsula and into Prosperous Lake.

The Cameron River ends on Prosperous Lake and paddlers continuing to Yellowknife will now follow the Yellowknife River. It's a 12 km (7 mile) paddle across Prosperous Lake to the Tartan Rapids on the Yellowknife River. Prosperous can be very windy and caution must be exercised. The Tartan Rapids portage is on river left and is marked by an old dock. These rapids are class 2 or 3 depending on water levels and should be scouted.

From here, the Yellowknife River winds slowly for 8 km (5 miles) to its mouth in Yellowknife Bay. There is a boat launch at the Ingraham Trail Bridge. This is the recommended finish point for canoes. Although only 8 km (5 miles) of paddling remain into the city itself, winds and the open water of Great Slave Lake can make this paddle extremely hazardous.

Yellowknife, with a population of 16,000, has all services available including restaurants, theatres, hotels and shopping centres.

MAPS REQUIRED: (read maps from left to right)

(1:250,000)	Hearne Lake 85 I	
	Yellowknife 85 J	
(1:50,000)	Gordon Lake South 85 I/14	Ross Lake 85 I/11
	Hearne Lake 85 I/6	Jennejohn Lake 85 I/5
	Prelude Lake 85 I/12	Prosperous Lake 85 J/9
	Yellowknife Bay 85 J/8	

AVERAGE GRADIENT: Gordon Lake to Prelude Lake – 1.2 metres per km (6.2 feet per mile). Gordon Lake to Yellowknife – 0.9 metres per km (4.7 feet per mile).

HYDROGRAPH: Cameron River below Reid Lake, 1975-1988

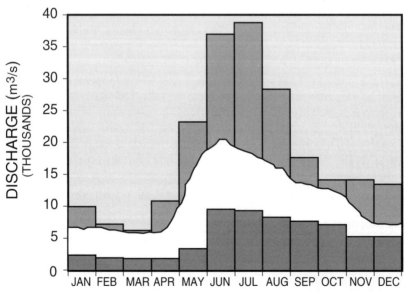

SOURCE INFORMATION:

1. Cameron River Trip Sheet, TravelArctic, GNWT, 1979.

2. Northwest Territories River Profiles, The Cameron River.

3. Johnson, Martha: Personal communication.

CUMULATIVE DISTANCES

Location	Kilometres	Miles
Gordon Lake Outlet	0	0
Saunders Lake Outlet	36	23
Reid Lake Inlet	76	48
Cameron Falls	86	54
Prelude Lake Campground	110	69
City of Yellowknife	157	98

Kim Poole

Negotiating the Cameron River

COPPERMINE RIVER

TOTAL DISTANCE:

A: 670 km (419 miles) from Lac de Gras to the Arctic Ocean

B: 665 km (416 miles) from Winter Lake to the Arctic Ocean

C: 561 km (349 miles) from Point Lake to the Arctic Ocean

D: 490 km (306 miles) from Rawalpindi Lake to the Arctic Ocean

DURATION OF TRIP:

A: 25 days from Lac de Gras to the Arctic Ocean

B: 26 days from Winter Lake to the Arctic Ocean

C: 21 days from Point Lake to the Arctic Ocean

D: 19 days from Rawalpindi Lake to the Arctic Ocean

START: The following are common starting points for canoeing the Coppermine River system:

A: West end of Lac de Gras

B: Ft. Enterprise on Winter Lake

C: Obstruction Rapids at the south end of Point Lake

D: Rawalpindi Lake

For longer trips, it is possible to begin at Fort Rae and ascend the Snare and Winter Rivers to the Coppermine. This trip takes about 6 weeks. Paddlers can also start in Yellowknife and ascend the Yellowknife and Winter Rivers. Again, this takes about 6 weeks.

FINISH: The community of Coppermine on the Coronation Gulf of the Arctic Ocean.

ACCESSIBILITY: Any of the starting points can be reached by air charter from Yellowknife. There are scheduled flights from Coppermine to Yellowknife. Canoes can be shipped as freight on a space available basis. Canoes can also be shipped by barge from Coppermine along the Arctic coast and up the Mackenzie River to Hay River with Northern Transportation Company Limited (NTCL). There are only 2 trips a year and it takes the barge about a month to reach Hay River.

Both Yellowknife and Hay River can be reached by highway or by scheduled flights from the south.

RIVER NOTES: From its headwaters at Lac de Gras, the Coppermine River flows swiftly to its mouth at the Coronation Gulf on the Arctic Ocean. On its way north, the river passes through a variety of landforms. Although there are several possible starting points, this report begins at Point Lake. From the stark tundra of Point Lake, the river passes through the dense spruce forests of the Redrock and Rocknest Lakes region and finally the low-lying mountains and rolling hills of the barrenlands. The Coppermine offers a combination of flatwater paddling and challenging whitewater, rugged landscapes, abundant wildlife and isolation. This is a trip for experienced river paddlers with a good knowledge of wilderness camping. Spray decks are recommended for the sections of heavy water, but are not a necessity.

GEOGRAPHY: The Coppermine flows through a series of different physiographic regions on its way to the Arctic coast. The lake portions on the upper part of the river are located in the barrens, dominated by rocky hillsides and boulder-filled lake and river beds. As the river flows north, these rock and boulder shorelines alternate with steep, eroded sand and clay embankments and low marshy flood plains. For the most part, the river valley forms a corridor of lush vegetation dominated by stands of stunted spruce. Beyond the river valley spectacular barren hills reach an elevation of 730 metres (2395 feet) above sea level. Eroded cliffs of sand and clay are found where the White Sandy River flows into the Coppermine. Big Bend marks another transition point as the terrain becomes rockier, with gravelly shores giving way to steep cliffs of sandstone. The September and Coppermine Mountains near Big Bend display impressive barren slopes scattered with low shrubs and rock outcrops. The red sandstone cliffs of Muskox and Sandstone Rapids change to white as Escape Rapids is approached. Beyond Bloody Falls near the river's mouth, the river flows through the sediments of an earlier delta.

Quantities of native copper have been found along the river near the Coppermine Mountains but no efforts have been made to exploit it. The greenish-coloured nodules can still be found in places along the river banks.

Mary McCreadie

The Coppermine River

CLIMATE: Although breakup on the Coppermine itself occurs in mid-June, many of the larger lakes remain ice-covered well into July. During John Franklin's journey in 1821 the frozen lakes presented extreme hazards. On June 30, 1821 he writes: "The river was about 200 yards wide and its course being uninterrupted, we cherished a sanguine hope of now getting on more speedily, until we perceived that the waters of Rocknest Lake were still bound by ice, and that recourse must again be had by the sledges. The ice was much decayed and the party were exposed to great risk of breaking through in making the traverse."

Drawing by Lieutenant Back of his expedition passing Pointe Lake

Canoeists should be sure to plan their trip after breakup to avoid serious ice problems. Freeze-up occurs in early October.

During the summer months, temperatures in the Point Lake area range from 13°C to 16°C. Temperatures can also fall below freezing and snow storms have been recorded in mid-summer. In the community of Coppermine temperatures as high as 32°C have been recorded; however, the average summer temperature is 10°C. Generally, the weather is warm and sunny, with little precipitation. However, wind and rain storms can blow up very quickly, especially on the big lakes, creating hazardous paddling conditions.

Warm clothing, rain gear, a good sleeping bag and tent are necessities on the Coppermine River.

This is "the Land of the Midnight Sun" and the long days favour paddlers wishing to travel in the evening. In the community of Coppermine, the sun doesn't set at all in June and it disappears for just over an hour in July.

FLORA: Although most of the river system flows through the tundra, the river valley itself is an oasis of lush vegetation. Downstream from Muskox Rapids the stunted

Coppermine River

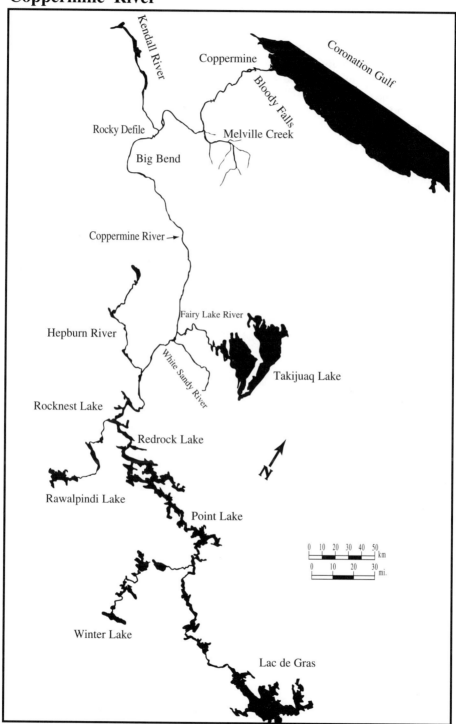

spruce stands give way to scrub willow and birch. Typical barrenlands vegetation includes cotton grass, sedges, various wildflowers and berries. Firewood for cooking fires can be found from the headwaters to Bloody Falls. A gas stove is a good idea.

FAUNA: The lush river valley is home to a variety of barrenground wildlife. Caribou, moose, wolves, Arctic fox and grizzly bears frequent the shores. Tundra swans and geese nest in the valley and the steep rock cliffs provide excellent nesting sites for raptors such as golden eagles, bald eagles, and gyr and peregrine falcons. Lake trout, grayling and northern pike are plentiful along the entire river system and Arctic char can be found in the river downstream of Bloody Falls in late August.

HUMAN HISTORY: The Inuit of the Coppermine region often used the river as a route inland to their caribou hunting and char fishing grounds. The Dogrib and Yellowknife Dene from the Great Slave Lake region also used the southern sections of the Coppermine for hunting. Ample reminders of the human history of the area are provided by artifacts at old campsites, graves and cabins.

Mary McCreadie

Barrenland paddling on the Coppermine River

Samuel Hearne is credited with being the first European to travel to the mouth of the Coppermine. In 1771 he reached the Arctic Ocean with the help of his Chipewyan guide Matonabbee and a party of Indians from northern Manitoba. He and his party travelled overland from Hudson Bay, reaching the Coppermine at the Sandstone Rapids only 64 km (40 miles) from its mouth. As they headed downstream, they came upon a sleeping camp of Inuit, traditional enemies of the Chipewyan. Under Matonabbee's direction, the Chipewyans massacred the entire group. Hearne named the rapids "Bloody Falls".

Fifty years later, John Franklin left Old Fort Providence on Great Slave Lake, guided by the Yellowknife Chief Akaitcho and headed for the Arctic coast. With his crew and officers Dr. John Richardson, George Back and Robert Hood, he explored the entire length of the Coppermine by boat. They portaged from the headwaters of the Yellowknife River over the height of land to Winter Lake where they were forced to spend the winter. There they built three log cabins which were grandly named Fort Enterprise. The following summer, 1821, they travelled to Obstruction Rapids and down the Coppermine, reaching the ocean in only 34 days.

RIVER PROFILE: This report describes the Coppermine River from Point Lake to the community of Coppermine on the Arctic Ocean. Canoeists who start at the south end of Point Lake rather than on Lac de Gras can avoid 142 km (95 miles) of lake paddling. Starting at Rawalpindi Lake requires several carries over shallow river sections but allows paddlers to avoid the paddle along Point Lake. Another advantage of starting at Rawalpindi is that it offers paddlers a chance to hone their river skills before reaching the Coppermine River itself.

Point Lake is 120 km (75 miles) long and is prone to large waves created by high winds. Paddlers should allow a few extra days in their schedule to allow for the possibility of becoming windbound. As winds often subside at night, it is often the best time to paddle.

There are two sets of rapids between Redrock and Rocknest Lakes which are easily navigable. The shores of both lakes are wooded with black spruce providing lots of firewood. Faster water is encountered downstream from Rocknest Lake near the confluence of the Coppermine and Napaktolik Rivers. This set of four rapids in an 8 km (5 mile) stretch is the first real whitewater challenge paddlers will encounter. The rapids are characterized by boulder fans which create hazardous shallows, large standing waves and ledges. This section requires technical paddling, lining and/or portaging. The level of difficulty of these rapids depends largely on water levels. Scouting is necessary for all sections. The last section, over a kilometre long, can be navigated with caution in the shallows around many of the boulders. A steep sand bluff on river right marks the end of these rapids and the beginning of a 14 km (9 mile) lake section. There are some ideal campsites on the beachy shores with plenty of black spruce for fires.

The next 30 km (18 miles) have few rapids and the current is often sluggish. Small lakes or widenings in the river can make wind a problem. The river then picks up speed and continuous rapids are found for about 40 km (25 miles), bringing paddlers to the confluence of the Coppermine and Fairy Lake River. Many of the rapids are unmarked on the maps and vary in difficulty, depending on water levels. The river splits around two islands just south of Fairy Lake River. The right channel is deeper and may offer a better route, although many parties have also followed the left channel. Good campsites are difficult to find due to the low, marshy floodplains surrounding the river.

Fairy Lake Rapids mark the last whitewater for the next 130 km (81 miles). The surrounding hills are impressive along this section. There should be lots of good opportunities to see wildlife. At Big Bend, the river turns sharply to the northwest and flows towards the Coppermine and September Mountains. Hiking in the surrounding hills offers spectacular views of the barrenlands.

After Big Bend, the current picks up noticeably and there are a number of rapids between here and Rocky Defile. Many of these rapids are not marked on the map. To avoid getting swept into the canyon at Rocky Defile, paddlers should pull out on river right well above the entrance to the defile. This rapid is 500 metres long and can be easily recognized by the impressive 60 metre (195 foot) rock cliffs. The well-used portage trail on river right starts from a rocky cove before the cliffs begin. It is a relatively good trail beginning with a steep climb over low shrubs and hummocks. Scouting this rapid is difficult from the heights of the canyon, and impossible from water level. Canoeists should remember that waves and drops look much smaller from above. Only expert paddlers should attempt this canyon because of the large standing waves, whirlpools and ledges. Several people have lost their lives in Rocky Defile and anyone who capsizes risks a long, cold and possibly fatal swim.

A fishing camp, apparently abandoned, is located at the mouth of the Kendall River. Early explorers used the Kendall River as a route to Great Bear Lake via Dismal Lake and the Dease Arm. The wide Kendall River Valley forms part of the caribou migration corridor and is a good spot for a short hike. Scenic limestone cliffs form the left bank just downstream from the Kendall as the river winds its way through the mountains. These cliffs provide excellent nesting sites for raptors and cliff swallows.

The landscape downstream from the Kendall is barren with steeply eroded rock outcrops. Scattered patches of snow may be found in the crevices of these slopes year round. Firewood is less abundant, but the dwarf willows and stunted spruce trees should still provide adequate fuel for cooking fires. Samples of native copper can be found in nodules along the cobble shores or wedged in crevices.

More unmarked rapids are encountered upstream from Muskox Rapids. Canoeists should be aware that the two Muskox Rapids are closer together than is shown on the map. The first can be scouted and portaged on river right, the second on river left. Both are runnable, but careful scouting is required. Paddlers are advised to run these rapids in empty canoes with spray decks. There is an excellent campsite on river left at the second rapid with a superb view of the river and its surroundings. The river is banked with beautiful red sandstone cliffs, which is prime habitat for birds of prey.

From here to Bloody Falls canoeists will encounter almost continuous whitewater, starting with the Sandstone Rapids. An inlet on river left, just upstream from these rapids, offers a safe exit for scouting. Advanced technical paddling skills are required to navigate this section of white water. The large standing waves and ledges that make up these rapids are the limit of navigability for open canoes. Scouting is recommended for all sections.

Rapids continue as the river flows towards Escape Rapids. An unmarked ledge extending almost the full width of the river just upstream from Escape Rapids can be avoided by staying to the extreme river left.

Depending on the water level, Escape Rapids is rated as either class 3 or 4. This is the most difficult rapid of the trip and should be carefully scouted. Scouting on river left is easiest, but the 2 km portage is on river right. Remember once again that it is difficult to get a proper assessment from above. The river flows through an S-curve gorge creating turbulence near the canyon walls on the outside curves. Two metre (6 foot) waves roll along the left limit at the first bend and a large ledge blocks passage on river right. Careful navigation is necessary throughout the entire canyon. Canoeists who decide to run this rapid are advised to do so in empty boats with spray decks.

From here to Bloody Falls there are more unmarked rapids and then a lake section with sandy banks. Five km (2 miles) downstream, a canyon entrance warns paddlers of the proximity of Bloody Falls. This is not a true falls, but two ledges separated by a short section of calm water. Neither of these ledges is runnable in open or closed boats and must be portaged. The one-kilometre portage is on river left up and over a steep, rocky embankment. The grassy hilltop provides an ideal campsite. This is where Samuel Hearne's Chipewyan guides massacred a group of sleeping Inuit in 1771. Bloody Falls is still a popular char fishing site for the people of Coppermine.

The final 16 km (10 mile) section of the river is silty and shallow. High winds may create large waves, especially on the ocean. Canoeists should exercise caution on the approach to Coppermine.

The community is located on the left bank of the mouth of the river. It has a population of approximately 900 people, with accommodation, groceries and scheduled airline services available.

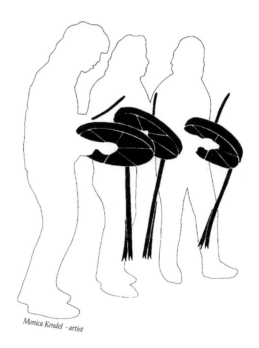

Monica Kendel - artist

MAPS REQUIRED: *(read maps from left to right)*

(1:250,000)		
Lac De Gras 76D	Winter Lake 86A
Point Lake 86H	Redrock Lake 86G
Hepburn Lake 86J	Sloan River 86K
Dismal Lake 86N	Coppermine 86O

AVERAGE GRADIENT: From Point Lake to the Arctic Ocean, the river drops 0.85 metres per km (4.5 ft. per mile).

HYDROGRAPH: *Coppermine River at Outlet Point Lake, 1965-1988*

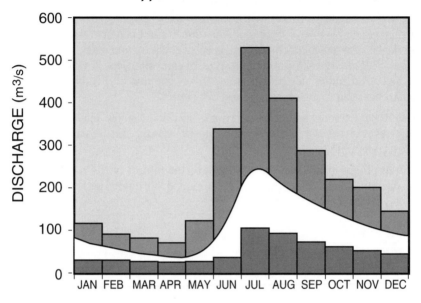

SOURCE INFORMATION:

1. Parks Canada Wild River Survey, The Coppermine River, 1972.
2. GNWT, Travel Arctic, Coppermine River Trip Report, 1979.
3. Cameron, Barbara: Personal Log, 1985.
4. Vermeulen, Fred: Personal Log, 1976.
5. Hodgins, Shawn: Camp Wanapitei, Personal Log.
6. Franklin, Captain John: *Narrative of a Journey to the Shores of the Polar Sea in the Years 1819, 20, 21 and 22.* New York: Greenwood Press, 1969.

CUMULATIVE DISTANCES:

Location	Kilometres	Miles
Lac de Gras Outlet	0	0
Point Lake Outlet	229	143
Redrock Lake Outlet	259	162
Big Bend	489	305
Rocky Defile	520	325
Muskox Rapids	592	370
Escape Rapids	635	397
Bloody Falls	652	407
Coppermine	670	419

HANBURY/THELON RIVERS

TOTAL DISTANCE:
A: Hanbury headwaters – 847 km (529 miles) from the Hanbury Portage to Baker Lake
B: Thelon headwaters – 916 km. (573 miles) from outlet of Lynx Lake to Baker Lake

It is 643 km (402 miles) from the Hanbury/Thelon confluence to Baker Lake.

DURATION OF TRIP: Either trip will take from 30 to 40 days.

START: The most common starting points are:
A: Deville Lake or Sifton Lake – approximately 400 km (250 miles) northeast of Yellowknife.
B: Southeast corner of Lynx Lake – approximately 400 km (250 miles) east of Yellowknife.

FINISH: The most common finishing point is the community of Baker Lake on Chesterfield Inlet.

ACCESSIBILITY: Air charter from Yellowknife to starting point. Air charter or scheduled flight from Baker Lake to Yellowknife, Rankin Inlet or Churchill.

RIVER NOTES: The Hanbury/Thelon is probably one of the most varied wilderness canoe routes in the world, as well as being one of the longest and most remote. The total trip, starting near the headwaters of either river is between 800 and 900 km (500 to 600 miles) and offers an incredible variety of landscape and wildlife.

For an even longer and more varied trip, intrepid adventurers can start on Great Slave Lake near Fort Reliance and travel up the historic 45 km (28 mile) Pike's Portage Route to Artillery Lake. The famous Hanbury Portage joins two continental drainage basins. To the east, the waters flow down the Hanbury/Thelon to Hudson Bay. To the west, the waters flow down the Lockhart River to Great Slave Lake and from there down the Mackenzie to the Arctic Ocean. This route would add another week to the paddling schedule and is not examined in this report.

For the most part, both the Hanbury and Thelon Rivers flow through very remote and isolated barrenlands. Paddlers must be very experienced in wilderness travel. There is no room on a trip like this for mistakes. Both routes offer a combination of flat and whitewater paddling. Major river hazards include several large rapids and falls, canyons and large, unprotected lakes that are subject to sudden and severe winds.

There is only one section of whitewater from the confluence of the two rivers to Baker Lake. Given this fact and the incredible wildlife viewing poss' ~~necially in the Thelon Game Sanctuary, paddlers with little whitewater expe؛ ؟؟d to the river. Keep in mind however, that the very remoteness an؛ it dangerous. Several outfitters guide trips on the Thelor wilderness experience should consider contacting them. included in Appendix E.

Because of the length of this trip and the possibility o؛ the lakes, paddlers should add several extra "weather" da

GEOGRAPHY: The headwaters of both rivers are loc a transitional zone between the subarctic spruce forest

-73-

gives way to rolling tundra, with long eskers or sand ridges being fairly common. The Hanbury is well known for its spectacular canyons and falls just upstream from the confluence of the two rivers. In the midst of the tundra, in the Thelon Game Sanctuary, a forest oasis rises out of a sandstone plain.

The Thelon Bluffs, located just upstream from Beverly Lake are the most prominent topographic feature of the river. Downstream from the Bluffs, the land flattens out considerably. As the Thelon nears Baker Lake, the Halfway Hills angle towards the river, rising to heights of about 200 metres. Finally, where the Thelon enters Baker Lake, there is a series of deltaic sand flats.

CLIMATE: Although spring breakup on the Hanbury/Thelon system occurs in mid-May, the larger lakes may not be ice-free until mid-July. Crossing ice covered lakes is hazardous and not recommended. Paddlers are advised to check with air charter companies to determine when the lakes are open. Freeze-up on the rivers takes place during October.

The weather in this region can be extremely variable. Paddlers may experience warm sunshine, heavy rain, snow and sleet in a single day. The predominately flat landscape

Max Finkelstein

Helen Falls, the last portage on the Hanbury River

offers little relief from the winds that seem to blow almost constantly. Paddlers may find themselves windbound several times. Average July temperatures are about 10°C (50°F); however, the temperature might easily slip below freezing at night. By August temperatures are already considerably colder.

Canoeists must be prepared for weather extremes by bringing warm clothing, a parka, good rain gear, a three-season sleeping bag and a good, wind-proof tent.

RA: Although the Thelon drainage begins in the taiga transition zone, most of basin is covered by barrenland vegetation. This includes several types of es and wildflowers as well as willow shrubs and alder. A few stands of ruce are found along the way.

Thelon System

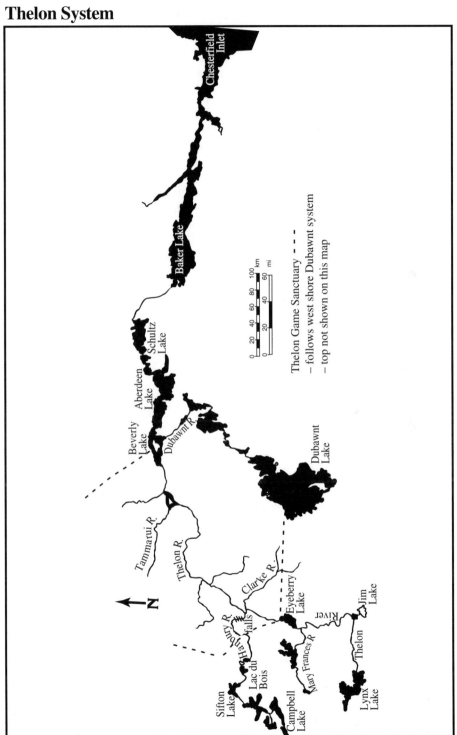

Chesterfield Inlet

Baker Lake

Schultz Lake

Aberdeen Lake

Beverly Lake

Dubawnt R.

Dubawnt Lake

Thelon Game Sanctuary - - -
– follows west shore Dubawnt system
– top not shown on this map

km
0   20   40   60   80   100

mi
0   20   40   60

Tammarui R.

Thelon R.

N

Clarke R.

Hanbury R.

Falls

Eyeberry Lake

Mary Frances R.

Thelon River

Jim Lake

Sifton Lake

Lac du Bois

Campbell Lake

Lynx Lake

An isolated oasis of forest growth is found in the Thelon Game Sanctuary. It consists of many old stands of spruce and larch as well as willows and birch.

Although firewood can usually be found along the Thelon drainage, the supply is limited. Canoeists should carry a small gas stove and fuel for cooking.

FAUNA: One of the biggest attractions of this canoe route is the wildlife. Most notable are the barrenground caribou, part of the Beverly herd which migrates through the area in July. Since this herd is made up of about 200,000 animals, chances are good that paddlers will see hundreds if not thousands of them either along the shores or crossing the river. While caribou movements are unpredictable, they often favour certain river crossings. On the Thelon, these include the areas of Warden's Grove, Lookout Point, Grassy Island, the junction of the Hanbury and Thelon Rivers, and the narrows in the Beverly-Schultz-Aberdeen lake complex.

The Thelon Game Sanctuary also has a very healthy muskoxen population. These prehistoric-looking animals can be seen individually or in groups of up to 30 grazing or resting along the shoreline. While photographers may be tempted to approach the muskoxen for close-up shots, they should keep in mind that they will charge and can cause serious injury.

Although it is not known how many barrenground grizzlies inhabit the region, virtually all trips have reported sightings. Aggressive bears have been reported, so extreme caution should be taken. It would be wise to contact the NWT Department of Renewable Resources in Yellowknife to get information on ways of detecting and deterring bears. They issue an excellent pamphlet on safety in bear country. Wolves, moose, foxes and other smaller mammals are also common in the area.

Late June and early July is a great time to see tens of thousands of tundra swans and Canada geese nesting along the Thelon in the swampy sections. High banks and cliffs along both the Hanbury and Thelon provide excellent nesting habitat for raptors such as gyr and peregrine falcons, rough-legged hawks and golden eagles.

There are plenty of fish in the faster moving sections of both rivers, as well as in the lakes, with lake trout and grayling being the most common catches. Arctic char is reported to be found in the lower reaches of the Thelon in late summer.

HUMAN HISTORY: Archaeologists have discovered evidence of man along the Hanbury and Thelon Rivers dating back to 6000 B.C., with the most notable site being located near Warden's Grove. It is believed that these people were part of a caribou-hunting culture.

Evidence of more recent Inuit and Chipewyan occupation of the area is evident in numerous old camps. Anthropologists believe that early Chipewyan hunters travelled north of the tree line every summer for the annual caribou hunt, returning south of the tree line for the winter. Caribou Inuit, who had initially occupied coastal regions along Hudson Bay, gradually penetrated the barrenlands of the Keewatin following the migrating caribou. By the late 1800s they were living year round along the entire Thelon basin, including the areas formerly occupied by the Chipewyan. Famine and starvation caused by the unreliability of the caribou migration were common. Ethnologist Knud Rasmussen reported the death of about 100 people due to starvation when he travelled through the area in the 1920s. In the late 1950s the Canadian government moved the people to permanent settlements along Hudson Bay to prevent further tragedy. Today, the Thelon River basin has no permanent population.

Samuel Hearne was the first European to pass through the area in 1771, when he made his overland journey from Churchill to the Coppermine River guided by the Chipewyan chief, Matonabee.

British adventurer David T. Hanbury ascended the Thelon and Hanbury rivers in 1899 and again in 1901. After the second trip, he wintered in Baker Lake before travelling north to the Arctic coast. This trip formed the basis of his book *Sport and Travel in the Northland of Canada.*

Around the same time, the area was surveyed by the Tyrell brothers for the Geological Survey of Canada. Accounts of their several trips through the area are published in the Canadian Geographical Journal in 1895 and '98. It was J.W. Tyrell who first recommended that the area be set aside for special protection. This didn't actually happen for another 30 years until after the infamous John Hornby, along with James Critchell-Bullock, surveyed the area in 1924-25 and recommended the establishment of a sanctuary for the dwindling muskoxen population.

Hornby achieved fame, not for his muskoxen report, but because he starved to death with two unlucky followers on the Thelon River in the winter of 1927-28. What is left of the cabin where he and his companions met their end can be seen at Hornby Point. Three graves are located behind the cabin.

Today, nobody lives permanently along the river; however, the Inuit of Baker Lake and the Dene of Snowdrift (called Lutsel'ke in Dene) on Great Slave Lake do hunt and trap in the area.

RIVER PROFILE: Because of the many lakes near the headwaters of both the Hanbury and Thelon Rivers, canoeists have several alternate starting points.

A) HANBURY RIVER: The actual headwaters of the Hanbury River are on Campbell Lake; however, most paddlers begin their trips on either Deville or Sifton Lakes. The Hanbury Portage, which spans the height of land between the Arctic and Hudson Bay drainage systems, enters Deville Lake from the west at the northwest corner of the lake. It is 41 km (26 miles) from here to Muskox Hill on Sifton Lake. Many paddlers choose to start at Muskox Hill because it is near the headwaters and easily identified. The terrain around Sifton Lake is mainly boulder-strewn sand hills and eskers. There is little or no firewood to be found.

As the river picks up speed, frequent boulder gardens and rapids make paddling tricky. Lining or portaging is necessary on most of the marked rapids on the Hanbury and all of them should be scouted. Malcolm Waldron, in his book "Snow Man", describes the Hanbury as "hardly a river at all, but rather a series of small lakes, rapids and falls. It is navigable only with many portages, some of them up or down the sides of steep cliffs....travel is only for the hardy."

Portaging around the first marked rapids is easy but the river is runnable along the left bank. The second marked rapid on the topographic map is a metre-high ledge that should be portaged. The 30 metre (100 foot) hike is easiest along river right.

As the river flows towards Grove Rapids the boulders become more prominent and require skilful manoeuvreing. Grove Rapids, named for a small group of trees found there, separates Lac du Bois from Hanbury Lake. These rapids have two sections. The first section follows a right turn and although some parties have lined and run this section, portaging is advised. The 1 km portage goes up over the hill on river right. A

Max Finkelstein

Over 300,000 caribou pass through the Thelon Game Sanctuary each year

Max Finkelstein

A log cabin at Warden's Grove along the Thelon River. The cabin was built in 1963 by Frank Riddel, a wolf trapper hired by the federal government

short paddle through some riffles brings you to the second section of rapids, which is divided into two channels by several rock islands. At some water levels this can be lined along the left bank, however most paddlers choose to portage for less than a kilometre along river left.

A third marked rapid is encountered upstream from where the river widens to form Hanbury Lake. Although this lake is relatively small, high winds can create waves large enough to swamp an open canoe. The Caribou Rapids mark the outlet of Hanbury Lake. It is possible to run these rapids along river right although many parties prefer to portage.

As the river approaches Hoare Lake, the landscape begins to open up. Many of the rapids are marked by stones and will require lining or portaging. During periods of low water unmarked boulder swifts may also require portaging. Just upstream from Hoare Lake there is a shallow canyon with swift water which can usually be run. A Water Survey cabin is located on the top of a ridge overlooking this rapid.

Downstream from Hoare Lake the river narrows considerably and loses its characteristic "lake, rapids and falls" pattern. This section of the river is very pleasant and the rapids are generally easy to run. About halfway to MacDonald Falls the river opens up in an area of sand dunes dotted with spruce. Muskoxen are often seen along the river in this section. Eight km (5 miles) upstream from the falls, the river does a U-turn and heads south.

There are two sets of rapids as the river approaches MacDonald Falls. Although both can be navigated, scouting is advised. A mistake here means big trouble. The first portage around the 5 metre (16 foot) falls is on river left and is fairly short.

The next portage starts across the river from the end of the first portage and bypasses the famous Dickson Canyon. This 3 km (2 mile) portage is the most gruelling on the river. It is marked by small cairns, but these are sometimes hard to see. There are several spots that are boggy and thick with willows and bugs. It takes a full day to complete this portage. It is advisable to carry your canoes right to the end of the portage but to camp about one half kilometre back, alongside the canyon. The view from these open spots is superb and the openness of the area tends to keep the bugs down.

Just past the end of Dickson Canyon is the portage around Ford Falls. It is on river right and is about 2 km (1 mile) long. This is a buggy and difficult trail. At some water levels this portage can be shortened considerably, but caution is advised.

It is about a 17 km (10 mile) paddle to Helen Falls, which, at 14 metres (46 feet), is the highest on the river. About 400 metres upstream from the falls is a rapid which can be paddled. The route through is on river right and the paddler must then quickly ferry across the river to river left to pull out for the portage. A mistake here could be deadly. For this reason, it is recommended that paddlers pull out on river left upstream from the rapid. The portage is about 3 km (2 miles) long and is fairly easy walking. There is a cairn at Helen Falls containing messages from the many parties that have passed this way since the 1960s.

From here to the confluence with the Thelon River is an enjoyable 15 km (9 mile) paddle without any serious obstacles. At the confluence of the rivers the landscape is wide open with a clear view up and down the Thelon. The water here is shallow, but deep enough for a float plane, should paddlers plan to either end or begin their trip at this point.

B) *THELON RIVER:* The headwaters of the Thelon River spring from Lynx Lake. This is a large and very confusing lake with numerous islands and bays. It is a good idea to ask the pilot to do a flyover before landing so that you can tell exactly where you are. It is also a good idea to land close to the lake's outlet to avoid spending days wind-bound (or lost). The landscape is typical of the tree line, with white sand hills and eskers as well as groves of large trees.

The first 17 km (10 miles) of the river are a fast but easy paddle. However, there is an unmarked rapid that needs scouting where the river turns northward after widening. Paddlers may choose to line down river left to bypass this 3/4 km (1/2 mile) rapid. There are 2 more unmarked rapids before you reach a long, narrow lake. The last rapids heading into the lake can be portaged on river right.

A series of rapids are located downstream from this lake where the river makes a U-bend south and then north. These rapids also require portaging. The first set can be portaged on river left, while the second, about 1.5 km (1 mile) downstream, can be portaged on river right.

The Thelon winds through shallows for the next 25 km (15 miles) until reaching the 18 metre (60 foot) falls, west of Jim Lake. These falls indicate the demarcation point between the Precambrian Shield and the Barrenlands. The portage is found on river right and paddlers are advised to pull off the river before the banks become too steep. This portage is about 1 km long and is very rough.

Downstream from Jim Lake the river widens and picks up speed, but is easily navigated until 12 km (7 miles) south of the Mary Frances River. This section is rock strewn and spotted with ledges, and requires very precise navigation.

There are many runnable rapids in this section of the river upstream from the Thelon Canyon. About 12 km (7 miles) north of Eyeberry Lake the channel is divided midstream by two islands. Both channels contain rapids; however, the left channel is usually the most navigable, depending on water levels.

The magnificent Thelon Canyon is located only a short distance upstream of the confluence of the Thelon and Hanbury Rivers. The portage, reputed to be 6.5 km (4 miles) long, is located on river right. A more dangerous alternative to portaging is to line along river left, although this alternative is not always possible. Two more rapids, both usually either runnable or linable, are situated downstream from the canyon and upstream from the Hanbury junction. The first is just south of the Clarke River mouth and the second is less than a kilometre upstream from the Hanbury.

The paddle from the confluence of the Hanbury and Thelon Rivers to Beverly Lake usually takes about 10 days to 2 weeks. There are no serious obstacles to worry about before the Thelon Bluffs. Generally, the best campsites are found on the north shore of the river. The wide and shallow 65 km (40 mile) stretch of river from the confluence of the Hanbury and Thelon to Hornby Point usually provides the best opportunity to observe wildlife.

Warden's Grove, 13 km (8 miles) downstream from Hanbury Junction is reputed to be the finest stand of trees on the river. Several cabins have been built on this site. One constructed in 1928 by the first warden of the Thelon Game Sanctuary, W.B. Hoare, still stands. In 1978, the Soviet satellite, Cosmos 954, crashed near this spot.

Past Grassy Island the cobble-lined river is wide and has a good current. It is another 51 km (32 miles) of flatwater to Hornby Point. Here, the remains of Hornby's cabin can be observed in a thick stand of trees about 45 metres (150 feet) inland. Three wooden crosses mark the graves of the unfortunate adventurers.

A swift current carries canoes 107 km (67 miles) downstream to Lookout Point, a traditional Inuit hunting spot. The river then flows towards the Thelon Bluffs, passing white, sandy beaches. The Bluffs look positively mountainous after nearly 3 weeks of paddling through flat country. The river bend that heads into the canyon is a good place to take out your canoe and camp. The view from the top of the bluffs is well worth the hike.

The paddle through the canyon of the Bluffs can be a little tricky. The safest way is to stay close to river right, avoiding some high standing waves and rock outcrops.

The three big lakes, Beverly, Aberdeen and Shultz are the bane of the Thelon River trip. Many paddlers choose to be picked up on Beverly Lake. Planes can land here safely in calm weather. The slightest breeze can create dangerous whitecaps on the open water. Canoeists must keep close to shore and should be prepared to spend a few days windbound. If time permits, it is worth paddling 16 km (10 miles) up the Dubawnt River to Loudon Rapids, where the river spills through a high gorge. The Dubawnt brings lots of driftwood from the tree line, so this is a good place to stock up on firewood for the treeless lakes ahead.

The 80 km (50 mile) paddle across Aberdeen Lake can also be hazardous because of winds and large waves. The shores of this lake are covered with boulders and cobbles and offer several sheltered campsites. Rock cairns and Inuit tent rings are found in this area.

Schultz Lake offers paddlers a change of scenery from the gently rolling tundra. The north shore is a rugged range of hills. Just downstream from the outlet of Shultz Lake are the Aleksektok Rapids. These can be very formidable at high water, although at other times they are described as easily navigable.

The entrance to Baker Lake is marked by deltaic sand flats. Paddlers have only another 13 km (8 miles) to the community of Baker Lake. This settlement of about 900 people is the approximate geographic centre of Canada and the only inland Inuit community in the NWT. Baker Lake is internationally renowned for its crafts. Accommodation and scheduled air service are available here.

MAPS REQUIRED: *(read maps from left to right)*

(1:250,000)   **Thelon River**

Beaverhill Lake 75 I	Lynx Lake 75 J
	Hanbury 75 P
Hanbury River	
Hanbury 75 P	Artillery Lake 75 O
Hanbury/Thelon to Baker Lake	
Clarke River 65 M	Tammarvi River 66 D
Beverly Lake 66 C	Aberdeen Lake 66 B
Schultz Lake 66 A	Baker Lake 56 D

AVERAGE GRADIENT:

A: Hanbury Portage to Baker Lake – 0.43 metres per kilometre (2.25 feet per mile).
B: Lynx Lake to Baker Lake – 0.38 metres per kilometre (2 feet per mile).

SOURCE /INFORMATION:

1. Thelon/Hanbury River Trip Sheet, TravelArctic (GNWT), 1979.
2. Hanbury-Thelon Rivers, Parks Canada Wild River Survey, 1972.
3. Canadian Heritage Rivers System, *Background Report in Support of Nomination of Thelon River*. Reid Crowther and Partners, 1984.
4. Hanbury/Thelon Canoe Route, Mithril Wilderness Programs, 1989.
5. Thelon River Trip Report, Dept. of Economic Development and Tourism, GNWT. 1990.
6. Northwest Territories Rivers Profile. The Thelon River; The Hanbury River; Pikes Portage/Artillery Lake/Lockhart River.
7. King, Bill: The Thelon River, *Nastawgan*, Summer, 1989.
8. Stephenson, John: Personal communication.
9. Bayly, John U., Notes on a Canoe Trip from Campbell Lake to Beverly Lake, 1973.
10. Whalley, George: *The Legend of John Hornby*. Toronto: Macmillan Company of Canada, 1977.
11. Waldron, M. Snowman: *John Hornby in the Barrenlands*. Boston: Houghton Mifflin, 1931.

HYDROGRAPH: *Hanbury River above Hoare Lake, 1971-1987*

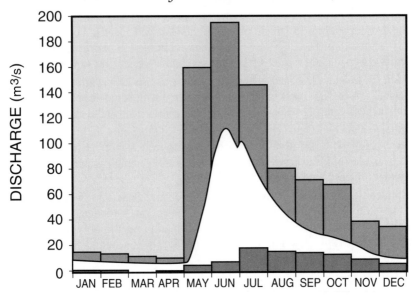

HYDROGRAPH: *Thelon River above Beverly Lake, 1970-1988*

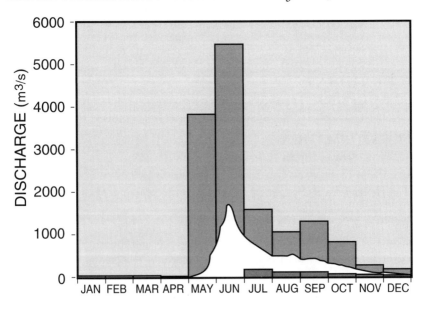

HYDROGRAPH: Thelon River above Baker Lake, 1973-1982

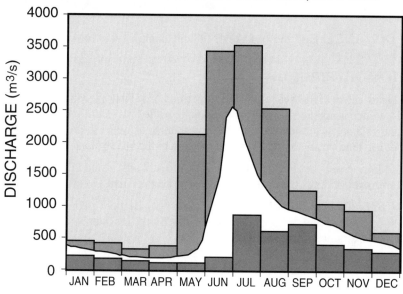

HANBURY RIVER
CUMULATIVE DISTANCES:

Location	Kilometres	Miles
Hanbury Portage	0	0
Muskox Hill	42	26
Grove Rapids	102	64
Hoare Lake Inlet	142	89
McDonald Falls	186	116
Helen Falls	203	127
Hanbury/Thelon Confluence	214	133
Community of Baker Lake	847	529

THELON RIVER
CUMULATIVE DISTANCES:

Location	Kilometres	Miles
Lynx Lake Outlet	0	0
Jim Lake Junction	89	56
Mary Frances River Confluence	195	122
Hanbury/Thelon Confluence	283	177
Hornby Point	354	221
Lookout Point	461	288
Thelon Bluffs	554	346
Dubawnt River Junction	617	386
Aberdeen Lake Inlet	647	404
Schultz Lake Inlet	767	480
Community of Baker Lake	916	573

HOOD RIVER

TOTAL DISTANCE: East end of Lake 414 (Tahikafaaluk Lake) to Arctic Sound is 295 km (183 miles).

DURATION OF TRIP: 16 days.

START: Headwaters of the river is at a lake identified only by its elevation (in metres) – Lake 414, which is just northeast of Lake Takijuak (called Napaktulik Lake on some maps). Lake Takijuak is located 480 km (298 miles) north of Yellowknife. For a shorter trip, parties can land on any of the lakes downstream of the headwaters.

FINISH: Many paddlers end their trip at Wilberforce Falls, while others prefer to paddle on the extra 45 km (28 miles) to Arctic Sound on the Arctic Ocean.

ACCESSIBILITY: The Hood River is accessible only by float plane, most easily arranged from Yellowknife. Yellowknife is accessible by the Mackenzie Highway, and by flights from Edmonton and Winnipeg.

Paddlers starting on Lake Takijuak (called Napaktulik Lake on some maps) must portage, paddle and pull their canoes for about 6 km (4 miles) to reach Lake 414, the headwaters of the river.

Planes on wheels will land on an esker near Wilberforce Falls to pick up canoeing parties. Paddlers continuing on to Arctic Sound can be picked up by float planes; however, wind can pose a problem there for planes trying to land. Be prepared to wait a few extra days for pickup.

From either of these finishing points, paddlers can go to the tiny community of Bathurst Inlet or return directly to Yellowknife.

RIVER NOTES: The Hood River flows from west to east across the Barrenlands of the central NWT, parallel to the Arctic coastline about 160 km (100 miles) inland from the Arctic Ocean. Before emptying into Bathurst Inlet, the river turns north and tumbles over spectacular Wilberforce Falls.

The Hood flows through classic tundra, a mixture of muskeg, bleak rock and sand eskers stretching on for miles. The canoeing season near the coast is a short 5 to 8 weeks, depending on ice and weather conditions. The first 100 km (62 miles) of the river is actually a string of narrow lakes which can still be ice-choked in July.

The river itself has a lot of whitewater, ranging from small rapids to falls. There are at least 4 or 5 mandatory portages and the same number of difficult rapids that may have to be portaged depending on water levels and paddling abilities. The scenery and abundant wildlife, especially caribou and muskoxen, combine to make the Hood River an unforgettable experience. It is a challenging whitewater river and this, combined with its remoteness and frigid waters, make it unsuitable for paddlers without extensive whitewater and wilderness experience. Spray covers are recommended and gas cook stoves are essential.

GEOGRAPHY: The Hood flows entirely through the tundra, with no trees to be found anywhere. The river begins on the Contwoyto Plateau. It is characterized by

The Hood River

Hood River

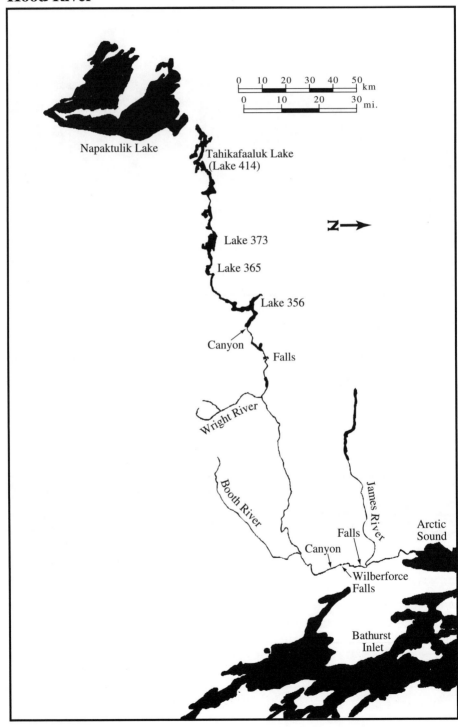

Napaktulik Lake

Tahikafaaluk Lake
(Lake 414)

N→

Lake 373

Lake 365

Lake 356

Canyon

Falls

Wright River

Booth River

James River

Falls

Canyon

Arctic
Sound

Wilberforce
Falls

Bathurst
Inlet

0 10 20 30 40 50 km

0   10   20   30 mi.

granite boulder till mixed with sand, and eskers which can extend for many kilometres. From the plateau, the river flows through the Wilberforce Hills and after dropping over several waterfalls, travels through the Arctic Coastal Plain and into the Arctic Ocean.

Forty-five km (28 miles) upstream from the Arctic Ocean, the Hood drops over Wilberforce Falls. The falls is the highest in the circumpolar world, dropping 50 m (160 feet) in two steps into the canyon below.

CLIMATE: Barrenlands weather is best described as unpredictable. During the short summer season, a day which started out sunny and warm can quickly deteriorate into driving rain (or snow) and biting winds. July temperatures in the region average about 10°C (50°F) in the daytime, dropping to near freezing at night. The upper part of the river has many good-sized lakes which must be crossed. Winds can render them extremely dangerous on short notice. Add a few extra days to your schedule to allow for the possibility of being windbound.

Ice can be a problem on the upper river, even in July. It's a good idea to fly over the area and find a landing site where there is enough open water to make some progress downstream. Warm clothing, good tents and rain gear are all essential on the Hood River.

FLORA: The vegetation along the Hood River is typical of the barrenlands. Plants are short and close to the ground, rarely being over a metre high. Lichen and moss carpet the ground, along with wildflowers, berries, dwarf willow and alder. Because of the scarcity of wood, paddlers should bring a gas stove for cooking.

FAUNA: One of the highlights of the Hood River is the wildlife. Caribou from the Bathurst herd, which numbers around 300,000 animals, cross the Hood on their way to and from their calving grounds east of Bathurst Inlet. Chances of seeing groups numbering in the thousands are good, especially early in July.

Muskoxen are also found singly or in groups along the entire river valley. While they seem docile, muskoxen will charge if alarmed, so photographers beware.

Both grizzly bears and wolverine are fairly common throughout the area, although the bears are more often seen. Wolves, who follow the caribou migration are also very common. White fox, although numerous, fluctuate drastically in numbers depending on the lemming and mouse populations.

A variety of birds, including golden eagles and peregrine falcons, are found along the river. Ducks, geese, ptarmigan, shorebirds, songbirds, gulls and swans all nest in the area.

Fishing on the Hood River is generally good, with lake trout being the main catch. Fishing is usually best in pools below rapids or falls.

HUMAN HISTORY: The Hood River does not seem to have been as widely used as the neighbouring Burnside River by the Inuit of the area. However, some tent rings and other signs of use can still be noted along the river valley.

The Hood's main historical claim to fame is its association with Captain John Franklin's First Arctic Overland Expedition. In 1820-21 he led an expedition north from Great Slave lake in search of the fabled "Northwest Passage". After wintering at Winter Lake on the upper Snare River, his 20-man expedition descended the Coppermine River

George Drought

Caribou on the Hood River

to the Arctic Ocean and paddled two ten-man canoes eastward along the coast toward a planned rendezvous with ships sailing west from Hudson Bay. These ships were thwarted by heavy ice in their attempt to travel west. As a consequence, Franklin and his men were forced to return overland to Fort Enterprise, their wintering place of the previous year.

On August 26, 1821, the crew began ascending the Hood River, which Franklin named for Lieutenant Robert Hood, a valued member of his expedition. The river proved to be impossible to ascend, and at Wilberforce Falls, the group halted and reorganized their equipment for the 400 km (250 mile) walk to Fort Enterprise. Franklin named the falls after William Wilberforce, the British Chief Justice who later abolished slavery in the Empire.

Before embarking on their overland trek, Franklin instructed his men to rebuild two small canoes from the big ones and to cache all non-essential equipment in order to lighten their load. Over the years, paddlers on the river have searched for Franklin's lost cache. To date, all that has been found are some axe heads and a cooking pot that are housed at the Prince of Wales Northern Heritage Centre in Yellowknife.

The trip across the barrens to Winter Lake is a chronicle of horror. Starving men were reduced to eating lichen and shoe leather to survive. Eleven of the 20 eventually perished, including Hood, who was murdered by a deranged Iroquois guide. An account of this trip can be read in Franklin's journal "Narrative of a Journey to the Shores of the Polar Sea in the Years 1819-22", or Dr. John Richardson's journal entitled "Arctic Ordeal".

RIVER PROFILE: This trip report begins at Lake 414 (its elevation in metres), located northeast of Lake Takijuak (called Napaktulik Lake on some maps), on the Arctic Circle. The first 100 km (62 miles) of the river is a series of long, narrow lakes, usually not more than 1 or 2 kilometres wide. None of these lakes, or the rapids between them, are named, so they are referred to by their height in metres above sea level.

Lake 414 meanders through high, rocky tundra for 34 km (21 miles) before spilling into a 5 km (3 mile) stretch of river that is a series of rapids and falls. The first rapid is shallow and rocky, but can usually be run (or portaged) on river right. This is quickly followed by a class 3 rapid with big standing waves at the end. This can be portaged on river left or run tight along the left shore. A picturesque falls is next and it can also be portaged on river left. This is followed by a fairly simple rapid which can be run on river left.

One kilometre downstream is a long rapid in two sections. The first section should be portaged along river left. The second section may be runnable along river right through a boulder garden. Another kilometre downstream is a class 4 rapid with a bad ledge near the end which makes it unrunnable. The portage is on river left. The last rapid in this group is a ledge falling into Lake 385. This ledge must also be portaged along river left.

Lake 385 is 10 km (6 miles) long and as it narrows it runs through a class 4 rapid which must be portaged on river left. Lake 373 is the widest lake on the route, being almost 4 km (2.5 miles) across at one point. There is an easy rapid in the connecting channel as the river drops 2 metres into Lake 371. This is the shortest lake on the trip, being only 7 km (4 miles) long. The river section joining this lake to the next consists of 2 rapids, each about 400 metres (1300 feet) long with about 300 metres between them. The first set can be run on river left, although there are some big waves. The second set is a shallow boulder field and should be run along river right. Three kilometres (1.5 miles) along this 11 km (7 mile) lake, is the first obvious change in topography. A large esker runs east and west on both sides of the river.

The river makes its first major change in direction on Lake 356 and heads north for 16 km (10 miles) before turning east again. Lake 356 is 24 km (15 miles) long and is the last real lake on the river. From here on the river narrows for its 195 km run to the ocean. There are some massive eskers at the end of the lake.

Four km (2.5 miles) downstream is a class 5 rapid which can be portaged on river right. Two km further downstream is an easy rapid. It is followed in another 2 km by a long and difficult class 3 rapid, which can be portaged on river right. If you decide to run these rapids, they can be negotiated most easily along river right. After these rapids there is some fast water running in channels among gravel beds, which shift from year to year.

About 5 km (3 miles) downstream, 120 km (75 miles) from the headwaters, is a class 5 rapid which must be portaged on river left. This portage is over a kilometre long.

Four km (2.5 miles) further downstream are two chutes about 200 metres apart which can be run with care. The first can be run on river right and the second along river left. Alternatively, both can be portaged along river right. These chutes are followed by a 25 metre (82 foot) waterfall which can be portaged on river right. Good campsites can be found on both sides of the river just after the falls.

The river slows down for the next 25 km (16 miles) as it passes through grassy hills. The Wright River joins the Hood on river right at km 147 (mile 92). It is well worth stopping here and hiking. There are old Inuit tent rings on the southwest plateau overlooking the confluence of the two rivers.

There are also some interesting geological formations at the falls on the Wright River.

Around km 148 (mile 92), the current increases again and paddlers will encounter a series of swifts and small rapids over the next 16 km (10 miles). These then turn into a series of class 2 rapids and care should be taken, especially around km 166 (mile 103) where the manoeuvring becomes more technical. There is a class 2 rapid at km 175 (mile 109) which is difficult to read from the river. It is normally run along river right. This rapid marks the end of the stretch of class 2 rapids.

From these rapids until about 3 km (1.5 miles) upstream from the confluence with the Booth River, the Hood returns to swifts and class 1 rapids. The rapid upstream from the confluence of the two rivers is a class 3 rapid about 1.5 km in length. It can be portaged or scouted on river left and is best run along river right. One group of paddlers reported seeing thousands of caribou crossing the river in this area.

From these rapids to Wilberforce Falls, the river drops continuously, with numerous swifts and class 1 and 2 rapids. The toughest stretch is found between km 233 and 235 (miles 145 and 146). The best route here is on river left. Downstream, the river becomes braided with a good current and a gravel bottom. There is a mineral exploration camp 6 km (4 miles) upstream from the falls on river left.

The takeout for Wilberforce Falls is on river left, 1 km south of the falls upstream from a set of rapids. Don't get drawn into these rapids. The portage is 3 to 4 km (2 miles) long with a good campsite at the bottom. Paddlers leaving the river here can be picked up by a plane which can land on a nearby esker.

This spectacular falls, which is almost as high as Niagara, tumbles 50 metres (160 feet) in 2 stages into the gorge below. This gorge feeds into a canyon which is about 2 km (1 mile) long, containing 8 or 9 sets of rapids. These rapids are difficult to scout from above. There is no way out of the canyon and these rapids are considered unrunnable, at least in high water.

Below the canyon, there are a few sets of class 2 or 3 rapids. Another falls is encountered 33 km (21 miles) from the ocean. This falls plunges 10 metres (33 feet) over a red sandstone cliff with an island in the middle. There is a short portage on river left and good fishing at the base of the falls.

The James River enters the Hood from the west about 3 km (1.5 miles) downstream from these falls, turning the river silty. The current here begins to slow down as the Hood passes through high sandy banks, covered with willows. Good campsites become hard to find.

The final set of rapids on the river is found 10 km (6 miles) upstream from the mouth. It is a series of ledges that can be run mostly on river left or portaged on the same side. There is a good campsite here.

For the last 3 or 4 km (2 miles) the river is shallow, with many sand bars. This is a poor place for float planes to land, so canoeists will probably have to be picked up south of the river's mouth in Baillie Bay. It should be emphasized that there is a good chance of being windbound anywhere along the coast while waiting for a plane to land. Finding fresh water can be a problem.

MAPS REQUIRED: *(read maps from left to right)*

(1:250,000) Takiyuak Lake 86 I Kathawachaga Lake 76 L
             Mara River 76 K   Arctic Sound 76 N

AVERAGE GRADIENT: Headwaters (Lake 414) to the Arctic Ocean: 1.4 metres per kilometre (7.4 feet per mile)

SOURCE INFORMATION:

1. Drought, George, Wilderness Bound Outfitting: Personal communication.

2. Scriver, Mark, Black Feather Wilderness Adventures: Personal communication.

3. Warner, Boyd and Paige Burt, Bathurst Inlet Lodge: Personal communication.

4. Lentz, John: "On Canada's Hood River", *National Geographic*, Jan. 1986.

5. Mason, Bill: "In Franklin's Wake", *Wild Waters: Canoeing Canada's Wilderness Rivers*. Edited by James Raffan. Key Porter.

6. Franklin, John: *Narrative of a Journey to the Shores of the Polar Sea in the Years 1819-22*. Everyman's Library.

7. Richardson, John: *Arctic Ordeal*. Edited by C. Stuart Houston. Kingston and Montreal: McGill-Queen's University Press.

CUMULATIVE DISTANCE:

Location	Kilometres	Miles
East end Lake 414	0	0
Outlet Lake 414 (Tahikafaaluk)	37	23
Outlet Lake 356	112	70
Confluence Wright River	147	92
Confluence Booth River	227	142
Wilberforce Falls	252	158
Confluence James River	268	168
Arctic Sound	295	184

HORNADAY RIVER

TOTAL DISTANCE: From the headwaters of the river to its mouth is approximately 300 km (186 miles). However, the first 50 km (31 miles) are too shallow in most years for canoes and the last 90 km (56 miles) are impossible to navigate. This leaves a stretch of approximately 160 km (100 miles) which can be paddled.

DURATION OF TRIP: 10 days to 2 weeks

START:
A: Latitude 67° 53', longitude 121° 24' (50 km or 31 miles downstream of the headwaters)
B: Outlet of Hornaday Lake about 60 km (37 miles) east of the river, the headwaters of a tributary. Latitude 68° 43', longitude 120° 46'.

FINISH: Latitude 68° 55', longitude 122° 45'. Twelve km (8 miles) upstream from the Hornaday River Canyon.

ACCESSIBILITY: Float plane charters from Inuvik or Norman Wells are closest. Both communities can be reached daily by air from Yellowknife and Edmonton. The community of Paulatuk lies approximately 15 km (9.3 miles) from the mouth of the river and has scheduled air service to and from Inuvik. Canoe rentals are available in Inuvik. Paddlers using their own canoes can fly them to Inuvik or Norman Wells, or can have them barged down the Mackenzie River from Hay River.

RIVER NOTES: The Hornaday is a shallow tundra river that flows 300 km (186 miles) northwest from its headwaters 160 km (100 miles) north of the Arctic Circle to the Arctic Ocean, 15 km (9 miles) east of the community of Paulatuk.

The river has two distinct sections giving it a definite Dr. Jekyll/Mr. Hyde character. The upper 210 km (130 miles) of the river flow through a wide shallow valley. Parts of the valley are characterized by vast sand fields dotted with tall willows, giving the overall impression of a desert with oases. The river flows very slowly here and is like a long narrow lake in some sections.

At latitude 68° 55', longitude 122° 42', the scenery and nature of the river change dramatically. The peaceful river quickly becomes a dangerous, raging torrent, culminating in a 45 km (28 mile) canyon that drops 300 m (984 feet) along its length. There are 150 to 200 rapids in the canyon, many of which are Class 5 and 6, including the 20 metre (66 foot) high La Ronciere Falls. The canyon is very narrow and in many places it is impossible to climb out or to set foot on the side of the river. Frequent stone avalanches make travel even more hazardous.

Although canoeists can't paddle beyond the canyon mouth, the countryside provides some spectacular hiking and several days can be spent in the area before pickup. A National Park, to be called Bluenose Lake National Park, is proposed for the area to protect the calving grounds of the Bluenose caribou herd.

Because this river is extremely remote and little visited, paddlers must be expert in wilderness camping.

GEOGRAPHY: The Hornaday lies in the tundra about 70 km (43 miles) above the tree line. At its headwaters, the river is about 500–600 m above sea level (1640-1969 feet). Over the next 220 km (137 miles), it declines gently to about 400 metres (1312 feet) above sea level. The landscape is flat or rolling and covered with numerous small lakes, tundra polygons, exposed rock and tundra grasslands. The river valley is shallow, and vast sand fields skirt much of it. Cliffs are almost entirely absent along the upper 160 km (100 miles) of the river.

During the final 80 km of the river, the elevation of the country declines steeply. The river drops approximately 300 m (984 feet) while cutting its way through a dramatic canyon. The exposed rock and cliffs are mainly hard sandstones, shales and dolomites. The canyon ends about 35 km (22 miles) upstream from the Arctic coast and is replaced by morainic hills and soft shale, silt and mudstone.

CLIMATE: The Hornaday is situated in an area of continuous permafrost where only a thin layer of soil ever thaws. Breakup on the river generally takes place in June, heralding the beginning of a short and cool summer. There can be long spells of rain and wind, and even snowstorms and frost are not rare in this region. Average summer temperatures are around 10°C (50°F). There is no natural protection in the open tundra and no firewood. Travellers must carry warm clothing, good tents and rain gear as well as gas stoves and fuel.

FLORA: The dominant vegetation of the region is the dwarf shrub, sedge and lichen typical of the tundra, with pockets of willow and dwarf birch. There are no trees, but some patches of tall willows can be found in the river valley. These few willows are important habitat for birds and wildlife and should not be used for fuel.

Part of this area was not glaciated during the last ice age. As a result, it was a refuge for several species of plants not normally found in this region. The flowering season starts the second week of June, reaches its peak in the first two weeks of July and ends in early August. The density and variety of flowers and vegetation during this brief summer is overwhelming.

FAUNA: Caribou are the predominant mammals of this area. Hundreds or even thousands of animals can be seen daily along the river. These caribou are part of the Bluenose caribou herd whose calving grounds are east of the river.

Other animals which occupy the region include muskoxen, grizzly bears, wolves, foxes, Arctic hares and lemmings.

Among the sixty or more species of birds on the river, the peregrine falcon is the most striking and noticeable. It breeds in abundance along the canyons and cliffs of the river and is easily observed. Other birds commonly seen include golden eagles, pacific loons, tundra swans and oldsquaw ducks.

Lake trout may be caught along the river but generally, fishing on the upper river is poor. The lower part of the river below the La Ronciere Falls is a well known spawning ground for Arctic char.

HUMAN HISTORY: The lower part of the river has been used by the Inuit for several centuries because of its importance as a major char spawning ground. Some archaeological sites have been located in the area.

The Hornaday remained unknown to Europeans long after the neighbouring rivers to the east and west had already been explored. The first known white man to explore this river was the missionary Abbe Emile Petitot. In 1868, he travelled from Fort Good Hope on the Mackenzie River to the Hornaday and mapped most of its course, although he never reached the mouth. Later explorers did not confirm the existence of the river and for several decades it remained a legend. The river was finally named in 1920, after the Director of the New York Zoological Gardens.

Hornaday River

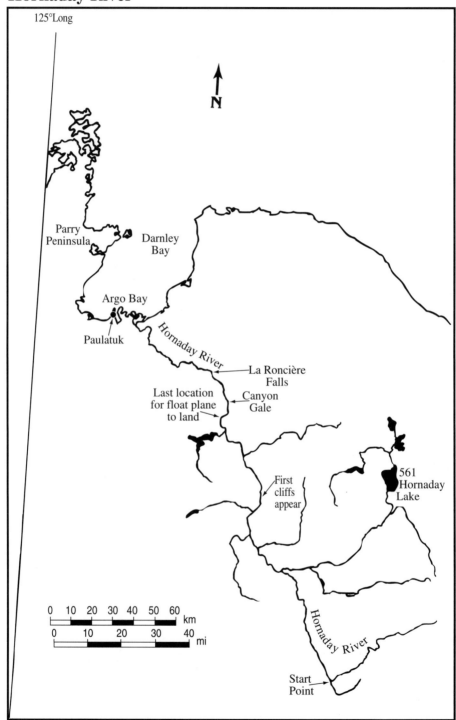

125°Long

N

Parry Peninsula

Darnley Bay

Argo Bay

Paulatuk

Hornaday River

La Roncière Falls

Last location for float plane to land

Canyon Gale

First cliffs appear

561 Hornaday Lake

Hornaday River

Start Point

0 10 20 30 40 50 60 km

0 10 20 30 40 mi

RIVER PROFILE: Breakup usually takes place on the Hornaday during the first week of June and float planes can land beginning in mid-June. The first 50 km (31 miles) of the river are too shallow for canoes, so the most suitable starting point for a canoe trip is at latitude 67° 53', longitude 121° 24', where the river turns sharply to the northwest. The river is 50 to 70 m (164 to 230 feet) wide and the valley is very shallow. From this point, the river flows slowly and gently for about 160 km (100 miles). Winds in this open country can make paddling very difficult.

Another possible starting point is at Hornaday lake, about 60 km (37 miles) east of the river (lat. 68° 43', long. 120° 42'). An 85 km (53 mile) tributary starts at this lake and joins the Hornaday at lat. 68° 20', long. 121° 58'. This tributary is fast flowing, narrow, rocky and shallow and contains six rapids. The last 5 km (3 miles) are 15 to 25 m (49 to 82 feet) wide. There, the deepest water on June 23, 1988 was 2 metres (6 feet). It is possible for water levels to drop significantly in July.

At lat. 68° 37', long. 122° 15', the first cliffs are noticed along the river and from here on they become increasingly common. At lat. 68° 55', long. 122° 42', the wide, tranquil river narrows quickly within a 900 metre (2953 foot) left turn. This is the last location for 60 km (37 miles) where float planes can land. Paddlers are advised to make arrangements to be picked up here. If paddlers enter the river canyon, they will be forced sooner or later to abandon their boats and hike for 80 or 90 km (50 miles) to the community of Paulatuk.

From the takeout point, a scenic 12 km (7 mile) hike will take you to the spectacular canyon gate. Several days can be well spent hiking along the canyon.

MAPS REQUIRED: *(read maps from left to right)*

| (1:250,000) | Bloody River 96 P | Erly Lake 97 A |
| | Brock River 97 P | Franklin Bay 97 C |

SOURCE INFORMATION:

1. Obst, Joachim: *A Canoeing Report on the Hornaday River.* Prepared for the Canadian Parks Service, Yellowknife, 1990.
2. Osgood, Lawrence: *The Hornaday River.* Prepared for TravelArctic, Yellowknife, 1978.

CUMULATIVE DISTANCES:

Location	Kilometres	Miles
Start: Latitude: 67° 53'		
Longitude: 121° 24'	0	0
Confluence of tributary from Hornaday Lake	63	39
First cliffs noticed:		
Latitude: 68° 37', Longitude 122° 15'	110	69
Last location for 60 km where float plane can land		
Latitude 68° 55' Longitude 122° 42'	157	98
Alternate start: outlet Hornaday Lake...............	0	0
Confluence of tributary from Hornaday Lake	85	53
First cliffs noticed:		
Latitude: 68° 37', Longitude 122° 15'	131	82
Last location for 60 km where float plane can land		
Latitude 68° 55' Longitude 122° 42'	179	112

HYDROGRAPHS: According to the Water Survey Office of Canada in Yellowknife, no hydrographs have been recorded on the Hornaday River.

HORTON RIVER

TOTAL DISTANCE : Horton Lake to Franklin Bay on the Arctic Ocean is approximately 600 km (373 miles).

DURATION OF TRIP: Three to four weeks.

START: Horton Lake near the headwaters of the river or at one of several landing sites along the river.

FINISH: Franklin Bay on the Arctic Ocean.

ACCESSIBILITY: A float plane from Inuvik or Norman Wells can land almost anywhere along the river. There are also a limited number of gravel bars where small planes with "tundra tires" can land.

Inuvik and Norman Wells have daily jet service to Yellowknife and Edmonton. Canoes may be rented, flown to Inuvik or Norman Wells, or barged down the Mackenzie River from Hay River with NTCL (Northern Transportation Company Limited).

RIVER NOTES: The Horton is one of the most remote rivers in the NWT. It has only recently become a destination for paddlers and given its natural attributes, it is only a matter of time until it becomes one of the most popular rivers in the north.

Perhaps the Horton's most outstanding feature is the abundance of wildlife that can be seen along its shores. Caribou, muskoxen, wolves, grizzlies and over 80 species of birds abound. The scenery is also exceptional – rolling tundra, cliffs, and canyons combine to make the journey a unique experience. Clear, swift flowing water with few obstacles will attract paddlers in search of wilderness rather than whitewater thrills. The few rapids along the way are primarily found in the three major canyons on the river, and are easily avoided.

Although the river valley itself is wooded for much of its length, the tundra surrounds it and is easily seen from any high vantage point. Hiking opportunities are plentiful and a few extra days should be scheduled to take advantage of this.

Water levels vary enormously on the river. In late June the water is extremely high and many rapids may be impassable. Water levels drop in late July and early August, making the rapids less dramatic.

Because of its isolation, paddlers planning to travel the river should be experienced wilderness campers.

GEOGRAPHY: Much of the Horton River lies within the Northern Interior Plains region of the Mackenzie Lowlands. It is generally low, hilly terrain marked by numerous lakes and streams. Horton Lake is characterized by highly calcareous, sandy till, with moderate to low relief. The Interior Plateau lies at the western extremity of the Pre-Cambrian Shield, and has developed from sedimentary rock deposited on top of the Shield.

The lower reaches of the river flow through an extensive badlands area. Exposed hills of yellow, pink, grey and black rock give the area an eerie but beautiful appearance.

The Horton River

Horton River

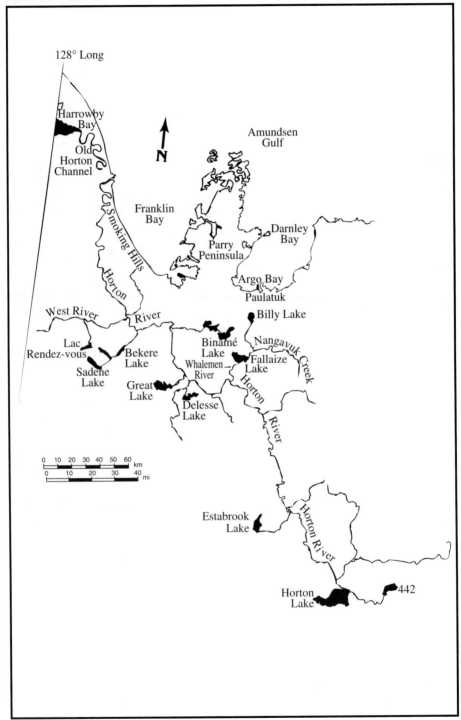

128° Long

Harrowby Bay

Old Horton Channel

Amundsen Gulf

N

Smoking Hills

Franklin Bay

Horton

Parry Peninsula

Darnley Bay

Argo Bay

Paulatuk

West River

River

Billy Lake

Lac Rendez-vous

Bekere Lake

Binamé Lake

Nangavuk Creek

Whalemen River

Fallaize Lake

Sadene Lake

Great Lake

Horton River

Delesse Lake

0 10 20 30 40 50 60 km
0 10 20 30 40 mi

Estabrook Lake

Horton River

Horton Lake

442

The coastal area east of the Horton is dominated by the Smoking Hills. These hills contain vast deposits of magnesium, sulfur and low grade coal, which spontaneously combust when exposed to oxygen. The constant wind in the area tends to maintain the combustion, giving the hills their well-deserved name.

Around 150 years ago, the Horton River was shortened by about 25 km (15 miles) when a new channel eroded the east bank of the river close to the mouth. The river now spills almost directly into the ocean without flowing through a delta like other rivers on the Arctic coast. Today, the old channel is a grassy valley wandering northwest from near the mouth of the river.

CLIMATE : The Horton River passes through 2 semi-arid climatic zones. The Horton Lake area and the upper part of the river are situated in the Continental Sub-Arctic, where mean summer temperatures range from 6°C to 13°C (43°F to 55°F). Temperatures can soar as high as 30°C (86°F), giving sunny, windless days more fitting for southern climates.

The lower sections of the river are located in the Arctic Coastal Plains region where mean summer temperatures range from 3 to 5°C (37°F to 41°F).

For much of the summer there is 24 hours of daylight. Although this area is very dry, frequent rain squalls, fog and even snow make good rain gear essential. Winds are also a factor along the river valley, often making travel very difficult. Warm clothing, good sleeping bags and tents are a must when travelling in this area.

FLORA: The headwaters of the Horton are located east of the tree line on the tundra, but the river flows southwest and then north, and follows this imaginary line for most of its length. To the east of the river lies the tundra, while to the west is the open forest transition zone. The river valley itself is wooded, and firewood is available along the entire length of the river, until the final 100 km (62 miles).

The growing season is about 60 days, giving life to a variety of plants. Willows, dwarf birch, wild flowers, sedges, moss and lichen cover the tundra. In the forest transition zone, tundra vegetation mingles with open forest, dominated by small, widely spaced spruce trees. Dense stands of willows and alder grow along creek valleys.

FAUNA: The Horton River offers spectacular wildlife viewing opportunities. The area is particularly well known for its population of peregrine and gyrfalcons which nest in the river canyons. A variety of water fowl, loons and shorebirds inhabit the area, along with songbirds, ravens, eagles and ptarmigan. About 80 species can be spotted in a good year.

If you are on the river in June or July, you stand a good chance of seeing hundreds, or even thousands of caribou during their post-calving migration from Bluenose Lake. This herd, known as the Bluenose herd, numbers about 115,000 animals. There is also a significant population of muskoxen in the region.

The Horton is prime grizzly bear country and it is not uncommon to see them along the river. They can be very dangerous, so it is always important to keep your camps clean to avoid attracting them. The NWT Department of Renewable Resources has an excellent pamphlet entitled "Safety in Bear Country", which it distributes free of charge.

A number of wolf packs work the area, usually following the caribou migration. Foxes, marten and various rodents are also common.

Fish are plentiful along most of the river, although they may be difficult to catch during spring floods. Arctic grayling and lake trout are the most common species, although there is an Arctic char run during the late summer.

HUMAN HISTORY: Several Inuit archaeological sites exist in the Horton-Anderson River region, including two Thule winter houses near the Cape Parry DEW Line station. Two other houses are reported to be located at Tom Cod Bay and another at Cape Bathurst. The earliest of these dates back to around 1350 A.D. Human habitation is likely to have begun much earlier, during the Paleo-Eskimo migration from Alaska and Siberia around 2500 B.C.

Most of the Horton River archaeological sites were inhabited by Thule people who migrated to the Canadian Arctic from Alaska between 1100 and 1400 A.D. The Thule people were very skilled at surviving and even thriving in the harsh Arctic conditions. They are famous for their skin boats, the umiak and the kayak, as well as for their use of dog teams, snow goggles and other adaptations to their environment.

Today most of the inhabitants of the region are Inuvialuit, descendants of the Inuit who migrated to the area with the 19th-century Euro-American whalers. The closest community is Paulatuk, located about 100 km (62 miles) east of the Horton River. The name Paulatuk means "coal or soot" and refers to the coal that the people once used for heating. The original community was established in the 1920's at Letty Harbour. It was moved to its present site in 1935, when the Roman Catholic mission established a post there.

Less is known about the Hareskin Dene who also hunted and lived in the area. It is believed that there were about 1000 Hareskins living in several bands throughout the region when the first Europeans arrived. Today, most of their descendants live at Colville Lake, a small community about 160 km (100 miles) west of Horton lake.

One of the first Europeans to explore the Horton River area was Captain Robert McClure, who was searching for the lost Franklin expedition. In September of 1850, his search party investigated what appeared to be a smouldering fire in Franklin Bay. The party found not flames from campfires, but what they described as "thick columns of smoke emerging from rents in the ground, and a smell of sulphur so strong that we could not approach the smoke pillar nearer than 10 to 15 feet."

Naturalist-explorer and Hudson's Bay Company employee Roderick MacFarlane was one of the first Europeans to explore the interior of the Horton-Anderson River area. Upon his recommendation, a trading post was established on the Anderson River in 1861. MacFarlane remained in charge there for 5 years. Each year he travelled on foot to the Horton, crossed it and then returned to the post. Fort Anderson was closed in 1865 after an epidemic of scarlet fever decimated the local population.

Missionary Father Emile Petitot, famous for his ethnological observations of the people of the north, travelled along the upper and middle sections of the Horton River in 1868.

Well-known Canadian explorer Vilhjalmur Stefansson also travelled the Horton River Valley extensively and documented his findings in a book written in 1913 called

The Horton River winding its way to the Arctic Ocean

"My Life With the Eskimo". The remains of his log cabin can still be found today near the Coal River.

Paulatuk remains the only permanent settlement in the Horton River area. Because of its remote location and the absence of industrial activity in the region, most of its residents still depend on hunting and trapping for a living. This may change somewhat with the creation of a proposed National Park in the Bluenose Lake area.

RIVER PROFILE: Horton Lake, 80 km (50 miles) north of the Dease Arm of Great Bear Lake, is one of the most popular starting places for a trip down the Horton River. Although not actually the headwaters of the river, it is large enough for any float plane to land. Horton Lake stays frozen into June, so it is wise to check the state of the ice with pilots before planning to land there. The Horton River can be reached by a small creek flowing north from Horton Lake. It may be difficult to paddle in low water levels.

Several small lakes, which may or may not be adequate for float planes, are located north of Horton Lake, closer to the actual headwaters of the river.

One hundred and sixty-five km (103 miles) from the headwaters, the first big cliffs make their appearance on the east bank. They are visible from quite a distance and are about 15 metres (50 feet) high. The water remains fairly calm with no major rapids reported here. A hike to the top of the river valley will reward paddlers with a view of tundra on both sides of the river.

The Whalemen River enters the Horton from the north, 293 km (182 miles) downstream from the headwaters. Here, the river makes an obvious arc, flowing first north and then south. Three km (1.5 miles) south of the Whalemen, on the west bank of the Horton, lie the remains of either an old Inuit camp or a hunting camp left by whalers – three tent rings and a stone fence used by hunters to herd the caribou into an area for slaughter.

About 11 km (7 miles) further downstream is a set of rapids that are usually runnable. The river is split by a gravel island which can be used to line canoes if necessary.

Approximately 17 km (11 miles) downstream from the Whalemen River, the first canyon on the Horton begins. Cliff walls on both sides of the river extend for 3.5 km (2 miles). The river flows south and then angles abruptly to the west. There are 4 rapids in this canyon and the first is encountered about 1.5 km downstream from the opening of the canyon. When water levels are high, these rapids can all be lined. Later in the year, when water levels have dropped, these rapids can usually be run. The water levels on the Horton vary from year to year and paddlers should be very cautious through the three canyons, always scouting before running any rapids, regardless of the time of year.

The canyon itself is very scenic, and fossils can be found on the right bank of the river. About 2 km downstream from the end of the canyon there is a very shallow spot where canoes may have to be dragged at almost any time of the summer.

Eight km (5 miles) downstream from the end of the canyon, there is a 2 km section of fast water, which, depending on water levels, might be a major rapid. Even in August, canoes may have to be lined. A point of interest 10 km (6 miles) downstream, is a small waterfall tumbling out of a cave on the right bank. Just 2 km downstream from the waterfall, there are 2 more sets of rapids which may be run or lined on river right. There are still cliffs along the river, although they are not continuous.

The second canyon begins 23 km (14 miles) downstream from the end of the first canyon. It is slightly longer than the first and contains 6 or 7 major rapids. Early in the year, they cannot be run at all; however, in August they might be, except for the last set. This canyon is easily identified by a stone tower in the middle of the river, between 2 major rapids. It is possible to portage or line along river left.

The third and final canyon starts 2 km downstream from the end of the second canyon and is about 2 km long. It has few rapids, and in fact, in August, is usually only fast water. After this final canyon, there are no more rapids on the river, although fast water and riffles will be encountered.

The 30 or so km (19 miles) downstream from the final canyon are characterized by frequent gravel bars braiding the river. It is very shallow in many places and the deepest channels seem to be those along river right. The cliffs start to diminish after the third canyon, and around Stefansson Creek, the landscape opens up.

At km 450 (mile 280), the West River enters the Horton and 4 km (2 miles) downstream, the Coal River enters from the east. This river comes from the Smoking Hills and its water is a bit muddy and may be bad tasting. From here on, the water of the Horton tends to be muddier and the fishing poor.

At this point, the Horton passes through what could be called the "Badlands". The vegetation is thin and gradually the country takes on a desolate tone. Hills of barren rock, banded in various colourful hues, give the landscape an eerie quality. If the wind is blowing from the right direction, you can smell the sulphur from the Smoking Hills on the coast. About 100 km (62 miles) upstream from the river mouth, the trees disappear from the river valley.

The old Horton River valley crosses the peninsula to Harrowby Bay, a distance of about 25 km (16 miles). The Horton River itself spills into Franklin Bay. Most paddlers end their trip at the DEW Line station about 5 km (3 miles) from the river mouth, because it has a good landing strip. It is very tricky to get there, however, because of fluctuating tides and ice. At low tide, the water is too shallow to paddle, and the muck is too deep for a person to stand in. The only alternative is to pole your canoe for 5 km. A better alternative is to arrange to be picked up by float plane on the river, upstream of the mouth.

MAPS REQUIRED: (read maps from left to right)
(1:250,000)   Horton Lake 96 O   Erly Lake 97 A
                 Simpson Lake 97 B   Franklin Bay 97 C

AVERAGE GRADIENT: Average gradient from Horton Lake to the Arctic Ocean is 0.53 metres per kilometre (2.8 feet per mile).

HYRDOGRAPH: According to the Water Survey Office of Canada in Yellowknife, no hydrographs have been recorded on the Horton River.

SOURCE INFORMATION:

1. The Horton River: Northwest Territories Rivers Profile.

2. Obst, Joachim and Cynthia Brown: Personal communication.

3. Poole, Kim and Louise: Personal communication.

4. Hoyt, William B.: Politician with a Paddle, Buffalo News, 1987.

CUMULATIVE DISTANCES:

Location	Kilometres	Miles
Horton Lake	0	0
Whalemen River	293	182
First Canyon	310	193
Second Canyon	335	208
West River	450	280
Franklin Bay	600	373

KAZAN RIVER

TOTAL DISTANCE:

A: Kasba Lake to Baker Lake – 854 km (534 miles).
B: Angikuni Lake to Baker Lake – 483 km (302 miles).

DURATION OF TRIP: 45 days (Kasba Lake to Baker Lake).

START : The most common starting point is at Kasba Lake near the NWT/Manitoba border. For a shorter trip, paddlers can start at Angikuni Lake.

FINISH: The most popular finishing point for this trip is at the community of Baker Lake. Canoeists can also paddle to the community of Chesterfield Inlet on Hudson's Bay.

ACCESSIBILITY: The closest community to either Kasba or Angikuni Lakes is Arviat, situated on Hudson Bay, 432 km (270 miles) northeast of Kasba Lake. This community offers air charter services and can be reached from Winnipeg by air via Churchill, or from Yellowknife via Rankin Inlet. Air charters can also be arranged from Fort Smith and Yellowknife, which are 496 km (310 miles) and 640 km (400 miles) respectively from Kasba Lake. Both of these communities are accessible via the Mackenzie Highway and scheduled jet service from Edmonton.

RIVER NOTES: The Kazan River flows north from Kasba Lake near the NWT/Manitoba border and continues across the barrenlands to Baker Lake on Chesterfield Inlet. This river valley is a favoured hunting ground of the Caribou Inuit and Chipewyan Dene peoples. Not only is it of considerable archaeological and historical importance, but it is also notable for its abundance and variety of wildlife.

There are no settlements along the river except at Baker Lake, the usual finishing point. Some maps show Ennadai as a settlement, but in reality it is an abandoned weather station. Because of its extreme isolation, length, rapids and huge lakes, canoeists planning to travel the river should have good paddling skills and wilderness camping experience. This is not a river for beginners. Spray decks are recommended for canoes. Because of limited firewood along the route, paddlers should carry a small gas stove and fuel.

GEOGRAPHY: Kasba Lake, the source of the Kazan, lies within the tree line in the Precambrian Shield. The countryside is typical of the northern boreal forest, covered by dense spruce forests, numerous lakes, scattered patches of muskeg and rocky outcrops. The relief is mainly hilly with some plateaux. As the river flows north, it gradually enters the treeless barrenlands. The tree line, which is the approximate northern limit of trees, crosses Ennadai Lake. Eskers, erratics and morainal material were deposited in this area after the advance of the last glacier. Near its mouth on Baker Lake, the Kazan passes through the Hudson Bay Lowlands.

CLIMATE: The Kazan flows across the barrenlands where changeable weather is the rule, not the exception. Although daytime temperatures in July average around

15°C (60°F), they can drop to freezing at night. Severe and sudden winds are very common, making lake paddling in particular very hazardous. Paddlers can be windbound for days. Even in mid–summer, snowstorms are not uncommon. Good rain gear, a warm parka, a good tent and a 3 season sleeping bag are essential.

Although spring break-up on the river itself occurs between mid-May and mid-June, many of the large lakes remain ice–covered until mid-July, making progress slow and hazardous. Because the river flows south to north, the lakes nearer the source usually become ice-free first. Freeze-up is in early October.

FLORA: Spruce trees dominate the boreal forest around Kasba Lake. Beyond the tree line, paddlers will encounter typical barrenland vegetation, including wildflowers, berries and dwarf willows. Some small clusters of dwarf spruce occur as far north as Yathkyed Lake. Fuel for cooking fires is very limited beyond this lake.

FAUNA: Caribou are the most common large mammals along the Kazan. Part of the migration route for the Kaminuriak caribou herd, which numbers over 300,000 animals, is found along the Kazan River Valley. Hundreds, or even thousands of caribou can often be seen along the shores and swimming across the river. Wolves, which tend to follow the caribou, are also abundant and there are many good denning sites along the river valley. Muskoxen have been spotted with increasing regularity downstream of Yathkyed Lake. Arctic foxes and hares are also common in the barrens, while moose and otters are frequently sighted along the upper reaches of the river.

The Kazan River Valley is a rich breeding ground for a wide variety of birds. An expedition in 1988 identified 54 different species including snowy owls, peregrine falcons, tundra swans and ptarmigan. Waterfowl abound along the lake and river shores, while birds of prey nest high in the cliffs along the river banks.

Fishing is excellent along the river, with lake trout and Arctic grayling the most common catch. Arctic char can be caught in Baker Lake late in August.

HUMAN HISTORY: Perhaps the most outstanding feature of the Kazan River is its rich human history. For thousands of years Inuit and Chipewyan people have travelled and hunted the river valley, drawn by the abundance of caribou. Archaeological evidence of their lives can be found all along the river. An archaeological survey of the river was done in 1988. Virtually every habitable section of the river has some evidence of human use. The majority of the approximately 250 sites surveyed relate to the Caribou Inuit habitation since the mid-19th century. Some evidence, however, suggests a Paleo-Eskimo occupation which may date as early as 3000 years ago. Tent rings, meat caches, graves, kayak stands and a wide variety of tools and hunting implements were found. Even today, inuksuit, piles of carefully arranged rocks, guide travellers along the shores of the huge lakes. According to the survey's summary, "Few, if any, other rivers in Canada have so much visible evidence of cultural adaptation or such a wealth of native heritage." Paddlers are reminded that artifacts and archaeological sites are protected under the law. Feel free to explore and examine them, but don't remove any "souvenirs" or disturb the sites in any way.

Samuel Hearne was the first European to cross the Kazan on his second attempt to find the Coppermine River in 1771. The first systematic geological survey of the Kazan

Kazan River

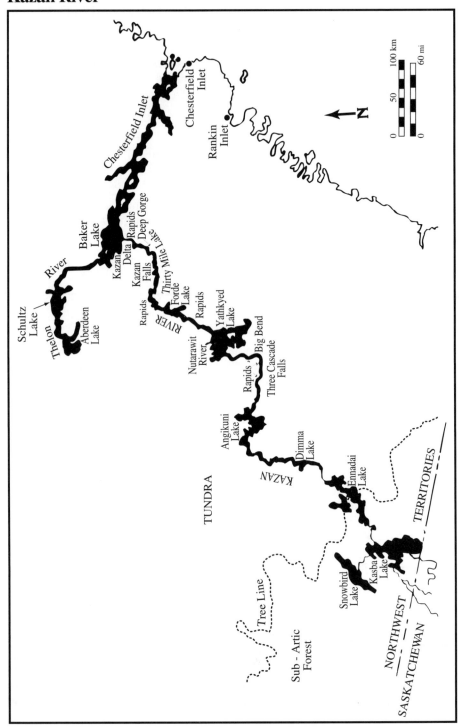

was done by J.B. Tyrell in 1894. He travelled the river for the Geological Survey of Canada. His journal records much about the people of the river. In all, he visited 39 tents, housing hundreds of people.

In the 1950s, a change in the caribou migration route spelled disaster for the Caribou Inuit. Many starved, and the survivors were forced to move to Baker Lake and other coastal settlements on Hudson Bay. Today the Kazan, once a busy highway, is a quiet river, little travelled.

RIVER PROFILE: The most common starting point for the Kazan trip is Kasba (Little Partridge) Lake. On the western shore of the lake is a fishing lodge (Kasba Lake Lodge). The run from Kasba to Ennadai Lake is a relatively easy one. The river is wide, with a fast current and few difficult rapids. The first marked rapid can be run, but must be scouted. Depending on water levels, paddlers may have to bypass four more rapids in this section. The first two are found at an 'S' bend just before a widening in the river, upstream from Tabane Lake. Two more rapids are located about a kilometre downstream from the Tabane outlet. Tabane Lake is characterized by very irregular shores and low wooded points and islands. As the river widens just upstream from Ennadai Lake, paddlers will notice a ruined cabin.

Fleming/NWT Archives

The first systematic geological survey of the Kazan was done by J.B. Tyrell in 1894 with the Geological Survey of Canada

The 60 km (38 mile) paddle along the length of Ennadai Lake takes paddlers across the tree line and into the barrens. Winds can be very strong here and travellers may be windbound for several days. On the northeast arm of the lake there is an automatically operated weather station and several buildings. One of these buildings is an emergency shelter supplied with food and clothing. In addition, a runway, in fairly poor condition, exists for aviation emergencies. The buildings were recently purchased by a private operator hoping to set up a fish camp there. An unmanned water monitoring station is located at the outlet of Ennadai Lake. There is also a cabin there, although there are no supplies or emergency equipment. A short distance downstream is a difficult stretch of rapids which, depending on water levels, can be run after careful scouting. The major hazard on Angikuni Lake is the wind.

For the next 50 km (31 miles), the Kazan winds through gravelly channels and wide stretches to Dimma Lake. Along this stretch paddlers must navigate around many islands. A rapid worth watching for is located at the entrance to a widening in the river upstream from Dimma Lake. At the outlet to Dimma Lake, maps indicate an island. Trip reports suggest taking the channel on river right, as the left channel apparently ends in a gravel bed.

Between Dimma and Angikuni Lakes, a distance of 118 km (74 miles), the Kazan flows through a long stretch of narrow lakes. Paddlers will spot many old Inuit camps in this section. There are some unmarked rapids in this section. Angikuni Lake, meaning "Great Lake" in Inuktitut, also has many Inuit sites along its shores. In 1894, Tyrell reported meeting many Inuit groups camped here. "Many Eskimos were camped in the vicinity, and at one time our Peterboro canoes were surrounded by 23 kayaks."

A long stretch of unmarked rapids occurs at the outlet of Angikuni Lake. Depending on the water levels, this section may be run, although it should be carefully scouted first. The river continues smoothly for about another 50 km (30 miles) until it is interrupted by 3 cascades. These should be portaged on river right. Misjudging the takeout could be fatal. Five km (2 miles) below the falls is another marked rapid. It should be portaged on river right. These rapids mark the beginning of a 32 km (20 mile) section of almost continuous rapids. Canoeists are advised to carefully scout all rapids in this stretch. The end of this stretch of rapids is signalled by a set that can be portaged on river right over an island and boulder field. The next 39 km (24 miles) are calm. A group of small islands fill the narrow channel. Paddlers should keep to river left here. Seven km (3 miles) downstream is another set of rapids which need scouting and may have to be portaged. On the approach to Yathkyed Lake, paddlers will see the last of the isolated spruce and tamarack trees on the river.

It is advisable to climb to the height of land on river right before reaching Yathkyed Lake, to check ice conditions on the lake. The word Yathkyed means "The Great Ice Filled One" in the Chipewyan language. Since winds on the lake can be daunting, paddlers should stay close to the protection of the north shore. Near the outlet of the lake there is a long point of land which can be crossed by portaging about 400 metres across its base.

There are two sets of rapids between Yathkyed and Forde Lake. Both can be paddled on river left. From the beginning of Forde Lake to its outlet is a distance of 25 km (16 miles). Two sets of marked rapids occur between Forde Lake and Thirty Mile Lake. The first, located 7 km (3 miles) downstream from Forde Lake, can be run on the far river left. The second set occurs 20 km (12 miles) further downstream where the river bends sharply to the left. It can be portaged on river left.

Thirty Mile Lake is notable not only for its length, but also for its excellent fishing and abundance of Inuit sites. In addition to several ancient gravesites, there are many inuksuit. The marked rapid at the outlet of the lake can be avoided by portaging through the small lake at the base of the point which makes up the left bank of the outlet. Alternatively, it can be portaged along either river bank.

Twenty-six kilometres (16 miles) downstream of Thirty Mile Lake are the Kazan Falls, a 25 metre (85 foot) cascade tumbling over red sandstone cliffs. The falls are preceded by 2 km of whitewater. While this can be run at least part way along river right, it is not recommended. An upset here will almost certainly take the paddler over the falls. The 2 km (1 mile) portage around the falls can be made along river right. At the falls, the river is channelled through a narrow, impassable gorge. The portage around the gorge is marked by an inukshuk. There is a cairn at the top of the falls with messages from paddlers over the years.

Beyond the gorge, the river splits into several channels and navigational skills are called upon. Just west of the 'Y'-shaped esker, paddlers will see the remains of an inukshuk fence used to channel caribou into position for hunters. There is a section of very fast water about 15 km (10 miles) past here where the river turns right. Paddlers are advised to keep to the inside. The landscape changes at this point from gravelly till to hard rock outcrop. Several marked and unmarked rapids can present challenges in this final stretch. About 8 km (5 miles) upstream from Baker Lake, there is an unmarked rapid with a large shelf on river left. The final several kilometres into Baker Lake are very fast.

Crossing Baker Lake to the community itself can be hazardous because of sudden high winds. The community of Baker Lake is the only inland Inuit community in the NWT. Accommodation is available at the Baker Lake Lodge or the Iglu Hotel. Scheduled air service is available to other communities.

MAPS REQUIRED: (read maps from left to right)

1:250,000	Snowbird Lake 65D	Ennadai Lake 65C
	Ennadai 65F	Kamilukuak 65K
	Tulemalu Lake 65J	Ferguson Lake 65I
	Thirty Mile Lake 65P	MacQuoid Lake 55M
	Baker Lake 56D	

Trips beginning at Angikuni Lake need maps from Kamilukuak to Baker Lake only.

AVERAGE GRADIENT: From Angikuni Outlet to Baker Lake, 0.8 ft per mile or 0.15 m/km.

HYDROGRAPH: Kazan River above Kazan Falls, 1965-1988

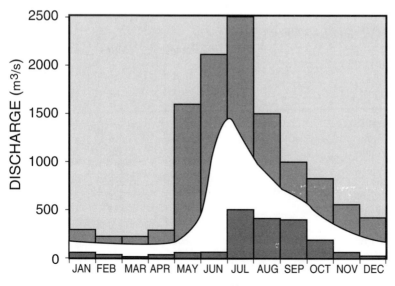

HYDROGRAPH: Kazan River at Outlet of Ennadai Lake, 1962-1988

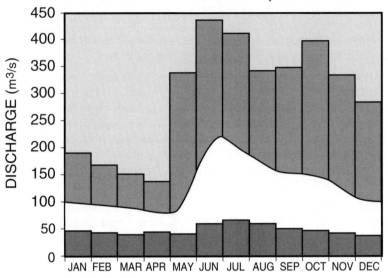

SOURCE INFORMATION:

1. MacKay, John W.: Arctic Adventure, A Kazan River Journal. Betelgeuse Books, 1983.

2. Tyrrell, J.B.: Report on the Doobaunt, Kazan and Ferguson Rivers and the Northwest Coast of Hudson Bay. Ottawa: Printed by S.E. Dawson, 1897.

3. The Kazan River Report, TravelArctic, 1979.

4. Pelly, David F.: Kazan: River of the Living Barrens, in *Wild Waters, Canoeing Canada's Wilderness Rivers*, edited by James Raffan. Key Porter Books, 1986.

5. McCreadie, Mary: Personal communication, 1988.

6. Summary, Operation Raleigh, Canadian Arctic Expedition, 1988.

CUMULATIVE DISTANCES:

Location	Kilometres	Miles
Kasba Lake outlet	0	0
Inlet Ennadai Lake	49	31
Ennadai Lake outlet	107	67
Inlet Angikuni Lake	308	195
Angikuni Lake outlet	371	232
Inlet Yathkyed Lake	506	316
Yathkyed Lake outlet	573	358
Inlet Forde Lake	612	382
Forde Lake outlet	637	398
Inlet Thirty Mile Lake	685	428
Thirty Mile Lake outlet	726	454
Kazan Falls Portage	752	470
Mouth of Kazan River	806	504
Community of Baker Lake	854	534

MACKENZIE RIVER

TOTAL DISTANCE: 1480 kilometres (925 miles) from Fort Providence to Inuvik.
DURATION OF TRIP: 3 to 4 weeks from Ft. Providence to Inuvik.
START: Most paddlers start at Hay River, Fort Providence or Fort Simpson.
FINISH: The most common finishing point is Inuvik.

ACCESSIBILITY: Hay River, Fort Providence, Fort Simpson and Wrigley are all accessible by road. Regularly scheduled air service is available to all communities along the river. Inuvik is accessible either by the Dempster Highway or by jet service from the south. Flying canoes south from Inuvik can be expensive. A cheaper alternative is to make arrangements with Northern Transportation Company Limited (NTCL) in Hay River. Their barges can backhaul canoes from Inuvik to Hay River. From Hay River, they can be trucked south.

RIVER NOTES: The Mackenzie River flows north almost 1500 km (950 miles) from Great Slave Lake to the Arctic Ocean. Along the way, several large rivers and lakes (notably Great Bear Lake) drain into the Mackenzie, making it Canada's largest river. Some of these tributaries, especially the Liard, carry great loads of sediment with them, giving the Mackenzie its murky character. Fresh drinking water can be taken from any of the streams emptying into the Mackenzie.

The Mackenzie is undoubtedly the most accessible river in the NWT. Paddlers without time to travel its entire length can put in or take out at any of the 9 communities along the way. The Mackenzie is also the only river in the NWT used by tugs and barges. Tugs pushing up to 10 barges supply the communities along the river with fuel and other necessities. Keep in mind that these large vessels do create large wakes and that a canoe is much more manoeuverable than a barge. Keep out of their way!

With the exception of two rapids, the Sans Sault and the Ramparts, the Mackenzie is a flatwater river. The river averages about 2 km (1.5 miles) in width and it is subject to strong winds which can make paddling very difficult, especially when the winds are blowing upstream.

The Mackenzie passes through some spectacular scenery and its numerous tributaries invite exploration. The small Dene communities along the way offer basic services, and are interesting to visit. Since most of the river flows through isolated country, paddlers should have good wilderness camping skills. Firewood is abundant.

GEOGRAPHY: The Mackenzie River begins in the low-lying lands on the southeastern shore of Great Slave Lake. This topography continues with few interruptions until past Camsell Bend, where the Mackenzie Mountains provide a spectacular backdrop to the wide, wooded river valley. An abundance of sand bars and islands offer good campsites for paddlers. Ever-shifting sand bars cause problems for large boats, necessitating a marked channel down the entire length of the river. The sand bars, however, are not a major problem for paddlers.

Most of the shoreline of the Mackenzie is made up of eroding clay beaches, bluffs and sand bars. Although the river itself is silty, clear water can be obtained at the mouth of the countless small creeks flowing into the river.

The Ramparts, just upstream from Fort Good Hope, form an 11 km (7 mile) long gorge carved through a limestone plateau. Coral fossils can be found along the face of these cliffs.

As the river approaches Arctic Red River, the Lower Ramparts provide the last relief in an otherwise flat terrain. These cliffs fade into lowlands and the river increases in width as it enters the Mackenzie Delta, a huge maze of channels and sandbars. The Big Rock Hills in the East Channel provide a striking contrast to the silty, alluvial soil of the Delta.

The town of Inuvik is situated on a flat, wooded plateau, overlooking the Delta, backed by the Caribou Hills.

CLIMATE: Spring breakup usually takes place in mid-May at the southern end of the river and in early June in the north, while freeze-up is in November. This means there is a fairly long paddling season.

Summer days are long and the farther north paddlers travel, the more daylight they will experience. Above the Arctic Circle, which crosses the river 27 km (17 miles) north of Fort Good Hope, paddlers can expect 24 hours of daylight during July and part of August.

The southern Mackenzie Valley has average daily maximum temperatures in July of about 21°C (69°F). At night, the temperature drops to about 10°C (50°F). Although rainfall is generally light, canoeists should bring good rain gear. Average temperatures in the northern region are approximately 3 to 8°C cooler. Rainfall levels are even lower near the Arctic coast.

FLORA: The Mackenzie River passes through two vegetation zones – the boreal forest in the southern part of the valley and the taiga or forest tundra in the Delta region.

The boreal forest is dominated by black and white spruce in the areas that have not been ravaged by forest fires in the last few decades. The more recently burned areas contain birch, aspen and poplar. Willow and alder thickets are found along the riverbanks. As you travel north, you will find that the trees gradually become shorter and less dense. Berries and wild flowers are common and a good book on the plants of the northern boreal forest is very useful (see Appendix G).

The forest tundra zone flanks the boreal forest and extends along the river as far as Inuvik. Black spruce dominate in the shelter of the river valley. The combination of warm summers and the rich silt in the Delta has fostered the growth of Canada's northernmost forest. On some of the islands near Inuvik, white spruce grow to heights of up to 15 metres (50 feet). Sedges, moss and other aquatic plants abound in and around the numerous lakes and small channels of the Delta.

FAUNA: The Mackenzie Valley is home to a wide range of wildlife. Approximately 39 species of mammals and 175 species of birds can be found in the area. The most commonly seen mammals are black bears, moose, beaver, and muskrat. Lynx, marten and wolves are more elusive. Nearly all of the birds found along the Mackenzie are migratory. The most common waterfowl are snow and Canada geese, tundra swans, and many types of ducks. Loons, gulls, sandhill cranes, bald and golden eagles, ospreys and falcons are also commonly seen.

Mackenzie River

Dempster Highway
Inuvik
Arctic Red River
Ramparts
Ft. Good Hope
Sans Sault Rapids

0   100 km
0   60 mi

Norman
Wells
Ft. Norman
Ft. Franklin
Great Bear Lake

Wrigley

New section of
Mackenzie
Highway
now open

N

Liard R.
Ft. Simpson

Jean Marie River

Edzo Rae
Ft. Providence
Yellowknife

Great Slave Lake

Enterprise

Hay River

Mackenzie Highway
road to
Ft. Smith
(Hwy. #5)

The Mackenzie Delta is a particularly rich area for wildlife. Its quiet channels are the nesting and staging area for countless waterfowl and it is considered to be one of the most productive muskrat trapping areas in the world.

Fishing with a rod and reel is best attempted in the rivers and streams emptying into the Mackenzie and paddlers have a good chance of catching Arctic grayling, dolly varden, northern pike, whitefish, inconnu, lake trout or walleye.

HUMAN HISTORY: For thousands of years, the Dene of the Mackenzie Valley have travelled "Deh Cho" (Big River). They lived a nomadic lifestyle, hunting and fishing along the valley and up the rivers and creeks on either side. It was only after a century of contact with fur traders, missionaries and government representatives, that the Dene began to settle in villages along the river.

There are four main groups of Dene along the Mackenzie: the north and south Slavey, the Hare and Mountain Dene, and the Gwich'in. The Delta is home to the Inuvialuit people.

The first European to travel the valley was Alexander Mackenzie, who paddled the river in 1789. In his search for a route to the Pacific Ocean, Mackenzie inadvertently opened up a new area for the fur trading companies who were expanding north and west across Canada.

Fur traders from the Northwest Company quickly took advantage of this new, untrapped area and opened posts at Fort of the Forks (Fort Simpson) and Fort Good Hope in 1804. Fort Norman was established in 1810. After the Northwest Company merged with the Hudson's Bay Company in 1821, more posts were added. Supplies, traps, and guns were traded with the Dene for beaver, muskrat, marten, lynx, fox, wolf and bear hides.

Missionaries, explorers and adventurers followed in the fur traders' footsteps,

An Inuvialuit whaling and hunt camp near Kendall Island

boarding steam-powered stern wheelers every summer to visit the north. Prospectors travelled the Mackenzie on their way to the Klondike, paddling up the Liard, Keele, Peel and Rat Rivers to cross the continental divide.

In 1919, Imperial Oil struck oil on the Mackenzie River near Norman Wells. This discovery prompted the first air flight into the north and marked the beginning of the industrial age in this remote northern valley. Two years later, the Government of Canada signed Treaty number 11 with the Dene of the Mackenzie region. During the Second World War, the Canol Pipeline was constructed from Norman Wells to the Yukon to supply oil to Alaska.

The discovery of oil and gas in the Mackenzie Delta and Beaufort Sea in the 1970's increased barge traffic on the river and eventually resulted in a pipeline from Norman Wells to Alberta. Today, there is still discussion about building a longer pipeline from the Delta down the Mackenzie Valley.

Anyone interested in Canadian history will be fascinated by a paddle down the Mackenzie. Old trader's cabins, ruins of abandoned posts, remnants of the Canol Road construction and many other sites can be found along the banks of the river. Several of the communities along the route are almost 200 years old. Historic sites, like the old Roman Catholic church in Fort Good Hope, are scattered along the river. It pays to do some reading on northern history before beginning your trip.

RIVER PROFILE: This report describes the Mackenzie River from Fort Providence, 72 km (45 miles) downstream from its beginning on Great Slave Lake, to Inuvik in the Mackenzie Delta. This trip is 1495 km (934 miles) long.

Fort Providence is a Dene community of about 600 people located on the north shore of the Mackenzie River on the highway to Yellowknife. There are two campgrounds here as well as several small stores and a motel. The local craft shop sells a variety of handmade items including moosehair tuftings, for which the community is well known.

The river is only about a kilometre wide in this first stretch and is surrounded by low and level countryside, covered with poplar and birch. About 19 km (12 miles) downstream, the river widens into Mills Lake, a large, shallow body of water which can be very hazardous in even moderate winds. It's a good idea to keep close to the south shore of the lake.

The abandoned Canol Camp of Axe Point can be found at benchmark (BM) 478, downstream from Mills Lake. The Sikhanni Chief, an old river boat, lies in the bush along the bank, and numerous trappers' cabins dot the shoreline in this area. The river narrows again flowing through low, wet swampland. The Trout River enters the Mackenzie from the south. It is well known locally for its excellent walleye fishing.

The first community on the river downstream of Fort Providence is the tiny village of Jean Marie River. This isolated Slavey community of less than 100 people is very traditional. Trapping is still the major source of employment and the women of the community are internationally renowned for their moosehair tuftings and porcupine quillwork. There are few services in this community, but it is nice to stop in and say hello.

About 19 km (12 miles) upstream from Fort Simpson are the Green Island Rapids. While there is little surface turbulence, the current is swift. Approaching Fort Simpson, paddlers are wise to keep to river right to avoid the fast water at the mouth of the Liard

River where it empties into the Mackenzie. You will notice a definite deterioration in the colour of the water downstream from the confluence of the Liard and Mackenzie Rivers, especially if there has been a lot of rain. Driftwood can also be a problem from here on down the river, especially during high water.

Fort Simpson is located on an island in the Mackenzie, just downstream from the mouth of the Liard. This town of about 1000 residents is an alternate starting point. It is located on the Mackenzie Highway and also has regular air connections with Yellowknife. It offers a wide variety of stores, services and accommodations.

Established in 1804, it is one of the oldest continuously occupied posts on the Mackenzie River. Because of the rich resources of the area, Fort Simpson quickly became a fur trading, transportation and service centre. The rich alluvial soil allowed the missions to grow vegetables and raise livestock. For many years Fort Simpson was home to an Experimental Farm run by the Government of Canada.

Hälle Flygare

Mackenzie River Delta

From Fort Simpson to the mouth of the North Nahanni, a distance of 118 km (74 miles), the river flows in a west-northwesterly direction. It is flanked by rolling, wooded plains punctuated by areas of muskeg. Both the landscape and the course of the river change quite dramatically at Camsell Bend, 5 km (3 miles) downstream from the mouth of the North Nahanni. A 900 metre (3000 foot) escarpment sharply deflects the river onto a northerly course and it breaks into several smaller channels. In the distance the Mackenzie Mountains provide a dramatic backdrop. There are many cabins along this stretch of the river and some of them are still used by local trappers. Downstream of the Bend the river slows and widens to about 3 to 5 km (2 to 3 miles).

North of the mouth of the Willowlake River, where there is a small camp, the Mackenzie enters a more mountainous region. Rising out of the lowlands on the east bank is the McConnell Range which parallels the river's right bank for nearly 320 km (200 miles). On the left bank, the river is flanked by the Camsell Range, a high wooded ridge, beyond which the land rises gradually to the Mackenzie Mountains. Immediately downstream from the mouth of the River Between Two Mountains, the Mackenzie narrows and the current increases. Old Fort Island is the original site of Fort Wrigley. It was referred to as Little Rapids Post by the Hudson's Bay Company and was moved several times before it became the permanent settlement of Wrigley.

Wrigley is a small community situated high on the bluff on the right bank of the river. A small store, cafe and nursing station are located here and the community has scheduled air service to Fort Simpson. The economy in this Slavey settlement is based on trapping, hunting and fishing.

Just downstream a 350 metre (1150 foot) high cliff face known as Roche qui Trempe a l'Eau, provides a nesting site for swallows and peregrine falcons. Thermal springs are found around this dome-shaped rock. The old settlement of Wrigley, which is still shown on some older maps, was located on the west bank and the remains of the RCMP station and several old cabins can still be found.

From here to the mouth of the Blackwater River, a distance of about 80 km (50 miles), the river flows fairly swiftly. The Ochre River, notable for its bright red colour in the early summer, joins the Mackenzie from the east.

Three kilometres (2 miles) downstream from the Blackwater River, the Mackenzie turns abruptly to the west for a few kilometres and then resumes its northerly course. The current becomes swifter and the river winds through islands and sandbars as it flows towards Fort Norman. Old Fort Norman was originally built near the confluence of the Redstone and Mackenzie Rivers. Although there are cabins at this site, the original buildings have long since disappeared.

Paddlers can travel 3.5 km (2 miles) up the Saline River to salt flats which attract a lot of wildlife. An abandoned oil camp is found at the mouth of the Saline River. There is rumoured to be good trout fishing in an eddy at the mouth of this river.

The Smoking Hills are located about 5 km (3 miles) upstream from Fort Norman. The smoke comes from smouldering seams of lignite coal along the river bank.

Fort Norman is located high on river right of the Mackenzie overlooking the mouth of the Great Bear River. Many services are available here including a store, nursing station, RCMP and scheduled flights to Norman Wells. The Hudson's Bay Company moved their post to this location in 1851. Father Grollier, OMI founded a mission here 8 years later. The Anglican church, built in the 1860's, is the oldest building in the valley.

Across the crystal clear waters of the Great Bear River, Bear Rock towers 450 metres (1500 feet) above the water. The Dene have a legend about the rock. A giant, after suffering through a long, cold winter, killed 3 huge beaver and stretched their pelts on Bear Rock. These pelts can be seen today as three red patches high on the rock face.

The original 1920 oil well that started the Norman Wells discovery is located near a creek just downstream from Bear Rock on river right. Some of the drilling equipment is still visible.

Downstream of Fort Norman, the river flows northwesterly between high clay banks. The 80 km (50 mile) stretch to Norman Wells contains many islands and is very wide, reaching over 5 km (3 miles) at some points.

Norman Wells is one of the newest communities on the river and is the site of the only oil refinery in the NWT. "The Wells" is located on a flat plain at the base of the Norman Range on river right. It has hotels, restaurants, stores and regular flights to Yellowknife, Inuvik and many smaller communities. The Canol Road, built beside the Canol Pipeline during World War Two, starts on the left bank of the river. It has become an increasingly popular hiking destination in recent years. A museum of local history has also opened recently and is well worth a visit. There is a fair amount of boat traffic on the river between the various artificial drilling islands, so canoeists are wise to stick close to shore.

The Mackenzie continues in a north-westerly direction, flowing between steep, sloping clay and gravel banks, interspersed with limestone cliffs. Downstream from Perry Island, the river turns sharply west for about 19 km (12 miles), flowing between sheer limestone cliffs. At the mouth of the Carcajou River, the Mackenzie again turns north, and then, just past the mouth of the Mountain River, constricts to about 1 km (3/4 mile) in width. It is here that the Sans Sault Rapids are encountered. These rapids are formed by a rocky ledge that extends from the east shore to midstream. These rapids are best approached along river left where they can be skirted with little difficulty. There is a sign above the rapids warning boaters to beware.

Downstream from the rapids, the river remains wide and dotted with islands and sandbars. Immediately upstream from the Ramparts Canyon, the river drops over a ledge known as the Ramparts Rapids. Paddlers must pass this ledge on river right. At high water it is not a problem. Please note that this ledge is not marked on topographic maps. The ramparts canyon, which is 12 km (7 miles) long, is the most spectacular part of the river. The limestone walls rise 80 metres (265 feet) straight out of the water and in some places jut into the sky like castle battlements. In days gone by, the tops of these cliffs were favoured camp sites for Dene fearing attack. Today, paths to the top can still be found along the banks. The current here is very fast and paddlers are probably wisest to follow the channel markers. Within sight of Fort Good Hope, a small statue of the Virgin Mary can be seen in a niche above the river, watching over travellers. She appeared here in a vision to a newly baptised Dene late in the 19th century.

Fort Good Hope is a Slavey community of about 500 residents. Accommodation and meals are normally available and there is a store, nursing station and scheduled flights to Norman Wells and Inuvik. One of the most interesting sites in the community is the interior of Our Lady of Good Hope Church, built in 1878. Paddlers may want to cross the Mackenzie and paddle up Fossil Creek (opposite the community) to Fossil Lake (16 km or 12 miles) to hunt for fossils. Ten to twelve thousand years ago, the Mackenzie River plunged over a huge falls and into this lake. The dried cliffs and plunge pool are all that remain today.

Twenty-seven km (17 miles) north of Fort Good Hope, the river crosses the Arctic Circle. A large sign on the right shore marks the occasion. First time circle crossers should go for a dip to commemorate the event! An abandoned trading post which is still in quite good condition can be seen along the right shore north of here.

The Grand View, a widening in the river, named for its open vista, begins downstream from the Ontaratue River. A small, family-run sawmill can be seen on the left bank of the river -- a good place to stop in and say hello. Little Chicago, located on the right shore, was the winter residence for prospectors travelling to the Klondike gold rush in the 1890's. It continued as a native community until it was destroyed by forest fires. Not much remains of it today.

Downstream from Thunder River, the Mackenzie turns sharply west and continues on this course for nearly 96 km (60 miles). At the Travaillant River, it swings back to the northwest. During periods of low water, sandbars and shoals may present a bit of a problem to paddlers.

Downstream from the mouth of Prairie Creek, the Mackenzie turns north again before entering the long horseshoe bend upstream from the settlement of Arctic Red River. This section of the river is known as the Lower Ramparts. This 13 km (8 mile) long canyon of shale cliffs is the last topographic relief on the river. Although the river narrows here, the current remains moderate.

The settlement of Arctic Red River is on the left bank of the Mackenzie at the mouth of the Arctic Red River. Located on the Dempster Highway that connects Inuvik, NWT and Dawson City, Yukon, this small Gwich'in community has been a traditional fishing camp for generations. It became a permanent settlement in 1868. Although it has a small store, no accommodation is available. A car ferry on the Dempster Highway crosses the Mackenzie here.

Twenty-four kilometres (15 miles) downstream from Arctic Red River paddlers will reach Point Separation. Here the Mackenzie splits into the many streams and channels forming the Mackenzie Delta. The Delta is a fascinating place, vibrating with life, but it is very easy to get lost here. The main channel to Inuvik, the East Channel, is marked for tugs and is the best route to take. The entrance to the East Channel is found about 16 km (10 miles) downstream from Point Separation.

Inuvik was established in 1955 by the government to replace the community of Aklavik on the west side of the delta, which experts felt was sinking into the river. Today Aklavik still stands, sporting a community motto of "Never Say Die".

About 3,500 residents live in Inuvik and all modern services are available. This is really the "Land of the Midnight Sun" for most of the summer. There are many interesting side trips that can be arranged from Inuvik for visitors wishing to see more of the north.

There is daily air service south and the Dempster Highway goes west to the Yukon from here.

MAPS REQUIRED: (read maps left to right)

(1:250,000)		
	Falaise Lake 85 F	Norman Wells 96 E
	Mills Lake 85 E	Sans Sault Rapids 106 H
	Fort Simpson 95 H	Fort Good Hope 106 I
	Bulmer Lake 95 I	Ontaratue Lake 106 J
	Camsell Bend 95 J	Travaillant Lake 106 O
	Wrigley 95 O	Arctic Red River 106 N
	Dahadinni River 95 N	Ft. McPherson 106 M
	Fort Norman 96 C	Aklavik 107 B
	Carcajou Canyon 96 D	

The following hydrographic charts would be helpful: 6381, 6410 to 6416, 6384 to 6387. These are available from the Dept. of Energy, Mines and Resources, Ottawa.

AVERAGE GRADIENT: The average gradient from Mills Lake near Ft. Providence to Inuvik is 0.1 metres per kilometre, or 0.5 feet per mile.

HYDROGRAPH: *Mackenzie River at Fort Simpson, 1938-1988*

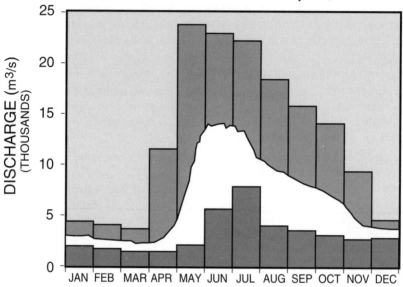

SOURCE INFORMATION:

1. Northwest Territories Explorer's Guide.

2. Mackenzie River Trip Report, TravelArctic. 1979.

3. Cuthbert, Gordon and Rick Morrison: Mackenzie River Canoe Trip Report, 1979.

4. Thompson, Keith: Small Boating on the Mackenzie River, 1973.

5. Hanks, Chris: Personal communication.

CUMULATIVE DISTANCES:

Location	Kilometres	Miles
Fort Providence	0	0
Fort Simpson	256	160
Wrigley	495	309
Fort Norman	740	463
Norman Wells	818	511
Fort Good Hope	1011	632
Arctic Red River	1350	844
Inuvik	1480	925

MOUNTAIN RIVER

TOTAL DISTANCE:
A. Dusty Lake to Fort Good Hope – 377 km. (236 miles).

B. Willowhandle Lake to Fort Good Hope – 359 km. (224 miles).

C. Shale Lake (Palmer Lake) to Fort Good Hope – 312 km (195 miles).

DURATION OF TRIP
A. 21 days

B. 19 days

C. 15 days

START :

A. Dusty Lake (also known as Perry Linton Lake)

B. Willowhandle Lake (a.k.a. Mountain Lake)

C. Shale Lake (a.k.a. Palmer Lake)

FINISH: Fort Good Hope

ACCESSIBILITY: The closest float plane base to the headwaters of the Mountain River is at Norman Wells, which is served by scheduled jet service from Edmonton and Yellowknife. Canoes may be rented, flown to Norman Wells, or barged down the Mackenzie River from Hay River. Return from Fort Good Hope can be either by scheduled small aircraft to Norman Wells or air charter.

Dusty Lake, also known as Perry Linton Lake, is a small lake high in the Mackenzie Mountains. By starting here, paddlers can extend their trip and spend more time in the high country. Because of its small size, only short takeoff and landing (STOL) aircraft like the Pilatus Porter can land here. At high water, it may be possible for a Twin Otter to land. A one–kilometre portage is required over hummocky terrain to reach the Mountain River from here.

Willowhandle or Mountain Lake is accessible by float plane charter from Norman Wells. The creek leading from here to the Mountain River may not be navigable in low water levels and paddlers are advised to check with pilots in advance for up-to-date reports on the level of this stream.

Starting at Shale Lake, or Palmer lake, offers paddlers a shorter trip. Palmer Lake Hunting Lodge is located on this lake. To reach the Mountain River, an 8 km (5 mile) portage is required. The first 3 km (2 miles) are relatively easy walking over distinct paths and horse trails. The last 5 km (3 miles) require hiking over hilly terrain, through spruce forests and frequent wet areas.

RIVER NOTES: The Mountain River is a major west bank tributary of the Mackenzie River. It begins high in the Mackenzie Mountains, just east of the NWT/Yukon border and flows northeasterly through the mountains and the

Mountain River

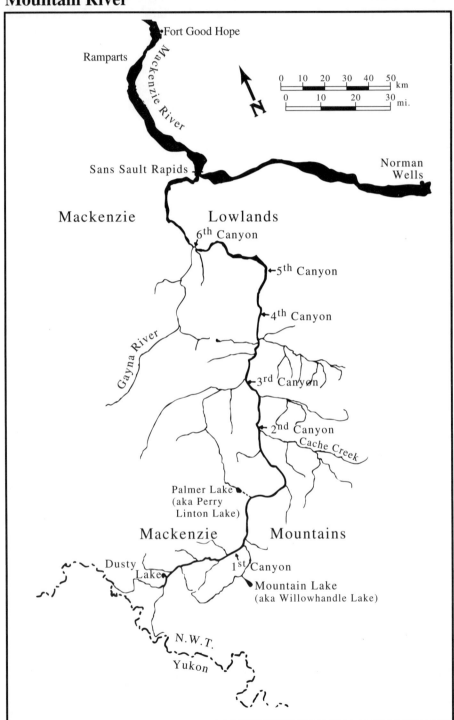

Mackenzie Lowlands, entering the Mackenzie River upstream from the Sans Sault Rapids. The settlement of Fort Good Hope is located on the Mackenzie, 80 km (50 miles) downstream from the mouth of the Mountain River. Norman Wells is 103 km (64 miles) upstream from the same point.

This is a true whitewater trip, with large volume rapids, fast current and six hazardous canyons. The river is frequently braided and its bed and bank materials are generally composed of gravel and cobblestones.

Paddlers should be experienced in whitewater canoeing and wilderness camping. This river is very isolated, with often continuous rapids, few eddies, and icy cold water. Like all mountain rivers, water levels can fluctuate drastically, sometimes rising over a metre in a few hours. It is wise to camp well above the high water line and secure boats well at night. The river is probably most easily navigated in August when water levels have dropped. Most of the large volume rapids and the canyons have to be portaged. Spray decks are recommended for open canoes.

The entire upper section of the river provides excellent opportunities for hiking and photography. Near the headwaters, peaks rising over 2500 metres (8000 feet) are common.

GEOGRAPHY: The Mountain River flows through two distinct physiographic regions – the Mackenzie Mountains and the Mackenzie Lowlands. The mountains mark the eastern front of the Western Cordillera and are a northern extension of the Rocky Mountain system. With the Ogilvie and Selwyn Mountains to the west, these mountains form the drainage divide between the Yukon and Mackenzie watersheds. Rising to heights of over 2700 metres (9000 feet), these mountains present an impressive topographic and climatic barrier.

Rivers in the Mackenzie Mountains cut through successive ranges of Paleozoic and Mesozoic rock formations. The names of many of these ranges – Backbone, Thundercloud, Sawtooth Canyon serve as reminders of the rugged and often unforgiving environment. Limestone and dolomites of buff, grey and cinnamon; black shales; green, grey and maroon siltstones and sandstones all provide the canoeist with vistas of rugged beauty.

The 96 km (60 mile) lower section of the Mountain River flows through the Mackenzie Lowlands. The wide valley here contrasts markedly with the mountainous section upstream. The river in this final stretch is bordered by low cutbanks and hills and contains numerous gravel bars.

CLIMATE: The weather in the Mackenzie Mountains is unpredictable. Moisture-filled air masses from the Pacific Ocean collide with the mountains throughout the summer, causing frequent, heavy rainstorms. Sudden drops in temperature may occur and snow and hailstorms are possible. Temperatures range from the mid-twenties C (70s F) during the day to freezing temperatures at night. Rain gear, warm clothing, and a good sleeping bag and tent are necessary.

FLORA: Black and white spruce cover the lower slopes of the mountains, with alpine tundra generally occurring above 1200 metres (4000 feet) of elevation. Willow, poplar and alder border the river, increasing in density and size towards the Lowlands. Vegetation in the lowlands section is relatively lush and dense. Firewood is available for the entire trip, although for hikers in the higher alpine region, it may take some scrounging.

FAUNA: The upper section of the Mountain River features an abundance of large game such as caribou, moose, Dall's sheep and grizzly bear, as well as wolves, wolverine, eagles, hawks and a variety of song birds. Lake trout are found in the mountain lakes and grayling abound in the major tributaries and creeks flowing into the Mountain. Because the Mountain itself is a very muddy river, fishing with rod and reel is best attempted where small, clear streams join the main flow. In the Mackenzie Lowlands, ducks, geese and black bears abound.

HUMAN HISTORY: The drainage system of the Keele and Mountain Rivers are the traditional lands of the Mountain Dene. Today there are no year round residents in the area, as most of the descendants of the Mountain people moved to the villages of Fort Norman and Fort Good Hope, earlier this century.

During the late 19th and early 20th centuries, the Mountain people hunted and trapped the headwaters on both sides of the Continental Divide. In the late spring, they built large mooseskin boats. These boats were loaded with families and the winter's catch of fur, and were navigated down the Keele and Mountain Rivers. Once trading was completed at Fort Norman or Fort Good Hope, the Mountain Dene walked back into the mountains where they spent the winter in small family bands. A mooseskin boat is on display at the Prince of Wales Northern Heritage Centre in Yellowknife.

RIVER PROFILE: Dusty Lake is the only accessible starting point for this trip close to the headwaters. The river is reached by a one–kilometre portage from the lake. The river is shallow, flowing around many sharp bends. Keep to the inside to avoid the faster outside corners. Canoeists should watch for submerged boulders along this upper stretch.

A canyon on the Mount Eduni topographic map (106 A), is the first of six canyons on the river. At the entrance to this canyon, the river makes a 90 degree bend to the right. In the middle of this bend is an undercut headwall, which paddlers must avoid to prevent entrapment. The next 3 km (2 miles) between the canyon walls is all fast water, with few eddies and no serious obstructions.

Good camping spots are easy to find along the entire river. Some of the better spots are located on the gravel deltas formed where small tributaries join the Mountain. Camping at creeks also offers the advantages of better fishing and clearer drinking water. The creek entering the river at grid reference 466N7125E is the one used by paddlers who begin their trip at Willowhandle or Mountain Lake.

It is about a 20 km (12 mile) trip down two icy creeks ("Pushmepull you" and "Blackfeather" creeks, respectively) from Willowhandle Lake to the main river. Paddlers are advised to take the first small creek that flows north out of the lake. Alternatively, you can walk north along the right side of the valley following a horse trail for about 1.5 km (1 mile) to where it crosses a tiny creek. Follow the creek to an ice field. This ice field obstructs the creek and care must be taken in passing it. Downstream from the ice field, this tiny creek joins a larger one which can be paddled, but requires caution. About one kilometre downstream from the junction, a small, narrow canyon can present some difficulties with class 2 or 3 rapids. Another similar canyon follows just downstream from the first. A third short canyon, not as narrow or difficult as the first two is located just before the creek turns north. From here to the Mountain River, the channel is quite braided, and care must be taken to avoid sweepers and to find a channel with enough water.

Shooting the rapids of Mini Canyon on the Mountain River

Six km (4 miles) downstream from the confluence of this creek and the Mountain River is a fascinating series of caves that can be explored in a day hike. At the caves, hikers are likely to find evidence of Dall sheep. This is also a well-used nesting area for many birds of prey.

The river volume increases after the first canyon. Red Mountain, on river left, is a major landmark to watch for. Further downstream, the river becomes braided with multiple channels. During periods of low water, it may be difficult to select the best route. This area is used by hunters from the Palmer Lake Camp as well as Dene from the Mackenzie Valley. Campsites and horse trails are abundant.

The river's volume increases as it turns north due to the increasing number of tributaries joining it. Turbulence and standing waves are encountered at these confluences and caution is advised. There are few eddies or calm stretches. The river makes several turns in this section and paddlers should be wary of unexpected sweepers and debris falling from eroded cutbanks on the outside of the bends.

The second canyon on the Mountain River begins at the mouth of Cache Creek. Paddlers should be reminded that there is no exit for approximately one kilometre as the river surges between the 100 metre (330 foot) canyon walls. The river narrows considerably as it enters the canyon. At the halfway point, the river makes a sharp turn to the right, creating turbulence at the inside corner and rough water on the outside where it hits the canyon wall on river left. Cache Creek offers excellent fishing for dolly varden and grayling. Tufa deposits and springs are located a short walk up Cache Creek, as is a naturally formed rock bridge.

Nineteen kilometres (14 miles) downstream from Cache Creek canyon, the river enters another range of mountains and a third, smaller canyon is encountered. At its entrance, an enormous house-sized rock, sometimes called "Battleship Rock", splits the channel with most of the river flowing to the right. This canyon is usually navigable along river right.

The river widens considerably downstream from the Stoneknife River. Paddlers will encounter sections of heavy whitewater in this stretch. There are many good hiking opportunities along the ridges surrounding the river valley.

The fourth canyon is found approximately 6.5 km (4 miles) upstream of Brunson Creek. In early summer, when melting glaciers send great volumes of water into the river, impassable 4 metre (13 foot) waves have been noted at the entrance to the canyon. Parts of the canyon have been run at the end of July, but paddlers must still contend with one to two metre (4 to 6 foot) standing waves. At medium water levels, the entrance to the canyon has standing waves and ledges which are best negotiated along river right. The main channel turns to the left and then to the right around a large boulder bar with a trickle to the right of the bar. This entire section becomes a giant chute at higher water levels. Even when the river is navigable, paddlers are advised to portage this section by walking the boulder bar. Caution is advised in crossing the eddy line at the outflow of the trickle. Large waves and huge boulders choke river right through the next section. The river then makes a sharp left turn. Scouting the remainder of this canyon can be done from the flat gravel bar on river left at the inside of this turn.

The fifth canyon marks the entrance to the Mackenzie Lowlands. It is shorter and can be run at medium water levels. There is a water survey station located here. Downstream from this point, there is a marked increase in the river's width and channels become numerous. Canoes should avoid getting separated.

The sixth and final canyon is found at the western end of the Imperial Hills. Fifty-four kilometres (34 miles) of braided channels snake through the wide open lowlands of the Mackenzie River valley before the Mountain River reaches the mighty Mackenzie.

Paddlers will hear the roar of the Sans Sault Rapids on the Mackenzie River as they approach the mouth of the Mountain. Stay river left to avoid the rapid's large waves. Those wishing to end their trip here can arrange to be picked up by float plane or boat from Norman Wells. Those paddling on to Fort Good Hope have an 80 km (50 miles) paddle ahead of them. High winds and barge and tug traffic can pose some problems. Upstream from Fort Good Hope, the river narrows to pass through the Ramparts, spectacular sheer cliffs, towering 150 metres (450 feet) above the river. Depending on water levels, a ledge at the head of the Ramparts can be very tricky. The safest route for paddlers is near the channel markers on river right. These rapids are not marked on topographic maps.

The settlement of Fort Good Hope marks the end of the trip for most canoeists, although you do have the option of continuing downriver to the Arctic Ocean. Fort Good Hope is the oldest fur trading post on the lower Mackenzie. Today it has about 500 residents and most modern services such as a store, hotel, nursing station, RCMP and scheduled air service.

Otto Schreiber

Second Canyon on the Mountain River

MAPS REQUIRED: *(read maps from left to right)*

(1:250,000)	Bonnet Plume Lake	106 B (Dusty Lake put in only)
	Mount Eduni	106 A
	Sans Sault Rapids	106 H
	Fort Good Hope	106 I

AVERAGE GRADIENT: From the headwaters to the mouth of the river, 4 metres per kilometre (20 feet per mile).

HYDROGRAPH: *Mountain River below Cambrian Creek, 1975-1988*

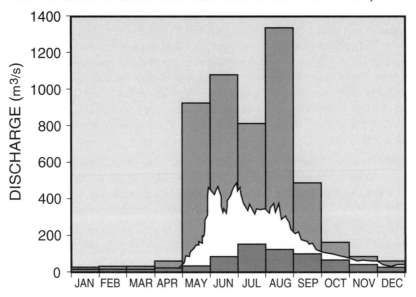

SOURCE INFORMATION:

1. Parks Canada Wild Rivers Survey, *The Mountain River*, 1972.
2. Andrews, Tom: *Personal Journal of the Mountain River*, 1984.
3. Scriver, Mark: Black Feather Wilderness Adventures, Personal communication.
4. Spaulding, Dick and Andrew: Personal communication.
5. Poole, Kim and Louise: Personal communication.
6. Wideman, Miriam and Mary McCreadie: Personal communication.

CUMULATIVE DISTANCES:

Location	Kilometres	Miles
Dusty Lake	0	0
First Canyon	35	22
Second Canyon	121	76
Third Canyon	143	90
Fourth Canyon	183	115
Fifth Canyon	204	127
Sixth Canyon	246	154
Mouth of Mountain River	299	187
Fort Good Hope	377	236

NATLA AND KEELE RIVERS

TOTAL DISTANCE: O'Grady Lake to Fort Norman – 490 km (306 miles).

DURATION OF TRIP: 17 to 21 days from O'Grady Lake to Fort Norman.

START: O'Grady Lake at the headwaters of the Natla River.

FINISH: Community of Fort Norman on the Mackenzie River. Some paddlers may prefer to continue 80 km (50 miles) further down the Mackenzie River to Norman Wells.

ACCESSIBILITY: O'Grady Lake is only accessible by float plane. Planes can be chartered from Norman Wells or Fort Norman, NWT or Ross River, Yukon. Some parties land downstream from the mouth of the Natla on the Keele River itself. There are several possible landing sites on the Keele as well as an old Shell airstrip at Caribou Flats. It is also possible to paddle another tributary of the Keele, the Tsichu, from its headwaters near mile 222 on the Canol road. This gives paddlers road access from the Yukon or an airstrip where a plane on wheels can land.

RIVER NOTES: The Natla/Keele River trip takes paddlers from high alpine meadows, through the tree line and across the Mackenzie Lowlands to the mighty Mackenzie River. The community of Fort Norman is located 97 km (60 miles) from the confluence of the Keele River and the Mackenzie.

Depending on the type of trip desired, paddlers have some choices of where to start. Starting at the headwaters of the Natla River at O'Grady Lake provides an advanced whitewater trip amidst spectacular mountain scenery. The Natla has a gradient of 3.75 metres per kilometre (20 feet per mile), making it both exciting and dangerous. Shorter trips starting on the Keele River itself will provide a challenging but less technically difficult trip. Paddlers starting from the Tsichu River on the Canol Road can expect continuous whitewater for most of its 40 km (25 mile) length. Like the Natla, it is a somewhat gruelling trip, which, depending on water levels, can take up to a week to paddle.

Excellent opportunities for hiking exist along both rivers, especially in the higher reaches and around O'Grady Lake. It is well worth adding a few days to your paddling schedule to allow for some exploration of the mountains.

Both the Natla and Keele Rivers are located in unforgiving, but beautiful terrain. Canoeists must have excellent paddling and wilderness camping skills. Like all mountain rivers, water levels can fluctuate daily depending on rain and meltwater. Flood peaks occur in June or early July and water levels become quite low towards the end of August. Spray covers are recommended for both of these rivers.

GEOGRAPHY: The Natla and Keele drainage system is a major tributary of the Mackenzie River. The headwaters of both rivers are located in the Selwyn Mountains, just east of the NWT/Yukon border. O'Grady Lake is located on a poorly drained plateau, surrounded by mountain peaks. During its 112 km (70 mile) course, the Natla drops from an elevation of 1300 m (4265 feet) to under 900 metres (2950 feet). In the upper reaches of the Keele, mountain tops rise to over 2250 metres (7380 feet) above sea level.

The Natla and Keele Rivers meet 297 km (185 miles) upstream of the mouth of the Keele. Downstream from the confluence of the two rivers, the Keele becomes broader and more braided. Mountain ranges and peaks parallel the river to within 80 km (50 miles) of the Mackenzie River.

Upon entering the Mackenzie Lowlands, the Keele becomes wider and slower, with frequent shallow stretches.

CLIMATE: The weather of the Mackenzie Mountains is unpredictable. In mid-summer (late June to early August), the weather is usually warm and sunny with frequent rain squalls. Daytime temperatures are around 20 C (68 F), dipping to just above freezing at night. Prolonged periods of rain can occur at any time during the summer, so good rain gear, warm clothing and a waterproof tent are essential.

FLORA: Alpine vegetation, consisting of dwarf birch and willows, moss, lichens and wildflowers surrounds O'Grady Lake and the first 24 km (15 miles) of the Natla River. The tree line extends to an elevation of roughly 1200 metres (4000 feet) along the upper reaches of both rivers. Below the tree line, 90% of the forest cover is spruce, with occasional stands of poplar. Larch, aspen and willows become increasingly common as the river descends to the Lowlands.

FAUNA: Caribou, moose, Dall's sheep, grizzly bears and wolves are common to the area. Salt licks along the Keele are excellent places for viewing sheep and caribou. Bald eagles and osprey are also commonly seen along the river.

Grayling and dolly varden provide excellent fishing in the river, while O'Grady Lake has good lake trout fishing.

HUMAN HISTORY: The drainages of the Keele and Mountain Rivers are the traditional home of the Mountain Dene. Today, most of the surviving Mountain people live in Fort Norman on the Mackenzie River. Prior to their move into villages in the mid 20th century, they roamed the mountains from the South Nahanni to the Mountain Rivers hunting sheep, caribou and moose, snaring rabbits and fishing. Their name for the Keele River was "Bacotyeh", meaning "meat drying river". It is also known as the Gravel River.

As the fur industry made its way down the Mackenzie Valley, the Mountain Dene began to trap and sell furs to the traders at Fort Norman and Fort Good Hope. After spending the winter trapping in the mountains, family groups would build large mooseskin boats of up to 10 metres in length and 2 metres in width. The frame was made of spruce trees, lashed together with raw moosehide strips. Ten or twelve raw hides were then stitched together and stretched over the frame. Seams were treated with spruce gum and sheep tallow. Extended families of a dozen or more people, along with their winter's catch and a full contingent of dogs then boated down the river, dodging boulders and gravel bars. The boats were dismantled at the trading post and after a few weeks of "civilization", the Mountain Dene would walk back into the mountains, packing all they needed for the winter.

An example of a mooseskin boat can be seen at the Prince of Wales Northern Heritage Centre in Yellowknife.

RIVER PROFILE: This report outlines a trip down the Natla River from O'Grady Lake to the Keele River and down the Keele to the Mackenzie River.

O'Grady Lake is 8 km (5 miles) long and 3 km (2 miles) wide, divided into two sections by a short, shallow stream 30 metres wide. Since the lake is located high on a plateau, the surrounding relief appears subdued. However, a hike up the highest peak to the south will bring the scenery into perspective. To the northwest are the Itsi Peaks and the Selwyn Range of the Mackenzie Mountains. To the west lie the headwaters of the South Nahanni River and to the east lies the Natla River Valley, 1000 metres below.

O'Grady Lake becomes ice-free by the end of June. Campsites and firewood are hard to locate but they are adequate. The best campsite is on a sandy peninsula on the eastern portion of the lake.

The Natla River leaves O'Grady Lake as a shallow and rapid stream. The first 40 km (25 miles) of the river are characterized by nearly continuous whitewater, flowing through 10 metre cut banks. These cut banks tend to limit the view of the surrounding mountains considerably and also make it difficult to see what's ahead on the river, making frequent scouting a must. Most of the rapids are class 2 and 3 and can be run by experienced paddlers. This can change, however, depending on the water level. Some portaging and lining is necessary. Sections of the river bed are strewn with boulders and rocks, which at times can obstruct the flow of the river.

As the Natla descends through the mountains, its banks diminish and the river valley widens, giving paddlers an unrestricted view of spectacular mountain country. The middle 72 km (45 mile) stretch of the river is much quieter than the top. The volume of water increases, but the speed slows down considerably as the river widens. Gravel bars and islands become more numerous and most of the chutes and rapids can be paddled. These conditions are usually a welcome relief to the tension experienced by most paddlers in the first 40 km.

This relief, however, is short lived. The final 8 km (5 miles) of the Natla is characterized by fast water and large rapids flowing through a canyon. Depending on water levels, this section of the river is often only runnable in closed canoes, handled by expert paddlers. Some trip reports indicate that difficult sections can be portaged and lined. The steep valley walls and ledges near shore could make lining difficult. Rapids in this section have been graded from class 3 to class 6 and are almost continuous for 7 km. Paddlers choosing not to try this part of the river will find a trail on river right high above the river, covering the entire 8 km. The trail ends near the confluence of the Natla and Keele and is used by outfitters with horses. The last kilometre of the Natla is braided and shallow and should pose no problem.

The Keele River upstream from its confluence with the Natla is narrow and fast. It is accessible only from the Tsichu River and a few ponds on either side of the Keele. Once the Natla and Keele join, the Keele quickly becomes much slower and more braided. In mid-July the water is at medium flow levels, making navigation in open canoes relatively easy. The river width varies from 200 to 400 metres with a velocity of about 8

The Natla/Keele River System

km per hour at medium water levels. As volume builds, the water becomes murky with suspended sediments and obtaining clear drinking water can be difficult. When possible, it is a good idea to camp near small tributaries where clean water is available.

Although the Keele is quieter than the Natla River, it is a large-volume river to be travelled carefully. Heavy rapids with large standing waves, small whirlpools and boils are found along the entire river. There are several canyons which, although not usually dangerous to paddle, are very fast and difficult to maneouver in. Frequent gravel bars can pose obstacles to navigation. It is usually advisable to choose the channel with the biggest volume of water, although these often have rapids.

Monica Kendel - artist

Portaging and lining are not normally necessary, but there are some areas that can pose difficulties depending on water levels. Twenty-one km (13 miles) downstream from the Natla/Keele confluence, near where the Shezal Canyon enters the river, there is a short portage on river left. Other possible problem spots include a place 2 km (1 mile) upstream from the mouth of the Ekwi River; the Flowerpot (a limestone pillar rising 10 metres above the river) located between the mouths of the Ekwi and Twitya Rivers; and a sharp left turn against a cliff that forms a whirlpool in the back eddy, 40 km (25 miles) downstream from the Twitya River.

A series of salt licks along the Keele attract large game like caribou and Dall's sheep. The first lick is located about 5 km (3 miles) upstream from the Shezal Canyon. A bit further downstream, near the Shell airstrip, licks are found on both sides of the river. Three more licks are located where the river passes through the Tigonankweine and Canyon Ranges.

Natla/Keele Rivers

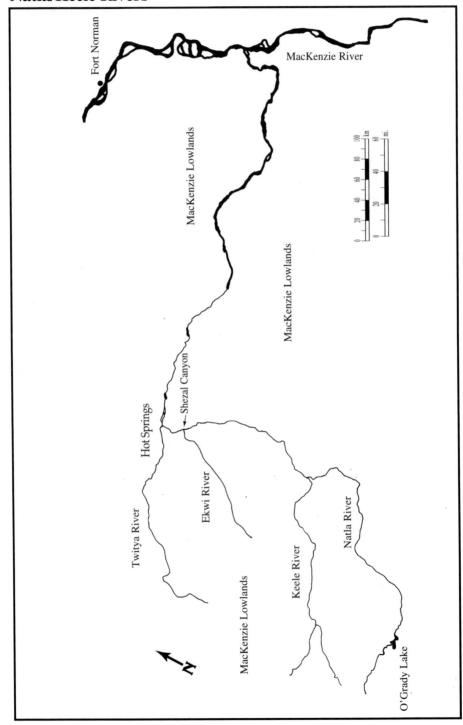

As the Keele enters the Mackenzie Lowlands, about 100 km (65 miles) upstream of its mouth at the Mackenzie River, it increases in width and slows down. Gravel bars and shallows become more frequent.

Two outfitters' camps are located on the Keele as well as a Canadian Wildlife Service cabin. An abandoned Shell Oil Camp downstream from the Shezal Canyon has an airstrip that is sometimes used to land canoeing and hiking parties. Fort Norman, at the mouth of the Great Bear River, was established in 1810 as a fur trade post. It is located on the Mackenzie River, 81 km (50 miles) from the mouth of the Keele and offers most basic services, including scheduled and charter plane service, RCMP, nursing station, accommodation and meals.

MAPS REQUIRED: (read maps left to right)

(1:250,000)	Sekwi Mountains 105 P	Nahanni 105 I
	Mount Eduni 106 A	Wrigley Lake 95 M
	Carcajou Canyon 96 D	Fort Norman 96 C

AVERAGE GRADIENT: The average gradient from O'Grady Lake to the Mackenzie River is 2.5 metres per kilometre (13 feet per mile).

HYDROGRAPH: According to the Water Survey Office of Canada in Yellowknife, no hydrographs have been recorded on the Natla and Keele Rivers.

SOURCE INFORMATION:

1. The Natla and Keele Rivers: Wild Rivers Survey. Parks Canada, 1980.

2. Hanks, Chris: Personal communication.

3. Beckett, Don: Trip Journal, 1976.

4. Coedy, Bill: Personal communication.

5. Stephenson, John: Personal communication

6. Hoyt, William B.: Call of the North, Sunday Courier-Express, Buffalo, N.Y., 1982.

CUMULATIVE DISTANCES:

Location	Kilometres	Miles
O'Grady Lake	0	0
Natla/Keele Confluence	112	70
Shezal Canyon	133	83
Ekwi River Confluence	183	114
Mackenzie Lowlands	304	190
Mouth of Keele River	408	255
Fort Norman	490	306

SLAVE RIVER

TOTAL DISTANCE: Peace Point (on the Peace River) to Fort Resolution (on Great Slave Lake) 561 km (351 miles).

DURATION OF TRIP:
Peace Point to Hay Camp – 3 to 5 days
Hay Camp to Ft. Fitzgerald – 1 to 2 days
Ft. Fitzgerald to Fort Smith – 1 to 3 days
Ft. Smith to Great Slave Lake – 4 to 10 days

START: Canoeists may start at Peace Point on the Peace River or Hay Camp, Fort Fitzgerald or Fort Smith on the Slave River.

FINISH: Paddlers can finish their trip at Fort Fitzgerald, Fort Smith or Fort Resolution.

ACCESSIBILITY: Fort Smith can be reached by an all-weather, gravel highway from Hay River or by scheduled air service from Edmonton or Yellowknife.

Peace Point, Hay Camp and Fort Fitzgerald can be reached by road or air charter from Fort Smith.

Fort Resolution, at the mouth of the Slave River, is located on Highway No. 6. It is also accessible by scheduled flights from Yellowknife or Hay River.

RIVER NOTES: The Slave River is a large river, second only to the Mackenzie in the NWT. It is a continuation of Alberta's Peace River with the addition of several large tributaries that drain into Lake Athabasca, including the Athabasca and Fond du Lac Rivers. The drainage basin of the Slave River includes three western provinces and part of the NWT.

The river winds its way between Precambrian Shield to the east and the sedimentary Alberta Plateau to the west. The Slave is part of the historic 2400 km (1500 mile) waterway from Fort McMurray to the Arctic Ocean. Smooth passage is interrupted only by the series of rapids on the Slave just south of the 60th parallel. Here, the giant river falls over a series of granite shelves, forming 4 sets of awesome rapids in the 30 km (18 mile) stretch between Fort Fitzgerald, Alberta and Fort Smith, NWT. Paddlers can portage this on a 12 km section of highway between Fort Fitzgerald and Fort Smith or can attempt the traditional fur trade portage system on the river's west bank. This should not be attempted without an experienced guide.

Except for this section, the Slave River is a massive but quiet paddle, with flat water all the way. The exposed and breezy ends of the many islands in mid-river are good campsites, especially during bug season. The water is very silty, making it unpalatable to many canoeists.

GEOGRAPHY: Canoeists beginning their trip at Peace Point on the Peace River pass through several diverse geographical regions on their way to Great Slave Lake. The

Peace River flows mainly through the Alberta Plateau en route to its junction with the three channels which drain Lake Athabasca. These rivers join to become the Slave River. This region is a vast and poorly drained plain, containing meandering streams, shallow lakes and bogs.

The Peace-Athabasca delta, the largest inland river delta in the world, has formed where the silt-laden waters of the Peace, Athabasca and Birch Rivers enter Lake Athabasca. The sediments deposited here have created a maze of marshes, shallow lakes, sedge meadows and wandering channels, which periodically reverse their flow depending on water levels in the main rivers. This delta forms a staging and breeding ground for migratory birds from four major flyways.

Downstream from this delta, the Slave River marks the natural boundary between the Precambrian Shield to the east and the Slave River Lowlands to the west. Extensive "salt plains" occur on the west side of the river, where springs containing salty water empty onto the flat, open ground. In contrast, the rivers entering the east bank of the Slave are clear and clean after their passage across the rocky Precambrian Shield. Downstream from Fort Smith, the river flows through the flat plains and prairies of the Slave River Lowlands.

Another large delta is found at the mouth of the Slave on Great Slave Lake near Fort Resolution. This delta is a 56 km (35 mile) wide fan of channels, sandbars and islands.

CLIMATE: The summers in this area are generally warm and dry. The average daily maximum temperature in July is about 21°C (69°F). At night temperatures drop to around 10°C (50°F). There are about 20 hours of daylight in June, decreasing gradually over the course of the summer.

Although rainfall is light, lightning storms do occur and this, combined with the dry land, can create an extreme fire hazard. Paddlers must be careful to ensure that their campfires are completely extinguished.

Break-up on the Slave River occurs in mid-May and freeze-up takes place in early November.

FLORA: White and black spruce, jack pine, tamarack, poplar, balsam and trembling aspen are all found in the boreal forest zone. The lowlands consist of jack pine and spruce forests mixed with sedge-covered open prairie, willow meadows and marshes.

FAUNA: The Slave River borders Wood Buffalo National Park, home of the largest free-roaming herd of bison in the world. About 4000 of these animals live in the park. The Park organizes "buffalo creeps" in the summer, allowing visitors to see the wood bison on foot. More information can be obtained from the Park Superintendent.

Also at home in the park is one of the rarest birds in the world – the whooping crane. They nest in the northern regions of the park, although their nesting grounds are closed to the public. The world's only colony of river-nesting white pelicans can be found on small rock islands mid-channel of the Mountain Rapids on the Slave River near Fort Smith.

Wood bison, moose, black bear, lynx, fox, mink, wolves, beaver and a host of other forest mammals live in the area.

Slave River

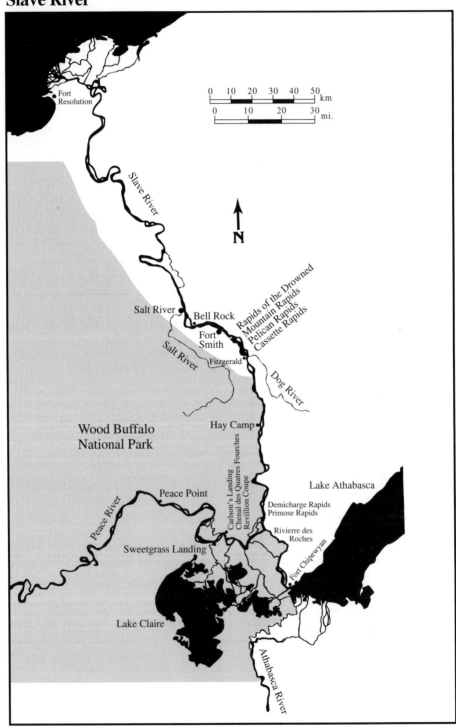

The Slave River is on a major flyway for nesting birds and the numerous lakes, ponds and marshes provide excellent nesting grounds for a wide variety of species.

The river is an important spawning ground for whitefish, inconnu, goldeye and northern pike.

HUMAN HISTORY: The waters of the Peace and Athabasca Rivers flow into the Slave River, which empties into Great Slave Lake. From here, the water flows unimpeded to the Arctic Ocean, over 1000 km (600 miles) to the north. As part of this huge aquatic highway system, the Slave River has always been historically important. The Dene and later the Cree have used the river traditionally for transportation and as a source of food.

The first recorded European to visit the area was Samuel Hearne of the Hudon's Bay Company. He walked along the Slave in the winter of 1771-72 with his Chipewyan guide Matonabbee on their way back to Hudson Bay from the mouth of the Coppermine River. A few years later, Peter Pond, a notorious fur trader working for the Northwest Company also travelled down the river on his way to Great Slave Lake.

In 1786 two rival fur traders, Laurent Leroux and Cuthbert Grant, descended the river looking for new areas to expand their trade, from their posts on the Athabasca River. Five of Grant's men drowned trying to shoot the "Portage de Noyes" opposite the site of Fort Smith. These rapids were later named the "Rapids of the Drowned". Both men built trading posts near the present day site of Fort Resolution, beginning a European expansion that would quickly engulf the Mackenzie Valley.

The Slave River became the "Gateway to the North" linking the resource-rich north with the rest of Canada. Fort Resolution, near the mouth of the river, quickly became a strategic post and later an administrative centre for the north. Schools, missions, trading posts and a hospital attracted trappers and their families.

Fort Smith later surpassed Fort Resolution as the government and trade centre because of its location at the end of the only portage on the entire water route north. York boats and tugs pulling large barges had to be transported over the portage road that bypassed the Slave River Rapids.

With the completion of the Mackenzie Highway and the railroad into Hay River in the 1960s, the river route north quickly lost its importance. Today there is little commercial traffic on the Slave River, but reminders of its hectic past can still be found along its banks.

RIVER PROFILE: Paddlers beginning their trip at Peace Point on the Peace River travel 112 km (70 miles) of mostly flat water to the beginning of the Slave River. A trip report on this section of the river is available from the Superintendent of Wood Buffalo Park. A side trip to Lake Claire in the Peace-Athabasca Delta is recommended. Two portages at Sweetgrass Landing lead to Sweetgrass Creek where paddlers can easily travel south to Lake Claire. Canoeists can also visit the Sweetgrass bison management station.

Further downstream, paddlers pass the fire tower at Carlson's Landing. A short distance downstream, three channels enter the Peace River from Lake Athabasca. This confluence marks the beginning of the Slave River. During the spring floods, the Peace

Mike van Duffelen

Rapids on the Slave River

pushes water back upstream through these channels into Lake Athabasca, reversing the natural flow of water.

Ten kilometres (6 miles) downstream from the beginning of the Slave River, paddlers will encounter two islands. These are best approached along river left before paddling between them. The river in this stretch is filled with rocks and sandbars, some of which are marked with navigational buoys. Primrose Rapids are located 13 km (8 miles) downstream from these islands. Again, paddlers should stay near river left for the best approach.

Navigational beacons will guide canoeists through the Demicharge Rapids which are located about 21 km (14 miles) downstream from the Primrose Rapids.

As paddlers approach Hay Camp, the location of the Park Warden's office, they will pass several large streams entering the Slave. Interesting side trips can be made up Ryan Creek, La Butte Creek or the Bocquene or Dog Rivers. From Hay Camp to Fort Fitzgerald is 43 km (27 miles) of flatwater paddling.

At Fort Fitzgerald canoeists can pull off the river and arrange vehicle transportation over the 12 km (7 mile) highway section to Fort Smith. For a fee to cover time and expense, transportation can usually be arranged with one of the residents of Fort Fitzgerald. Paddlers wishing to continue on the river to Fort Smith should contact a guide at Fort Fitzgerald, as the Slave Rapids are much too dangerous and confusing to be paddled without an experienced guide. Guides can be arranged through the Fort Smith Paddling Club.

At the Slave River Rapids, the river widens to several kilometres with countless small channels flowing through hundreds of wooded islands and innumerable granite outcrops and rocks. The rapids offer an incredible diversity of paddling opportunities, from the relatively easy traditional portage route to massive whitewater, where virtually all the river's water funnels through a 100-metre wide chute through the Pelican Rapids.

The rapids are spectacular and beautiful, with massive whitewater in the main channel and smaller waterfalls and chutes in the side channels. The whitewater varies from class 3 to class 6 and because of changing water levels and the countless channels created by the islands, it would be possible to paddle the area for several seasons without canoeing every possible route.

Large volumes of water flowing over wide ledges create incredible "surfing" waves, up to 100 metres wide and 3 to 4 metres high. In recent years the Slave River Rapids have become a focal point for NWT competitive canoeists, and they are also attracting international level competitors. The traditional portage route is appropriate for intermediate paddlers provided they are guided.

The complexity of the navigable channels through the Slave Rapids precludes route description in this report. Because of the extreme danger presented by taking the wrong channel, a guide is mandatory for first time paddlers. Anyone unfamiliar with the Slave who is considering unguided descent should be aware that there are class 6 sections in all four rapids.

The end of the portage route from Fort Fitzgerald to Fort Smith is below the Rapids of the Drowned, locally referred to as "the boat launch". Downstream from Fort Smith the river meanders on a winding 280 km course (175 miles) to its delta. Thirteen km (8 miles) downstream from the boat launch is Bell Rock, the end of the original portage for river barges. It was built by the U.S. Army during the Second World War. Northern Transportation Company Limited used this base for barges on their way to the Arctic until the railroad reached Hay River.

The settlement of Salt River, 16 km (10 miles) downstream from Bell Rock, is one of the oldest Metis settlements in the North. The Salt River is a good place for a side trip during high water periods in June.

Downstream of Salt River, the Slave zigzags for 176 km (110 miles) through the range of the Hook Lake Buffalo herd. As the river approaches its delta, its wandering ways become more pronounced. The shortest way for paddlers to reach Ft. Resolution is to leave the Slave River on the Resdelta Channel. When this channel splits, take the Old Streamboat Channel, and when that divides, take the Sawmill Channel. The Sawmill Channel splits into the Nagle Channel which empties into Nagle Bay on Great Slave Lake. It is a 13 km (8 mile) paddle across Nagle Bay and around the point to Fort Resolution. Paddlers should be careful on Great Slave Lake as wind and huge waves can come up very quickly.

Fort Resolution is a Chipewyan/Metis community of about 500 people. Two general stores, a motel, nursing station and the RCMP are located here. Highway 6 connects Fort Resolution with the Hay River/Fort Smith highway. There is also scheduled air service to Yellowknife and Hay River.

MAPS REQUIRED: *(read maps from left to right)*

(1:250,000)   Peace Point 84 P   Fort Chipewyan 74 L
               Fitzgerald 74 M   Fort Smith 75 D
               Little Buffalo River 85 A   Fort Resolution 85 H

Navigational charts are also recommended for this trip.They are available at most map offices.The following charts are recommended:

#6321 Peace River
#6301 Fort McMurray to Fort Smith
#6302 Fort Smith to Great Slave Lake

AVERAGE GRADIENT: Slave River from Lake Athabasca to Fort Resolution is 0.11 metres per km (0.6 feet per mile).

HYDROGRAPH: *Slave River at Fitzgerland, 1921-1922, 1930-1931, 1953-1988*

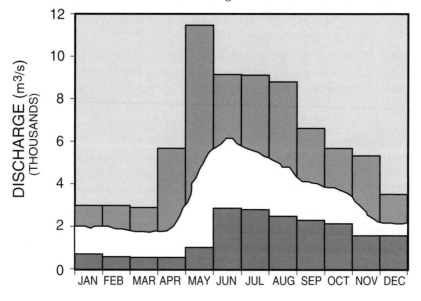

SOURCE INFORMATION:

1. Darkes, James: Personal communication.

2. Slave River Trip Report: TravelArctic.

3. Parks Canada: Wood Buffalo National Park Brochure.

4. Smith, Bruce: Personal communication.

CUMULATIVE DISTANCE:

Location	kilometres	miles
Peace Point	0	0
Peace and Slave River Junction	11	70
Fort Fitzgerald	221	138
Fort Smith	246	154
Fort Resolution	561	351

SNARE RIVER

TOTAL DISTANCE: 350 kilometres (219 miles) from Winter Lake to the community of Fort Rae.

DURATION OF TRIP: 15 to 17 days from Winter Lake to Rae.

START: Winter Lake is probably the most popular starting point for this trip; however, paddlers can start at several other lakes further downstream or at Jolly Lake, near the headwaters of the system. The village of Snare Lake, located on Snare Lake itself, is also a good starting point for a shorter trip.

FINISH: The community of Fort Rae is the usual finishing point. Some paddlers choose to end their trip at the dam site on Big Spruce Lake.

ACCESSIBILITY: Winter Lake, 160 kilometres (100 miles) by air north of Yellowknife, is accessible by float plane from Yellowknife. Jolly Lake is the closest that float planes can land to the actual headwaters of the system. The village of Snare Lake has regular scheduled air service from Yellowknife.

Several overland access routes have also been used both historically and in recent times. One such route goes up the Lockhart River system from the east end of Great Slave Lake and through Clinton-Colden, Aylmer, Mackay and Jolly Lakes. Another route goes up the Yellowknife River and overland to Winter Lake. This is the route used by John Franklin in 1820. Both of these routes are time consuming and arduous, and should be attempted only by expert paddlers with advanced navigational and survival skills.

Fort Rae is located on Highway 3 between Yellowknife and Fort Providence. Float planes can land here, but it is more economical to arrange transportation by highway to Yellowknife.

RIVER NOTES: The headwaters of the Snare system lie in the barrenlands, two kilometres (1 mile) northwest of Jolly Lake. From there the river flows through a string of lakes and empties into the North Arm of Great Slave Lake. Most of the rapids and falls are easily portaged or lined depending on water levels. Because of the variety of rapids and the isolation of the river, this trip should only be undertaken by paddlers with at least intermediate paddling skills and wilderness camping experience.

The Snare is one of the few rivers in the NWT to be dammed. The NWT Power Corporation operates a series of dams on the river downstream from Big Spruce Lake. Staff are always on site at the dam and will be able to advise paddlers about water levels and portage routes. A radio telephone is also located here.

The village of Snare Lake is located around the mid-point of Snare Lake. It is small (just over 100 people), but has scheduled air service and radio telephones. A small store stocks basic goods.

GEOGRAPHY: Most of the Snare flows through the rugged and lake-filled Precambrian Shield. The stretch of the river upstream from Winter Lake flows through

Snare River

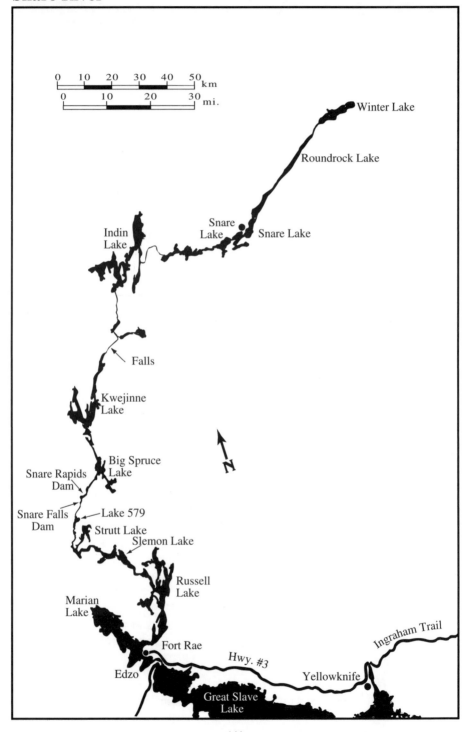

0 10 20 30 40 50 km

0 10 20 30 mi.

Winter Lake

Roundrock Lake

Indin Lake

Snare Lake

Snare Lake

Falls

Kwejinne Lake

N

Big Spruce Lake

Snare Rapids Dam

Snare Falls Dam

Lake 579

Strutt Lake

Slemon Lake

Russell Lake

Marian Lake

Fort Rae

Hwy. #3

Ingraham Trail

Edzo

Yellowknife

Great Slave Lake

the barrens. The tree line actually crosses the river near Winter and Roundrock Lakes. Upstream from Slemon Lake, the Snare tumbles down a series of rapids into the sedimentary Great Slave Plains, where the landscape is generally flat.

CLIMATE: The Snare River breaks up in May, but most of the lakes remain ice-covered until June. July is the best month for this trip to avoid spring runoff and low water levels in August.

Summer temperatures are generally warm, with the average daily maximum temperature in July being about 21°C (69°F). This drops to around 10°C (50°F) at night. Rainfall is usually light and the days are long and sunny. There are only 4 hours of twilight in June, allowing canoeists to paddle well into the evening.

FLORA: Although the upper reaches of the river are above the tree line, some stunted spruce groves can usually be found in sheltered areas. Downstream, tree size increases and spruce, jack pine, poplar and birch forests predominate. Willow and alder line the river banks and ground cover consists of mosses and lichen. There is abundant firewood for cooking along the entire route.

FAUNA: The upper reaches of the Snare Valley are part of the wintering grounds for barrenground caribou from the Bathurst herd. Wolves, moose and black bear are also common along the way, as are smaller mammals such as beaver, muskrat and marten.

The Snare River provides a nesting area for a variety of ducks, loons, terns and gulls. Bald eagles are often spotted in tree tops and rocky outcrops along the river bank.

Lake trout, whitefish, northern pike, Arctic grayling and pickerel can all be caught in the river.

HUMAN HISTORY: The Dogrib Dene of Fort Rae and Yellowknife have traditionally used the Snare River as an access route to their caribou hunting grounds on the barrenlands. In the early 1970's a group of families from Fort Rae built cabins on Snare Lake, where they spent winters trapping. By the late seventies, the number of people wintering on Snare Lake justified the building of a school and from there, the community of Snare Lake has continued to grow into the permanent settlement it is today.

Over the years, parts of this canoe route have been used by various European adventurers and explorers, including George Back and David Hanbury.

In the fall of 1820, John Franklin and his men built Fort Enterprise on Winter Lake. They spent the winter there, en route from Great Slave Lake to the mouth of the Coppermine River. The "Fort" consisted of three rather modest log buildings, none of which are still standing today. Franklin offered the following description of his living quarters: "It was merely a log building, fifty feet long and twenty-four wide, divided into a hall, three bedrooms and a kitchen. The walls and roof were plastered with clay, the floors laid with planks rudely squared with the hatchet, and the windows closed with the parchment of deerskin. The clay, which, from the coldness of the weather, required to be tempered before the fire with hot water, froze as it was daubed on, and afterwards cracked in such a manner as to admit the wind from every quarter; yet compared with the tents, our new habitation appeared comfortable..."

RIVER PROFILE: A chain of lakes northwest of Jolly Lake marks the beginning of the Snare River system. Canoeists wishing to start here can fly to Jolly Lake and portage 1500 metres (5000 feet) over the height of land into the Snare River. There is no set trail, but it is relatively easy walking from the northwest corner of the lake through low-lying terrain to the river.

The 53 km (33 miles) from Jolly Lake to Winter Lake is quite arduous, requiring lining and dragging of canoes through boulder-strewn shallows. Short portages occasionally have to be made as well. Canoeists should allow 4 days for this section of the river. The lake at elevation 1262 (1:250,000 86-A) has unmarked rapids at both ends, which, after scouting, can usually be run.

From lake 1262, the Snare increases in volume, and generally the rapids can be run. Some may require short portages at the bottom of the rapids where the river often fans out into boulder gardens.

Winter Lake is the first of several long, thin lakes on the Snare system. Two rapids at the outlet should be portaged. The first set can be portaged on river left, while the second portage is on river right.

Roundrock Lake is a 22 km (13 mile) long, finger-like lake which narrows to a small channel as it approaches Snare Lake. There are some good campsites on the sandy, sloping right bank. Small spruce trees line the shore, but thin out inland from the river.

The community of Snare Lake is located on the north shore, about halfway down Snare Lake, which is the longest of the lakes on the river. The outlet of Snare Lake marks the beginning of 29 km (18 miles) of canyons, falls and rapids, some of them unmarked on the maps. The average gradient for this section is 3.75 metres per kilometre (19.6 feet per mile). In this section of the river all rapids should be carefully scouted.

The first rapid encountered marks the beginning of a nearly continuous 3.5 km (2 miles) section of whitewater which ends in a 2.5 km (1.5 mile) long lake. Downstream from this lake is a 3 km (2 mile) canyon. Trip reports suggest that wherever portaging is required within the canyon, there is sufficient footing along the riverbank, although this may not be the case at high water levels. At map reference NB9926 the rapids marked are a series of cascades which must be portaged. After this section the river is flat to Indin Lake, with only one set of rapids to negotiate at the entrance to the lake. The portage for these rapids is on river right.

Canoeists can avoid this hazardous stretch of river by taking an alternate route covering 8 km (5 miles) and requiring 10 portages. This route begins in a bay at the outlet of Snare Lake and heads northwest through a chain of lakes. A string of 5 little lakes connected by short portages brings paddlers to the north end of a long, narrow lake which lies 2.4 km (1.5 miles) east of the south bend of the Snare and downstream from its rapids. By walking west from here, paddlers will eventually meet the river 2 or 3 km upstream from Indin lake. There are no set portage trails between these lakes but the woods are open and the footing dry.

Indin Lake twists in a north-south direction and has many bays and islands. The shores are lined with cliffs and rocky outcrops which offer good trout fishing at their bases. Despite the rough shoreline there are lots of good campsites.

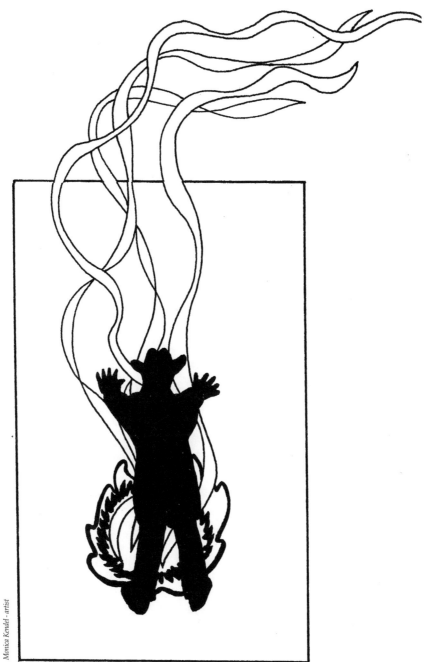

Between Indin and Kwejinne Lakes there are several rapids and falls. Canoeists are advised to scout all rapids and be prepared to line or portage most of them. In some places the shoreline has very difficult footing. The river drops a total of 50 metres over 22 km in this section. There is a falls (Wecho River topo map 85 O, grid 7697) which is marked as a rapid and is best portaged on river left. Downstream the river heads south for 2 km (1.25 miles) before making a sharp left turn through a valley bordered by spruce covered, rounded hills. The double rapids past this section can be portaged on river left. A short distance downstream another falls and set of rapids can also be portaged on river left. Depending on water levels, the rest of the rapids upstream from Kwejinne Lake are usually runnable.

The 32 km (20 mile) paddle down narrow Kwejinne Lake may be delayed because of winds, but there are many good campsites along the shores if this happens. Because of the Snare Hydro dam, both Kwejinne and Big Spruce have the same elevation.

The Snare Rapids dam, which supplies power to Yellowknife and Fort Rae, is located near the outlet of Big Spruce Lake and is operated by the NWT Power Corporation. There are always a few employees there and the radio telephone can be used by canoeists wishing to charter a plane from here to Yellowknife or Fort Rae. Those wishing to paddle downstream have two alternatives. One is to continue downriver, portaging around the dams. The other is to bypass the dams by taking a portage route that extends from the southern tip of Big Spruce Lake through a series of small lakes and portages along the winter road to Slemon Lake. This route is marked on the Wecho Lake topo map. From Slemon Lake, it's a short paddle to Russell and Marian Lakes and Fort Rae. Paddlers continuing downriver are well advised to contact the NWT Power Corporation in Yellowknife for up-to-date information on water levels downstream from the dams. Another alternative is to talk to employees at the Snare Rapids dam site on Big Spruce Lake. Canoeists should be careful to avoid the spillways at all three dams and should also be wary of turbulent water near the dam sites.

The short portage around the Snare Rapids dam is located on river left. Thirteen km (9 miles) downstream is the Snare Falls hydro dam which is also portaged on river left. About 4 km (2.5 miles) downstream is a set of rapids which can be lined, run or portaged depending on water levels. The portage is on river left.

A short distance downstream an island splits a set of rapids which can be portaged along the island itself. Just over a kilometre further downstream is the section of the river known as the Snare Cascades which requires a portage of about 200 metres along the rocks on river right. Another 2.5 km (1.5 miles) downstream is another set of rapids with a short portage on river right.

Judd Lake (unnamed but numbered 579 on some maps) forms a small pool before entering the next part of the river. Here, the last of the three dams on the river, the Strutt Lake Dam (officially known as the Snare Forks) has changed the character of the river. There are two marked rapids on the older maps which may have disappeared. The river splits around a large island. The left channel will bring paddlers to the dam itself. Portage around the hydro plant on river left. From here, the river winds for 24 km (15 miles) to Slemon Lake. At the inlet to Slemon, paddlers will encounter the last set of rapids on the route. The portage is on river left.

The last 64 km (40 miles) of the trip is flatwater paddling across Slemon, Russell and Marian Lakes to Fort Rae. Both Russell and Marian Lakes are widely used by residents of Rae. Don't drink the water in Marian Lake as it is very shallow and turbid.

Fort Rae was established in the last century as a fur trade post and has grown today to become one of the largest native settlements in the NWT. It offers most services and is connected to Yellowknife and the rest of the southern NWT by the Mackenzie Highway.

MAPS REQUIRED: *(read maps from left to right)*

(1:250,000)	Winter Lake 86 A	Indin Lake 86 B
	Wecho Lake 85 O	Marian River 85 N
	Yellowknife 85 J	Rae 85 K

AVERAGE GRADIENT: The average gradient from Winter Lake to Marian Lake is 0.6 metres per kilometre (3 feet per mile).

HYDROGRAPH: *Snare River at Bigspruce Lake, 1949-1976*

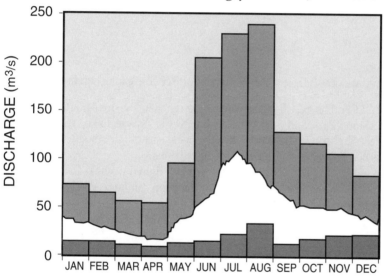

SOURCE INFORMATION:

1. Snare River Trip Sheet, TravelArctic. GNWT, 1979.
2. Wild Rivers: The Barrenlands. The Snare River. Parks Canada.
3. Bayly, G.H.U.: Notes on a canoe trip from Aylmer Lake to Rae, 1964.
4. NWT Power Corporation: Personal communication.
5. Stirling, Bill and Greg: Personal communication.

CUMULATIVE DISTANCES:

Location	Kilometres	Miles
Winter Lake	0	0
Snare Lake Outlet	97	61
Dam at outlet of Big Spruce Lake	230	144
Slemon Lake Outlet	301	188
Fort Rae	350	219

SOUTH NAHANNI RIVER

TOTAL DISTANCE:
A. Moose Ponds (headwaters of the South Nahanni) to Fort Simpson – 703 km (439 miles)
B. Flat Lakes (Little Nahanni River) to Fort Simpson – 693 km (433 miles)

DURATION OF TRIP:
A. Moose Ponds (headwaters of the South Nahanni) to Fort Simpson – 21 days
B. Flat Lakes (headwaters of the Little Nahanni) to Fort Simpson – 21 days

START:
A. Moose Ponds
B. Flat Lakes
   Another common starting point for a shorter trip (about 14 days) is Rabbitkettle Lake (just inside the Park boundary).

FINISH:
A. Fort Simpson
B. Fort Simpson
   Paddlers may also finish their trip at Nahanni Butte or Blackstone Landing.

ACCESSIBILITY: The South Nahanni can be reached by float plane from Fort Simpson, Blackstone Park and Fort Liard in the NWT; Watson Lake, Yukon or Fort Nelson, B.C. Fort Simpson is about 308 km (185 miles) east of Rabbitkettle Lake, while Watson Lake is about 224 km (135 miles) to the southwest.

Watson Lake and Fort Nelson are on the Alaska Highway, while Fort Laird and Blackstone Park are on the Liard Highway. Fort Simpson can be reached either by the Liard Highway or the Mackenzie Highway.

On the upper reaches of the river, float planes usually land at the Moose Ponds or Broken Skull. Further downstream, landings are made at Island and Rabbitkettle Lakes. In both cases, a portage to the river is required. Twin Otter aircraft on wheels can land on a gravel bar on the river, 10 km (6 miles) upstream from Rabbitkettle Lake, except when water levels are extremely high. Aircraft can also land at Virginia Falls. Canoeists with limited time might consider a shorter trip from Virginia Falls to Nahanni Butte which takes about 5 days. Access to the South Nahanni is also possible from two overland routes. One follows the Little Nahanni River from Tungsten, NWT while the other begins where the Canol Road crosses the Macmillan River. Although these alternatives will eliminate the cost of an air charter, they involve vehicle shuttles and extremely difficult river navigation through shallow, rocky water.

RIVER NOTES: The legendary Nahanni River begins as an insignificant stream high in the Selwyn Mountains. Over 500 km (310 miles) later it empties into the Liard River at the community of Nahanni Butte. Along its course, it offers the paddler spectacular scenery as well as more than its share of challenging whitewater. Because of the geological uniqueness of the land, the federal government created the Nahanni National Park Reserve in 1972 and in 1978, the Park was formally dedicated as a World Heritage Site by UNESCO.

Although its rapids and rugged wilderness terrain make the Nahanni unsuitable for beginning canoeists, it is certainly one of the most popular paddling rivers in the country. The 90-metre high (294 foot) Virginia Falls, numerous rapids, four canyons, several natural hot springs and unlimited hiking opportunities are some of the highlights of the river.

The character of the river varies drastically with the season, which extends from June to September. High water levels from the spring runoff in mid–June, and summer rain storms, can cause extreme fluctuations in water levels. Canoeists should always be careful to camp in safe locations, well above the high water mark.

Spray decks are essential for open canoes to reduce the risk of swamping in major rapids.

GEOGRAPHY: The South Nahanni begins in the Selwyn Mountains, flows through the canyons and gorges of the Mackenzie Mountains, and ends in the wide valley flats near its mouth. Geographers describe the Nahanni as an antecedent river, meaning one whose direction of flow was established before the mountains rose. Before the mountains in this area were created, the Nahanni wandered across a wide plain. When the rock uplifts occurred, the river maintained its course by cutting through the rock strata. This resulted in the formation of canyons believed to be 1.4 million years old.

Unlike most of Canada, this region was not completely covered by ice during the last ice age. Because of this, parts of the South Nahanni River Valley have not been affected by glaciation for at least 300,000 years. It is believed that the scouring and widening of the river valley was caused by advancing glaciers 2 million years ago.

This wilderness region contains rugged mountains and one of the deepest river canyons in the world. It also hosts one of the most remarkable karst limestone landscapes found anywhere. Caves, hot springs, tufa mounds, sand blowouts, spectacular plateaux, fossils and countless other geological phenomena are evident along the Nahanni valley.

CLIMATE: The weather in this mountainous region is unpredictable. Warm, moist Pacific air masses collide with cold, dry Arctic air, creating heavy summer rainstorms. Low-lying clouds may prevent aircraft from reaching the river valley for days on end. Canoeists should have flexible schedules to accommodate these delays. During the summer, temperatures can rise into the high 20s°C (80s°F) during the day and drop below freezing at night. Snow and hail are possible at any time. Rain gear, a good sleeping bag and tent, and warm clothing are essential.

FLORA: The flora of Nahanni National Park may be more diverse than that of any other region of comparable size in the NWT. Although white and black spruce predominate, there is a fascinating variety of other vegetation in the region. This is primarily due to the existence of highly specialized habitats like hot springs, mist zones near waterfalls, unglaciated terrain and areas of discontinuous permafrost.

FAUNA: Moose, woodland caribou, wood buffalo, Dall sheep, and grizzly and black bears frequent the South Nahanni River valley, as do porcupine, beaver and a number of smaller rodents. Because the river is often silty, fishing is not great. Dolly varden, lake trout and grayling can be caught in the clearer waters of the many tributaries that join the river. One hundred and seventy species of birds have been recorded in the park including trumpeter swans, bald eagles, golden eagles, gyr and peregrine falcons.

The Nahanni River (and surrounding area)

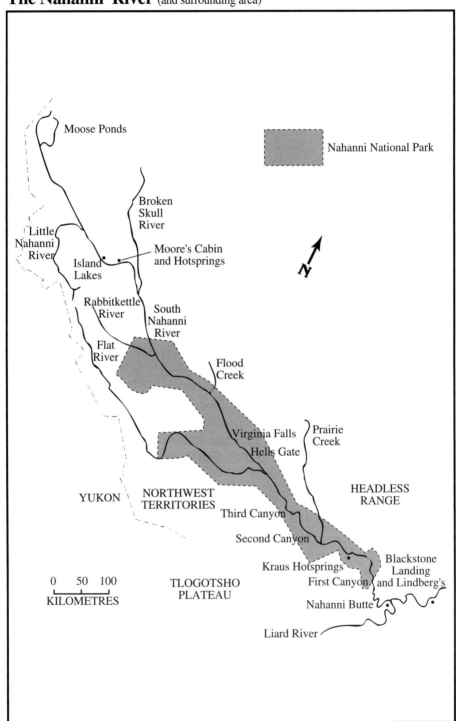

Moose Ponds

Nahanni National Park

Broken
Skull
River

Little
Nahanni
River

Moore's Cabin
and Hotsprings

Island
Lakes

N

Rabbitkettle
River

South
Nahanni
River

Flat
River

Flood
Creek

Virginia Falls

Prairie
Creek

Hells Gate

YUKON

NORTHWEST
TERRITORIES

HEADLESS
RANGE

Third Canyon

Second Canyon

0   50   100
KILOMETRES

TLOGOTSHO
PLATEAU

Kraus Hotsprings

First Canyon

Blackstone
Landing
and Lindberg's

Nahanni Butte

Liard River

HUMAN HISTORY: For perhaps thousands of years, the ancestors of the modern day Dene of the region lived and hunted in the Nahanni. Over time, 3 distinct regional bands of native people became established in the area. Along the shores of the Mackenzie and Liard rivers lived the Slavey people. The mountainous country to the west was home to two nomadic bands of natives, the Mountain Indians and a small group of Kaska Indians known to the Slavey as the "Nahaa". These were the mysterious Indians referred to as the "Nahannies" by the white fur traders who came into the country in the 1800's. The South Nahanni River is named after this group.

Alexander R. McLeod, the Chief Trader at Fort of the Forks, a Hudson's Bay Company post soon to be renamed Fort Simpson, was the first recorded European to venture into the land of the Nahaa in the year 1823. Others seeking furs and gold soon followed, Macabre incidents and traditional native lore intertwined to weave legends about the region. In 1908, the headless skeletons of the McLeod brothers were found along the river in what is today known as Deadmen Valley. Other skeletons and corpses followed and the Nahanni became fertile ground for lurid tales – a place where brave men and women feared to go.

It wasn't until the late 1920s, when prospector Albert Faille and adventurer/author R.M. Patterson ventured up the river, that some of the myths were dispelled. Patterson's book, *Dangerous River*, brought world-wide attention to the region. Although rumours of gold in the Nahanni still abound, it has never been found in any quantity.

RIVER PROFILE: There are several possible starting points for this trip. This profile describes trips starting at three of those most commonly used:

A. *MOOSE PONDS* – The Moose Ponds, at the river's headwaters, is one of the most popular starting locations, especially for experienced whitewater paddlers. Numerous class 2 and 3 rapids characterize the 190 km (119 mile) stretch from the Moose Ponds to the confluence of the South Nahanni and Rabbitkettle Rivers. A minimum of one week is required to complete this section, known as the "Rock Gardens", although 10 days is preferable so paddlers can explore and hike the high country above the river. Spray covers are necessary for open canoes on this upper stretch of the river.

The South Nahanni leaves the Moose Ponds as little more than a creek. Eight km (5 miles) downstream, the first rapids begin, just downstream from where the first major tributary enters the Nahanni on river left. After a couple of sets of rapids that can usually be run, the river bends sharply to the left and flows through a rock garden. A second big creek joins the river from the left about 10 km (6 miles) downstream from the Moose Ponds. There is a gravel bar campsite on river left where the tree line comes down to the river. The rapids there begin with a couple of little ledges as the river bends left and then right, flowing into a series of ledges and boulders.

Two kilometres downstream is another set of rapids which begin with a tight turn to the right and continue with a long straight stretch with big drops and rocks. From here, there are continuous class 3 rapids for a few kilometres.

About 20 km (12 miles) downstream from Moose Ponds is a very tricky, boulder-choked rapid. There is a narrow gate through the boulders, centre right at the bottom. Two hundred metres downstream, the main channel goes to the right of an island which has a nice campsite. Campsites are not plentiful for the next few kilometres.

A few kilometres downstream, the river divides around a rock pile and peters out on river right. The left channel is a steep drop with boulders, but may be runnable on river right.

Thirty kilometres downstream from the Moose Ponds, a major creek enters on river left. Rapids start immediately below the junction. There are two wide ledges separated by a pool, followed by 150 metres of big standing waves and rocks. The rapids now become relatively continuous, increasing in difficulty to class 3. About 4 km downstream, an island on river left of the main current offers a resting point. Downstream of this island is a constriction with big standing waves followed by a short pool and then two more islands. The main channel flows to river left around the first island and then the river divides evenly around the second island. Both sides are difficult, but the left channel is less steep, with fewer boulders. The river bends to the right at this point, making it difficult to see ahead to the openings between rocks. As the two channels join downstream from the island, difficult rapids continue with boulders and standing waves. There is a good campsite on river right immediately downstream of the island. The next 7 km (4 miles) are class 1 rapids, building to class 3.

About 5 or 6 km (4 miles) upstream from a river entering on the left, the Nahanni bends left towards a cliff and then sharply right. A trail on river left leads to a dry boulder field from which the rapids can be scouted. Two ledges extend almost across the river but a small channel on river right can often be negotiated.

One hundred metres downstream from these rapids is another set. The easiest route is usually to take the left channel around the first island and right channel around the second. This right channel goes into a cliff and then makes a sharp left turn. The sandy beach on this island is a good spot to stop. The next 4 to 5 kilometres (3 miles) have more rapids with standing waves but there are lots of options for manoeuvring around them.

The large river entering the Nahanni from the north, 50 km (31 miles) downstream from the Moose Ponds, signals the end of the technical rapids. From here paddling is easier, although there is still a strong current. There are lots of gravel bars for camping. It takes about 3 days to get to this point from the Moose Ponds, allowing time to enjoy the whitewater and take photos. It is another day of paddling yet to the mouth of the Little Nahanni, one more to Island Lakes and two more to the Park boundary at Rabbitkettle Lake.

B. *LITTLE NAHANNI* – Paddlers wishing to start their trip at the headwaters of the Little Nahanni must be extremely skilled whitewater paddlers. Although smaller than the South Nahanni, the Little Nahanni has similar volume to the "Rock Gardens" and is generally narrower, with steeper drops. Sixteen km (10 miles) downstream from Flat Lakes the Staircase Rapids begin – 18 km (11 miles) of almost continuous class 2 and 3 rapids. There is a steep gradient with only short pools between the rapids. The river here is narrow with few eddies.

About 40 km (25 miles) downstream from Flat Lakes is the first canyon. This canyon is dangerous and very difficult to get out of. A large hole stretches across the river at the end of the last rapids in the canyon. The canyon should be portaged on river left along a cart track. There is a good campsite below the canyon.

Downstream from the First Canyon are 4 or 5 km (3 miles) of class 2 and 3 rapids with large pools in between them. A class 1 rapid leads into "The Step", which is a large hole across the river. Paddlers can portage or lift over along river left. Just downstream is another good campsite on a sandy beach on river right. Downstream of the campsite the second canyon begins with class 2 and 3 rapids.

The third canyon begins 8 km (5 miles) upstream of the confluence of the Little Nahanni and the South Nahanni. There are several tight left bends with a cliff on river right. At the final bend paddlers can line or walk along river right to avoid some difficult class 3 and 4 rapids. From here to the South Nahanni is fairly easy paddling with some class 1 and 2 rapids.

C. *NAHANNI NATIONAL PARK* – About 3 days downstream of the confluence of the Little Nahanni and the South Nahanni is the border of Nahanni National Park. A clearly visible sign on river right indicates the portage to Rabbitkettle Lake. Parties must land and hike the 600 metres into the lake to complete mandatory park registration. Upon registration, the park warden will conduct a guided tour of the nearby Tufa mounds and hot springs, an area otherwise off limits to park visitors. Two hot springs have formed cream-coloured structures of tufa (calcium carbonate) 27 metres (90 feet) high. The average water temperature in these springs is 21°C. Visitors must remove their footwear to avoid damaging the brittle tufa and unfortunately, swimming is prohibited.

Downstream from Rabbitkettle River the South Nahanni widens slightly and breaks into several different channels. The smaller channels are shallow and may contain sweepers. Downstream from Flood Creek the valley widens, and bog and marsh areas encroach upon the river. Roughly 40 km (25 miles) downstream from Flood Creek, the Nahanni turns sharply to the left and one metre (3 foot) standing waves may be encountered.

Sixty-two km (39 miles) downstream from Flood Creek is Virginia Falls, the most spectacular waterfall in Canada. Immediately upstream from the falls is a short but wild set of rapids known as the Sluice Box. The combined height of the rapids and the falls is 117 metres (385 feet), over twice that of Niagara Falls. The falls is split mid-channel by a massive rock spire. The stretch of river upstream from the falls at the base of Sunblood Mountain is wide and quiet. Care must be taken to stay to river right where the park kiosk and campground are located. The portage trail begins 300 metres downstream from these buildings. Canoeists should be warned that just 30 metres (98 feet) below the trail the Sluice Box Rapids begins, funnelling down to the falls. The 1250 metre boardwalk is a good trail although the final bit can be slippery. The trail ends on a cobblestone beach at the foot of the falls.

Just downstream from the falls is the entrance to Five Mile Canyon, also known as Painted Canyon, an 8 km (5 mile) long gorge lined with attractive yellow and orange rock cliffs. The current here is very swift and turbulent, usually with large standing waves. Rapids are almost continuous through the canyon with a range of difficulty from Class 1 to 3. These increase in difficulty at higher water levels. Fortunately the gorge contains several small beaches where rest stops can be made safely. Five Mile Canyon ends at Marengo Creek, but the river remains rough until Clearwater Creek.

Two large islands are located mid-stream, just downstream from Clearwater Creek. These are well situated vantage points from which paddlers can plot their course through Hell's Gate or Figure 8 Rapids. Located at the next right angled bend in the river, Hell's Gate contains the river's best known rapids, generally acknowledged to be the most difficult on the lower South Nahanni. At the start of the rapid the river turns to the right and comes up against a cliff face creating irregular standing waves of up to 1.5 metres (3 to 6 feet). The river then makes a sharp, left turn and enters a short gorge. The current crosses the channel to pile up against a rock wall. Large whirlpools are created on either side of the main current. At high water levels, even expert paddlers are

Canoes on the beach below the cliffs of Painted Canyon

required to portage here. Since these rapids vary in difficulty from Class 2 to 4, paddlers must exercise good judgement when deciding whether or not to run them. The short portage trail along river right provides an excellent vantage point from which to scout the river or take photos.

After Hell's Gate, the 17 km (11 mile) stretch to the Mary River seems tame. It is initially shallow and braided, then narrows with short stretches of rapids. Paddlers should be wary of the tricky currents, whirlpools and boils at the Wrigley Creek confluence. Just downstream from the confluence of the Mary and South Nahanni Rivers, the landscape changes dramatically as the Nahanni begins its journey through 48 km (30 miles) of canyons. The first canyon paddlers encounter is called Third Canyon, followed by Second and First Canyons. In the Third and Second Canyons, the river is guarded by 100 metre cliffs. These in turn are backed by the 700 to 1000 metre high (2 to 3000 foot) mountains of the Funeral and Headless Ranges.

While the river is only an average of 150 metres (490 feet) wide in this section and the current fairly swift, there is little whitewater. Several small beaches are found at the base of the cliffs and can be used as resting places. At The Gate, about 13 km (9 miles) into Third Canyon, the water is essentially flat. Here the Nahanni makes a sharp, hairpin turn and flows through a narrow gap flanked by two vertical rock faces over 300 metres (1000 feet) high. Surprisingly, the waves created are no more than 30 cm (1 foot) high, except in extremely high water. The river will try to push canoes into the rock wall on river left. Pulpit Rock, a thumb-shaped pinnacle reaching 100 metres (300 feet) above the water, towers over paddlers as they pass through The Gate.

Downstream from Headless Creek, the river leaves the Second Canyon and enters a broad river valley, known as Deadmen Valley. This area provides a respite for paddlers before they tackle the next section of canyon. The current here slows considerably and care should be taken to avoid running aground on the many shoals and sandbars, particularly downstream from the Meilleur River junction. The surrounding countryside is marshy with many deciduous trees. Good campsites abound on either side of the river. The valley's dominant feature is the great alluvial fan created by Prairie Creek. An abundance of wildlife, including Dall sheep, is attracted to the salt licks here making it a great place to hike. Paddlers should be careful to avoid disturbing the wildlife.

At the Nahanni's confluence with Sheaf Creek, a few rotting base logs from three cabins remain as evidence of previous inhabitants. Raymond Patterson and his partner built the first structure here in the 1920's and two prospectors built the others in 1939-40. Behind the old Northwest Lands and Forests cabin are the remains of another cabin built by trappers in 1945.

Deadmen Valley offers prime hiking opportunities, providing access to the Tlogotsho Plateau from Sheaf Creek. Dry Canyon Creek also offers access to spectacular alpine tundra on the Nahanni Plateau.

A short distance downstream from Dry Canyon Creek is the entrance to First Canyon. For the next 9 km (14 miles) the Nahanni winds through a spectacular canyon flanked by 1000 to 1300 metre (3000 to 4000 foot) limestone and dolomite cliffs. Unlike Third and Second Canyons which were backed by mountains, First Canyon has been deeply incised in a plateau. The current is swift here and paddlers must navigate carefully through the entire length of the canyon. George's Riffle (a.k.a. Cache Rapids) is found at the entrance to the canyon. A cobble island diverts most of the water to the right channel. High standing waves are created by a low band of rock extending into the channel. There is no established portage around these class 3 to 4 rapids and they must be run with caution. At high water levels the best route is along river left, while at lower levels, river right is recommended.

Another very hazardous stretch occurs about 13 km (8 miles) downstream, where the river turns to the left and splits around an island. The two channels meet at the apex of the island, creating tricky currents and whirlpools. As paddlers exit the canyon, they are greeted with one final challenge, Lafferty's Riffle, located just downstream from Lafferty Creek. High standing waves are found on river right. These can be avoided by running along river left.

After First Canyon the river slows in its descent towards Yohin Ridge.

Kraus Hot Springs can be found on river right immediately downstream from the canyon. The main springs are about 300 metres south of the river and can be detected at some distance by their sulphurous odour. Hot water of 35°C bubbles up through fine mud, filling two pools. Gus and Mary Kraus resided here intermittently between 1940 and 1971.

Downstream from Yohin Ridge the river is braided, shallow and slow. This section is known as "The Splits". Ten km (6 miles) south of Twisted Mountain is the southeastern boundary of the Park. From here it is 33 km (53 miles) to the community of Nahanni Butte, where the South Nahanni enters the Liard River. This area is mountainous and dominated by the dolomite and limestone outcrops of the Nahanni Butte mountain. Canoeists can finish their trip at Nahanni Butte by pre-arranging pickup with an air charter company. Other options include paddling another 40 km (25 miles) downstream on the Liard River to Blackstone Territorial Park where pick-up by truck can be arranged, or continuing still further downstream to Fort Simpson. Three to five days should be allowed for travelling the 184 km (114 miles) from Nahanni Butte to Fort Simpson.

If canoeists choose to paddle the Liard River, caution is advised when negotiating the Beaver Dam Rapids. These are a series of limestone ledges extending across the 1 km width of the river in four distinct sets. Starting 3 km (1.9 miles) downstream from the confluence with the Poplar River, they extend some 20 km (12 miles) in length and at moderate water levels are Class 2 or 3 rapids. Given the width of the river and the power of the current, they should be approached with caution. The best route is to paddle as close as possible to river right.

Fort Simpson, which was established in 1804, is one of the oldest trading posts on the Mackenzie River. A National Park office is located there, as well as a Visitor Information Centre, hotel accommodation, a major airport and a campground.

NAHANNI NATIONAL PARK REGULATIONS: Canoeists travelling through the park must obtain a back country permit from park officials at the start of the trip. Travel registration offers a service similar to the R.C.M.P. Wilderness Trip Registration. At the completion of the trip paddlers are required to notify the park office or warden. A park entry fee has come into affect as of the 1995 paddling season. The fee for 1995 is $50 per person and will probably rise from year to year. Be sure to contact the Nahanni National Park administration office to obain current entry fee costs.

A National Park fishing permit must be obtained if you plan to fish within the park boundary. It is valid in all national parks for one season. Fishing regulations as well as information on other park regulations are given out at the administration office in Fort Simpson or at any other National Park information office.

Firearms must be broken down, cased and stowed with other gear. Hunting or discharging of firearms is strictly prohibited.

Removal of natural or historical objects from the park is prohibited. This includes fossils and antlers.

Ministry of Transportation (MOT) regulations require that one approved life jacket must accompany each paddler. Spare paddles should also be carried.

Camping is permitted at any suitable site along the river except where there are designated sites. In Nahanni Park, there are designated sites at Rabbitkettle Lake, Virginia Falls and Kraus Hotsprings.

Access to the caves is prohibited for environmental and safety reasons.

It is incumbent on visitors to ensure that prospective guides have been duly licenced by the Nahanni Park Superintendent.

MAPS REQUIRED: (read maps from left to right)

(1:250,000)   Nahanni 105 I   Glacier Lake 95 L
                   Flat River 95 E   Virginia Falls 95 F *
                   Sibbeston Lake 95 G   Fort Simpson 95 H
* Hell's Gate is not indicated on the second edition map series

AVERAGE GRADIENT: The gradient from Rabbitkettle Lake to Virginia Falls is 0.7 metres per km (3.7 feet per mile). From Virginia Falls to Kraus Hotsprings, the drop is 1.7 metres per km (8.9 feet per mile). The average gradient from Kraus Hotsprings to the Splits is 1.1 metres per km (5.8 feet per mile).

HYDROGRAPH: South Nahanni R. above Virginia Falls, 1962-1988

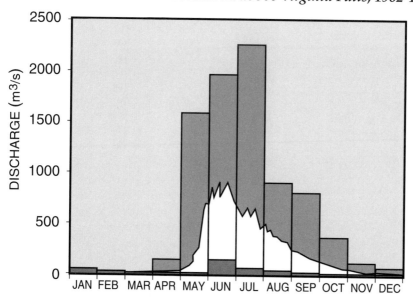

SOURCE INFORMATION:

1. Parks Canada, South Nahanni Canoe Trip Report, (from Glacier Creek to the Liard River).
2. Parks Canada Superintendent, Nahanni National Park: Personal communication.
3. Hartling, Neil, Nahanni River Adventures: Personal communication.
4. "Guide to the South Nahanni and Flat Rivers". Parks Canada Brochure, 1980.
5. Keough, Pat and Rosemary: *The Nahanni Portfolio*, Stoddart Publishing Company Ltd, Toronto, 1988.
6. Keough, Rosemary: Personal communication.
7. Scriver, Mark, Black Feather: Personal communication.
8. Hodgins, Shawn, Camp Wanapitei: Personal communication.

CUMULATIVE DISTANCES: *South Nahanni River*

Location	Kilometres	Miles
Moose Ponds	0	0
Confluence with Little Nahanni	79	49
Island Lakes	107	67
Glacier Lake	183	114
Rabbitkettle Lake	196	123
Virginia Falls	311	194
Hell's Gate	327	204
Park Boundary	480	300
Nahanni Butte (community)	519	324
Blackstone Landing	560	350
Fort Simpson	703	439

CUMULATIVE DISTANCES: *Little Nahanni River*

Location	Kilometres	Miles
Flat Lakes	0	0
Confluence with Little Nahanni	69	43
Island Lakes	97	61
Glacier Lake	173	108
Rabbitkettle Lake	186	116
Virginia Falls	301	188
Hell's Gate	317	198
Park Boundary	470	294
Nahanni Butte (community)	509	318
Blackstone Landing	550	344
Fort Simpson	693	433

WECHO RIVER

TOTAL DISTANCE: 230 km (144 miles) from Wecho Lake to Fort Rae.

DURATION OF TRIP: Twelve to fourteen days.

START: Wecho Lake

FINISH: Community of Fort Rae

ACCESSIBILITY: Wecho Lake, which is located 160 km (100 miles) north of Yellowknife, can be reached by air charter from Yellowknife.

The community of Fort Rae is on Highway 3, 100 km (62 miles) from Yellowknife. Fort Rae has regular bus service to Yellowknife and points south. Although it has no air strip, float planes serve the community from Marian Lake.

RIVER NOTES: The Wecho River flows south from Wecho Lake through rocky, forested Precambrian Shield to Russell and Marian Lakes, which drain into the North Arm of Great Slave Lake. This is not a frequently travelled river but it is easy and relatively inexpensive to reach from Yellowknife. While the Wecho has lots of rapids and falls, few are navigable in loaded canoes. The rapids near the headwaters are shallow and filled with boulders, while those further downstream tend to be the short, sharp drops often typical of Canadian Shield rivers.

Because it is seldom travelled, chances of seeing wildlife are good. The isolation of the river makes good wilderness camping skills a must, but paddlers need not be whitewater experts. Assuming that the most difficult rapids are portaged, the overall grade of rapids on the river is 1 and 2. Depending on water levels, there are approximately 35 portages, often over rugged terrain, so a good level of fitness and a compact outfit are a good idea.

Those who have paddled the river have found that its variety of lakes, sandy beaches, waterfalls, and rapids make it an enjoyable experience well suited to canoeists without the time, money or interest to tackle a major whitewater wilderness river.

GEOGRAPHY: The Wecho flows in a southerly direction into Great Slave Lake through the Canadian Shield. Igneous and metamorphic rocks formed by intense pressure and heat are dominant in the region. Lakes and rivers are plentiful and shorelines can vary from rock to sandy beaches or marsh. Some of the area surrounding the upper part of the Wecho has been ravaged by forest fires, a common occurrence in this part of the country. This trip takes place entirely within the tree line.

CLIMATE: The season for paddling the Wecho extends from June to late September. Although the river begins to break up in May, the larger lakes may still be frozen until the first week of June. Because the water levels drop over the season, paddlers are well advised to make this trip in June or July. Summers in this area are generally hot and dry. The daily temperature in July averages about 21°C (70°F) and may go as high as 30°C (86°F). In the evening, temperatures drop to about 10°C (50°F). In June and July there are about 20 hours of daylight.

**Marsh paddling
on the Wecho River**

Whitewater on the Wecho River

FLORA: Spruce forests and pine groves dominate this route, with willow and alder thickets often lining the shores of the river. Ground cover includes boreal forest species such as Labrador tea, cranberry, bearberry, lichens and mosses. Old burns near the headwaters of the river can make portaging difficult.

FAUNA: Moose, wolves, Black bear, beaver and marten are the most common wildlife along the route. Because this river is little–travelled, canoeists stand a better than average chance of seeing wildlife. Eagles, loons, and a variety of waterfowl and songbirds are also common. Lake trout and northern pike abound in the lakes along this route, while Arctic grayling can be caught in eddies and at the mouths of smaller creeks entering the river.

HUMAN HISTORY: The Wecho is one of several rivers traditionally used by the Dogrib Dene to gain access to caribou hunting grounds on the barrenlands. Family groups travelled upstream in late summer or early fall to seasonal camps within the treeline, near the barrenlands. From these base camps, hunters travelled to the barrens to hunt the caribou that group together during the fall breeding season. These camps were also used during the winter as bases for trapping. In the spring, people travelled downstream to spend the summer at Fort Rae or other trading posts.

RIVER PROFILE: The upper reaches of the Wecho, south of Wecho Lake, flow through an area of sandy glacial till laced with boulders. There is little exposed bedrock. The river is small here and the narrow sections between lakes are shallow boulder rapids that require wading and portaging. Much of this section of the river runs through an extensive burned area which can make portaging difficult and has eliminated most traces of old trails. There are more rapids than are indicated on either the 1:250,000 or 1:50,000 scale maps. Caution is advised while navigating the narrow chutes, and large boulders are encountered at the outlet of Wecho Lake. The upper part of the river shows little sign of having been canoed in recent years.

Rock outcrops reappear as the river flows south to Wheeler Lake. There continue to be more rapids than indicated on the maps. Jumbles of boulders and willows make footing awkward for many of the portages and the old burn areas continue to make trails impossible to locate, especially at the outlet of elevation 342 lake. Downstream from the burned area around elevation 289 lake (1:50,000 map), faint but discernable portage trails can be found around most rapids.

The 1:50,000 map does not show the river leaving the lake identified by elevation 284. The outlet is found in a series of rapids just south of the large peninsula on the east side. In the narrow section upstream from Wheeler Lake there is a scenic canyon containing many rapids which must be portaged. While there are stretches of smooth water in the top part of the canyon, there are also rapids which are not navigable for an open boat. The best portage route is on the west shore along a ridge. Paddlers have the choice of portaging the entire rapids along the ridge or crossing the river to the east shore in a small quiet area located just upstream from more unnavigable rapids. The east portage route goes through dense bush. Wheeler Lake is the approximate halfway point of the trip and it is a good idea to stick close to shore to avoid getting caught in sudden strong winds.

Several more rapids are encountered between Wheeler and Inglis Lakes. About 8 km (5 miles) upstream from Inglis is another burned area. This complicates portaging the series of rapids found there. The last rapid upstream from Inglis Lake is basically large standing waves and can probably be run in canoes with spray decks. There is a water survey station at the outlet of Inglis Lake measuring the daily discharge of the river. The rapids there are quite impressive and can be portaged on the south side. From here on, the portage routes, are still overgrown, though easier to locate. A longer portage begins upstream from the third marked rapids downstream from Inglis Lake, bypassing a series of drops and ending below the next marked rapid. Just downstream from where the power lines from the Snare Hydro dams cross the river, is another impressive set of rapids. This is the last marked rapid upstream from Mosher Lake. The portage begins on river right just upstream from the falls. This trail is good and easily followed.

Monica Kendel - artist

Mosher Lake is a very attractive, well-treed lake with high, rocky shores and no sign of recent fires. There is a small, unmarked falls where the river leaves the lake. Caution is advised as it is almost invisible from the lake. The first marked set of rapids downstream from Mosher Lake must be portaged on river right, beginning above a small, easy rapid. The trail is good and offers a view of the river. Just downstream from this is another unmarked rapid which can also be portaged on river right, starting about 50 metres upstream from the rapids in a quiet bay.

Just upstream from the marked falls is another unmarked falls on both sides of a small island. A well-used trail on river right bypasses both sets of falls. Just downstream another small falls requires a short lift over an island in the centre of the channel. "EDZO" is scraped on a large rock here, and there are signs of cooking fires and camping. Before the river enters the last small lake upstream from Russell Lake there is another small rapid to be run. On the other side of the lake is a tiny, well kept Dene graveyard.

One last rapid upstream from Lajeunesse Bay marks the end of the whitewater for the trip. There is a portage trail on river left. The abandoned chimneys of an old fur trade post can be seen on the east shore as you paddle south on Lajeunesse Bay.

The stretch of Marian Lake on the way to Fort Rae includes many small islands and reefs not indicated on the map. It is easy to run aground here as the rocks are almost invisible in the murky water.

Wecho Lake

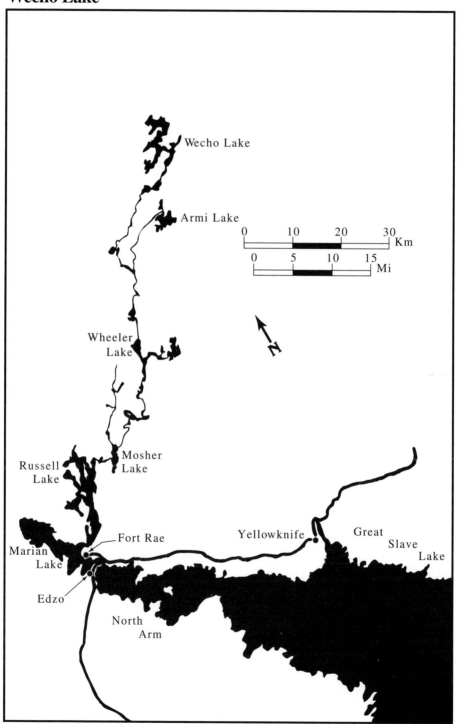

The communities of Fort Rae and Edzo on Marian Lake mark the end of the trip. Most modern conveniences are available here. Because these communities are situated on Highway 3, they are easily accessible either from Yellowknife or points south.

AVERAGE GRADIENT: The river drops 1 metre per kilometre (5 feet per mile) between Wecho Lake and the community of Fort Rae.

HYDROGRAPH: Wecho River at outlet of Inglis Lake, 1983-1988

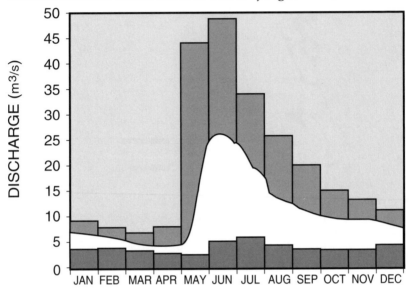

MAPS REQUIRED: (read maps from left to right)
(1:250,000)   Carp Lakes 85 P   Wecho River 85 O
              Yellowknife 85 J   Rae 85 K

SOURCE INFORMATION:
1. McInnes, John: Wecho Lake to Rae, Personal Journal, 1985.
2. Andrews, Ed: Personal communication.

CUMULATIVE DISTANCES:

Location	Kilometres	Miles
Wecho Lake	0	0
Wheeler Lake Inlet	108	68
Inglis Lake Outlet	152	95
Lajeunesse Bay	183	114
Russell Lake	199	125
Fort Rae	230	144

YELLOWKNIFE RIVER

TOTAL DISTANCE:

A. Greenstocking Lake to City of Yellowknife:
260 kilometres (163 miles).

B. Upper Carp Lake to City of Yellowknife:
175 kilometres (109 miles).

C. Fishing Lake to City of Yellowknife:
100 kilometres (63 miles).

DURATION OF TRIP

A. Approximately 2 weeks.

B. Approximately 10 days.

C. Approximately 4 days.

START: Paddlers can start at the river's headwaters at Greenstocking Lake, 200 air km (125 miles) north of Yellowknife or at a number of other lakes further downstream. Upper Carp and Fishing Lakes are two other popular starting points.

FINISH: Paddlers can paddle right into the City of Yellowknife by paddling across Yellowknife Bay on Great Slave Lake. This potentially dangerous stretch of water can be avoided by stopping at the Yellowknife River Bridge and hitchhiking into town, a distance of only a few kilometres.

ACCESSIBILITY: Any of the lakes along the Yellowknife River can be reached by air charter from Yellowknife. Paddlers can also retrace Sir John Franklin's 1820 route by travelling upstream on the river.

The City of Yellowknife is accessible by the Mackenzie Highway as well as by regular scheduled flights from Edmonton and Winnipeg.

RIVER NOTES: The Yellowknife River can be described as a series of about 15 lakes joined together by narrow, fast sections of river. It begins in the barrenlands at Greenstocking Lake and descends quickly into the boreal forest, spilling finally into Great Slave Lake.

The Yellowknife is a scenic river that offers a bit of everything – challenging whitewater, wildlife viewing, good fishing, and easy and relatively inexpensive access from Yellowknife. There are many portages along the route, especially on the section upstream from Upper Carp Lake. Paddlers with little whitewater experience might want to start their trip downstream from there to avoid some of the more demanding whitewater.

Caution is advised when crossing the larger lakes. Sudden winds can whip a calm, placid expanse of water into a whitecapped menace very quickly. Paddlers are also advised to scout rapids thoroughly to avoid surprises. Large fluctuations in water levels greatly affect the location and size of rapids on the river. In a dry year, the upper sections of the river can be very shallow.

Although the river is close to Yellowknife, it is only on the lower part that you are likely to see other boats. Prosperous Lake, the last lake on the river, is cottage country for Yellowknifers, so be prepared.

GEOGRAPHY: The headwaters of the Yellowknife River at Greenstocking Lake are located at the southern boundaries of both the Arctic tundra and discontinuous permafrost. The river descends quickly into open woodland and boreal forest country. The entire drainage is part of the Canadian Shield.

The landscape of the headwaters is typical of the Canadian barrenlands. Glacially polished granite ridges and hills protrude from boulder-clay drifts. The largest boulders measure more than 6 metres (20 feet) in diameter. Muskeg and tiny lakes dominate the low areas along the upper reaches of the river.

In the boreal forest, glacial erratics continue to dominate the shorelines. The spruce and tamarack increase in size, but muskeg still dominates the landscape.

CLIMATE: The ice on the Yellowknife River usually breaks up in May, but the lakes often remain frozen well into June. Check with air charter companies to find out when lakes are ice free.

Temperatures over the summer are generally warm, averaging between 13°C (55°F) and 16°C (60°F), although highs of 32°C (90°F) have been recorded. The weather is a little colder at the tree line. Canoeists should bring rain gear, a good tent, a three season sleeping bag and warm clothing.

In Yellowknife, there is no total darkness and only 4 hours of twilight on the summer solstice. Later in the summer the angle of the setting sun provides long hours of twilight, allowing daylight activities most of the night.

FLORA: In the Greenstocking Lake area, the only trees to be found are stunted spruce and dwarf birch growing in sheltered nooks along the lakeshores and river valleys. This area is along the fringe of the tundra and vegetation is sparse and characteristic of the barrenlands. Mosses, lichens and low shrubs, and a variety of wildflowers that bloom in June and July characterize the upper reaches of the river.

A mere 40 km (25 miles) south of Greenstocking Lake the river enters the boreal forest. The spruce and tamarack that dominate the forest are small and spindly but increase in size further south. Poplar, willow and birch become common along the river shore. Many edible plants and berries can be found along the way. A good guide to plants of the northern boreal forest is recommended.

FAUNA: Although barrenground caribou of the Bathurst herd are common in the area in the winter, it is unlikely that paddlers will see any during the summer. Along the high cliffs that line the river early in the journey, bald and golden eagles as well as a variety of hawks and falcons can be seen. This region is also the nesting ground for a wide variety of loons, swans, ducks and geese. A good bird guide will come in very handy.

In the boreal forest moose, black bear, otters and beaver are common. Grizzlies are not common along this river, but they may be occasionally seen in the tundra region.

Yellowknife River

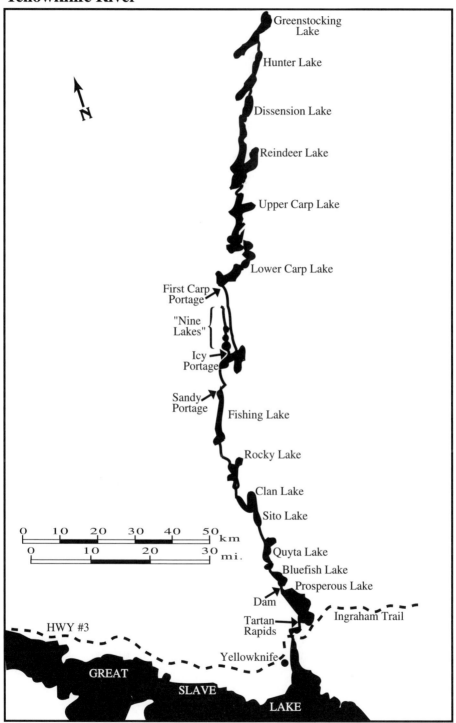

Greenstocking Lake

Hunter Lake

Dissension Lake

Reindeer Lake

Upper Carp Lake

Lower Carp Lake

First Carp Portage

"Nine Lakes"

Icy Portage

Sandy Portage

Fishing Lake

Rocky Lake

Clan Lake

Sito Lake

Quyta Lake

Bluefish Lake

Prosperous Lake

Dam

Ingraham Trail

Tartan Rapids

Yellowknife

HWY #3

GREAT SLAVE LAKE

N

0 10 20 30 40 50 km

0 10 20 30 mi.

Extra care should be taken to avoid both black and grizzly bears as they can be extremely dangerous.

The upper reaches of the river are filled with lake trout and grayling. Fishing is especially good in the pools below the frequent chutes and waterfalls. As you head south, pike become more common. Whitefish are also plentiful in the pools below waterfalls, but are difficult to capture with a rod and reel.

HUMAN HISTORY: The Yellowknife River is named after a tribe of Dene who lived and hunted in the area from Yellowknife Bay, east to Artillery Lake and north to Contwoyto Lake. The name stems from Sir John Franklin's observation that they possessed hunting implements made of copper. By the end of the nineteenth century, warfare and disease had greatly reduced the population of the Yellowknife people. Survivors joined with the Dogrib and Chipewyan Dene.

Sir John Franklin was the first European known to use the Yellowknife River. In August of 1820, his party was led up the Yellowknife River by the famous Yellowknife chief Akaitcho. The group arrived at Winter Lake, 24 km (15 miles) north of the river's headwaters, three weeks later. They built three log cabins which were named Fort Enterprise. After a long, hard winter the party travelled down the Coppermine River the next spring. It was a difficult trip which included near drownings and a murder. Franklin and his men struggled back to Fort Enterprise in October, where they nearly starved to death because their supplies didn't arrive.

Gold was first discovered in Yellowknife Bay by prospectors on their way to the Klondike in 1898. These finds were overlooked until 1934, when a large vein of gold was found on the shores of the bay. Within 2 years, the town of Yellowknife was a booming bustle of tents, cabins, floatplanes and rumours. Six mines were started in the region, attracting people from all over the country. The war put a temporary hold on development in 1940, but by 1947 there was renewed activity and the town site expanded rapidly. In 1967 Yellowknife became the capital of the NWT and today is Canada's most northerly city, boasting a population of 16,000. Several gold mines still operate in the area and evidence of mineral exploration can be found along the Yellowknife River route.

RIVER PROFILE: The Yellowknife River begins at Greenstocking Lake, 200 km (125 miles) north of Yellowknife. The lake is 24 km (15 miles) south of the abandoned Fort Enterprise on Winter Lake. Many of the rapids in the first 12 km (8 miles) must be portaged or lined. Water levels can vary drastically and will determine which sections are navigable. At Hunter Lake the river is still in the tundra, but trees become more common. The outlet of Hunter Lake is difficult to find because of thick willows. The portage past the rapids is on river left. Rapids at the outlets of lakes are very common on this route.

The short paddle to Dissension Lake is strewn with boulders. A combination of very technical paddling, portaging and lining is required. There are also several boulder rapids between Dissension and Reindeer Lake, which can be bypassed more quickly by portaging than by lining.

The 15 km (10 mile) long Reindeer Lake can become very rough when it is windy.

The outlet is at the most easterly bay at the south end of the lake.

Downstream from the second marked rapid between Reindeer and Upper Carp Lakes, there is an unmarked 10 metre (33 foot) cascade. From there to Upper Carp Lake, the paddling can be tricky depending on water levels.

Upper Carp Lake is a series of roundish lakes joined by narrow straits. When water levels are low these narrows can become rapids. There are several sets of rapids of varying difficulty leading into Carp Lake. The first Carp portage (on Carp Lakes 85 P 1:250,000 map) marks the beginning of a hazardous but scenic section of river characterized by many beautiful falls and rapids. The beginning of the rapids is deceiving and looks like little more than a riffle. Hidden downstream is a two foot ledge followed by large standing waves.

For the next 20 km (13 miles) the river tumbles through a narrow valley surrounded by 150 metre hills. The main channel is 20 metres wide and only those with extremely strong whitewater skills should attempt paddling this stretch. There is an alternate route called the "Nine Lakes" by Franklin, which parallels this section on river right. Although it requires more portaging it is much safer. The portages along this route are sometimes hard to find, but with a bit of bushwacking, map reading and patience, it is not a bad route. This route will bring you back onto the Yellowknife River at Icy Portage, just west of Lake 950.

In the stretch below Icy Portage there are three major portages all marked on the map. The Sandy Portage, just upstream from Fishing Lake, is a series of lifts around two rocky ledges. Depending on the time of year the water may be very shallow downstream from the portage.

Dave Nutter

Rapids on the Yellowknife River

Lining on the Yellowknife River

There is an old burn area at the outlet of Fishing Lake which creates difficult walking conditions on the portages. Paddlers should scout the rapids between Fishing and Rocky Lakes. Depending on water levels these rapids can be very deceptive. The last section upstream from Rocky Lake is about 2 km (1.25 miles) long and contains a series of drops and ledges which must be portaged. Rocky Lake is well named for the numerous rocks found just below the surface of the water at the northern end of the lake. Paddlers are advised to carefully scout the rapids found downstream from the lake.

The first sign of civilization, a power line, is encountered on Clan Lake. A portage around the waterfalls begins upstream from where the line crosses the river. Clan Lake is surrounded by an old burn and good campsites are impossible to find, so plan to camp either upstream or downstream from Clan Lake.

There are several falls and rapids between Clan and Quyta Lakes. Most of them should be portaged or lined. There is a winter trail on river left that can be used as a portage to Sito Lake (also known as Green Tree Lake on some maps). One of the better campsites in the area is located at the end of this lake on river right.

There are 4 portages between Sito and Quyta Lakes, the longest being about 400 metres. Quyta is one of the prettiest lakes on the final section of the trip. There is an island in the middle of the lake that is a good campsite. A word of caution again about sudden winds that can make the lake very dangerous.

There is an unmarked rapid and falls between Quyta and Bluefish Lakes. There is a short portage around them with the takeout point located on river left, just upstream from the chutes. From there on, the maps shouldn't be trusted because of the hydro dam located downstream and water levels that can change dramatically. Bluefish Lake was created by the dam, so paddlers should watch out for submerged trees.

There is a well-marked trail around the hydro dam on river left that is about 1.5 km (1 mile) long and ends at the caretaker's house. The base of the cascade is a good spot to fish for grayling.

Prosperous Lake is large (16 km or 10 miles long) and can get very rough on short notice. Paddlers are advised to keep to the right shoreline. There are few good campsites along the way to Tartan Rapids. These are the last rapids of the trip and are located at the outlet of Prosperous Lake. There is a well-used portage on river left. Depending on water levels the Tartan Rapids can be fun to run. However, scout them first, as there are some nasty holes at the bottom and the high standing waves can easily swamp an open canoe.

From the Tartan Rapids the river meanders peacefully to the Yellowknife River Bridge. High winds can make Yellowknife Bay very dangerous and many trips end at the bridge. Paddlers can easily hitchhike to Yellowknife to get transportation for their canoes and gear. If paddling across the bay to the city, be very aware of the wind and stick close to shore.

Yellowknife is a modern city with shopping centres, theatres, hotels, etc. If you have the time, there are many day trips to be made from the city. Information can be obtained from the Northern Frontier Visitors Association.

AVERAGE GRADIENT:

A. Greenstocking Lake to Yellowknife Bay: 0.9 metres per km (4.7 feet per mile).

B. Upper Carp Lake to Yellowknife Bay: 1.1 metres per km (6 feet per mile).

C. Fishing Lake to Yellowknife Bay: 1.2 metres per km (6.2 feet per mile).

HYDROGRAPH: Yellowknife R. at Inlet to Prosperous L., 1939-1970, 1972-1981, 1988

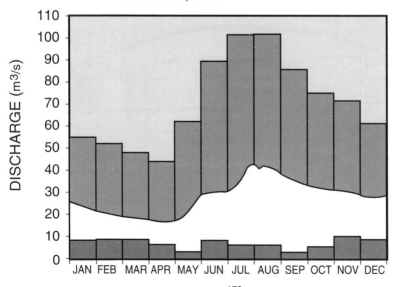

MAPS REQUIRED: *(read maps from left to right)*

(1:250,000)   Winter Lake 86 A   Carp Lakes 85 P
                     Wecho River 85 O   Yellowknife 85 J

SOURCE INFORMATION:

1. Yellowknife River Trip Report, TravelArctic, GNWT, 1979.

2. Franklin, Capt. John: *Narrative of a Journey to the Shores of the Polar Sea in the Years 1819, 20, 21 and 22.* New York: Greenwood Press, 1969.

3. Northwest Territories River Profiles: Yellowknife River.

4. Backhouse, Rob: Trip Report, Yellowknife River, 1983.

5. Smith, Bruce: Personal communication.

CUMULATIVE DISTANCE:

Location	Kilometres	Miles
Greenstocking Lake Outlet	0	0
Upper Carp Lake Inlet	66	42
Fishing Lake Inlet	142	89
Clan Lake Inlet	193	121
Tartan Rapids	244	153
Yellowknife River Bridge	253	158
City of Yellowknife	260	163

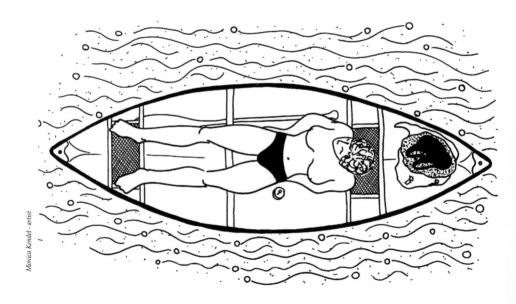

Monica Kendel - artist

INTERNATIONAL RIVER RATING SCALE

The International River Rating Scale rates the paddling difficulty of rivers and rapids. While useful, it should be treated with caution since it can be very subjective and does not take into account such factors as remoteness, air temperature, water temperature, and individual paddling skill. These factors must be considered along with the technical difficulty of a rapid when deciding whether to take the portage or run the whitewater.

GRADE 1: Moving water with a few riffles and small waves. Few or no obstructions.

GRADE 2: Easy rapids with waves up to one metre high and wide, clear channels that are obvious without scouting. Some manoeuvring is required.

GRADE 3: Rapids with high, irregular waves often capable of swamping an open canoe. Narrow passages that often require complex manoeuvring. May require scouting from shore.

GRADE 4: Long, difficult rapids with constricted passages that often require precise manoeuvring in very turbulent waters. Scouting from shore often necessary and conditions make rescue difficult. Generally not possible for open canoes. Paddlers in covered canoes and kayaks should be able to do the Eskimo roll.

GRADE 5: Extremely difficult, long and very violent rapids with highly congested routes which nearly always must be scouted from shore. Rescue conditions are difficult and there is significant hazard to life in event of a mishap. Ability to do the Eskimo roll is essential for kayaks and closed canoes.

GRADE 6: Difficulties of Grade 5 carried to the extreme of navigability. Nearly impossible and very dangerous. For teams of experts only, after close study and with all precautions taken.

Monica Kendel - artist

TRIP REPORTS

The NWT Canoeing Association and Canadian Recreational Canoeing Association are interested in making available accurate information on as many rivers as possible. Information which will improve the accuracy of any of the trip reports in this book, or reports on rivers in the Northwest Territories which might be included in future editions is appreciated.

The information that would be helpful includes, but is not restricted to:

* Total distance travelled
* Duration of trip
* Starting place
* Finishing place
* Accessibility
* Maps required and their scale
* Information about the geography, ice conditions, flora, fauna, human history, camping conditions, points of interest, etc.
* A river profile, noting rapids

SEND INFORMATION TO:

Canadian Recreational Canoeing Association,   or   *NWT Canoeing Association*
1029 Hyde Park Rd., Suite 5,   Box 2763
Hyde Park (London), Ontario, Canada N0M 1Z0   Yellowknife, NWT X1A 2R1
Phone (519) 473-2109/641-1261 Fax (519) 473-6560

(Please note that the Canadian Recreational Canoeing Association will be moving as of December, 1996 to its Outdoor Education Centre in Merrickville, Ontario.)

The Canadian Recreational Canoeing Association publishes Canada's only canoeing and kayaking magazine, *KANAWA* (trilingual for canoe). Quarterly subscriptions are \$20/year (4 issues) + 7% GST *(\$20 U.S. for USA and international subscribers).* The CRCA also produces the most comprehensive *"Paddling Catalogue"* of Canadian canoeing, kayaking and sea kayaking information anywhere, on paddling Canada. For a subscription to *KANAWA MAGAZINE* – contact the Canadian Recreational Canoeing Association and make cheques payable to C.R.C.A. Visa and Mastercard accepted.

"Canada's Paddling Information Specialists"

APPENDIX C

INFORMATION SOURCES

PADDLING INFORMATION:

CANADIAN RECREATIONAL CANOEING ASSOCIATION,
1029 Hyde Park Rd., Suite 5,
Hyde Park, Ontario N0M 1Z0
Phone: 519-473-2109/519-641-1261 Fax: 519-473-6560

NWT CANOEING ASSOCIATION
Box 2763, Yellowknife, NWT X1A 2R1
Phone: 403-873-3032 (c/o Sport North) Fax: 403-920-4047
Toll Free: 1-800-661-0797

Several NWT communities have local canoe and kayak clubs. Please contact the
NWT Canoeing Association for further information.

GENERAL TOURISM INFORMATION:

DEPARTMENT OF ECONOMIC DEVELOPMENT AND TOURISM
Box 1320, Yellowknife, NWT X1A 2L9
Phone: 403-873-7200 Fax: 403-873-0294
toll free: 1-800-661-0788

TOURISM INDUSTRY ASSOCIATION OF THE NORTHWEST TERRITORIES
4807 49th St., Yellowknife, NWT X1A 3T5
Phone: 403-873-2122 Fax: 403-873-3654

REGIONAL TOURISM INFORMATION:

ARCTIC COAST TOURISM ASSOCIATION
Box 91, Cambridge Bay, NWT X0E 0C0
Phone: 403-983-2224 Fax: 403-983-2302

BAFFIN TOURISM ASSOCIATION
Box 1450, Iqaluit, NWT X0A 0H0
Phone: 819-979-6551 Fax: 819-979-1261

BIG RIVER TOURISM ASSOCIATION
Box 185, Hay River, NWT X0E 0R0
Phone: 403-874-2422 Fax: 403-874-2027

TRAVEL KEEWATIN
Box 328, Rankin Inlet, NWT X0E 0G0
Phone: 819-645-2618 Fax: 819-645-2320

NAHANNI-RAM TOURISM ASSOCIATION
Box 177, Fort Simpson, NWT X0E 0N0
Phone: 403-695-3182 Fax: 403-695-2511

NORTHERN FRONTIER VISITORS ASSOCIATION
#4 – 4807 49th St., Yellowknife, NWT X1A 3T5
Phone: 403-873-3131 Fax: 403-873-3654

SAHTU TOURISM ASSOCIATION
Box 115, Norman Wells, NWT X0E 0V0
Phone: 403-587-2054 Fax: 403-587-2935

WESTERN ARCTIC TOURISM ASSOCIATION
Box 2600, Inuvik, NWT X0E 0T0
Phone: 403-979-4321 Fax: 403-979-2434

ARCHAEOLOGICAL SITES:
PRINCE OF WALES NORTHERN HERITAGE CENTRE
Senior Archaeologist,
Box 1320, Yellowknife, NWT X1A 2L9
Phone: 403-873-7551 Fax: 403-873-0205

FLORA, FAUNA, HUNTING, FISHING:
DEPARTMENT OF ECONOMIC DEVELOPMENT AND TOURISM
Box 1320, Yellowknife, NWT X1A 2L9
Phone: 403-873-7200 Fax: 403-873-0294
Toll Free: 1-800-661-0788

CONSERVATION EDUCATION, RENEWABLE RESOURCES, GNWT
Box 1320, Yellowknife, NWT X1A 2L9
Phone: 403-920-8716 Fax: 403-873-0221

There are local and regional Area Offices of the Department of Renewable Resources in many communities in the NWT. Information about where offices are located and how to contact them is available from either of the above.

WILDLIFE AND BIRD SANCTUARIES:
CANADIAN WILDLIFE SERVICE
Box 637, Yellowknife, NWT X1A 2N5
Phone: 403-920-8531 Fax: 403-873-8185

CANADIAN PARKS SERVICE:
AULAVIK NATIONAL PARK, BANKS ISLAND
Parks Canada, Box 1840, Inuvik, NWT X0E 0T0
Phone: 403-979-3248 Fax: 403-979-4491

AUYUITTUQ AND ELLESMERE ISLAND NATIONAL PARKS
Parks Canada, Eastern Arctic District
Box 1720, Iqaluit, NWT X0E 0H0
Phone: 819-979-6277 Fax: 819-979-4539

NAHANNI NATIONAL PARK
Bag 348, Fort Simpson, NWT X0E 0N0
Phone: 403-695-2310, -3151 Fax: 403-695-2446

WOOD BUFFALO NATIONAL PARK
Box 750, Fort Smith, NWT X0E 0P0
Phone: 403-872-2349 Fax: 403-872-3910

MAPS:

CANADA MAP OFFICE
130 Bentley Ave., Nepean, Ontario K2E 6T9
Phone: 613-952-7000 Fax: 613-957-8861

CANADA MAP COMPANY
63 Adelaide St., Toronto, Ontario M5C 1K6
Phone: 416-362-9297 Fax: 416-362-9381

MAP SALES OFFICE, YELLOWKNIFE
(under contract with the Federal Government)
Tgit Geomatics Ltd.
Box 244, #204 – 5110 50 Ave., Yellowknife, NWT X1A 2N2
Phone: 403-873-8438 Fax: 403-873-8439

AIR, LAND, WATER TRANSPORTATION
SCHEDULED AIR SERVICES TO THE NWT:

ALKAN AIR LTD.
Service between Inuvik, NWT and Whitehorse, YK.
Phone: 403-668-2107 Fax: 403-667-6117

CALM AIR
Schedule and charter air service between Thompson, Winnipeg and Churchill, MB
and Rankin Inlet, Chesterfield Inlet, Baker Lake, Arviat, Whale Cove, Repulse Bay,
and Coral Harbour, NWT
Phone: 204-778-6471 (Thompson) Fax: 204-778-6954

CANADIAN NORTH
(Division of CANADIAN AIRLINES INTERNATIONAL)
Service between many places in southern Canada and the NWT.
Phone Toll Free: Eastern Arctic 1-800-665-1177; Keewatin 1-800-665-1430;
Western Arctic 1-800-661-1505; United States 1-800-426-7000
Phone: 403-873-5533 Fax: 403-873-8077

FIRST AIR
Service between southern places in Eastern Canada and the Eastern Arctic and
Yellowknife.
Phone: 819-979-5810 (Iqaluit) or 403-873-6884 (Yellowknife)
Fax: 819-979-6760 (Iqaluit) or 403-920-7540 (Yellowknife)
Toll Free: 1-800-267-1247

NORTHWESTERN AIR LEASE
Service between Fort McMurray and Fort Chipewyan, AB and Fort Smith, NWT.
Phone: 403-872-2216 Fax: 403-872-2214

NWT AIR AND AIR CANADA
(Air Canada Connector)
Service between many places in southern Canada and the NWT.
Phone: 403-920-2500
Toll Free: 1-800-661-0789

PTARMIGAN AIRWAYS
Service between Yellowknife and Fort Simpson, NWT and Whitehorse, YK.
Phone: 403-873-4461 Fax: 403-873-5209
Toll Free: 1-800-661-0808

SCHEDULED AIR SERVICE WITHIN THE NWT:

AIR TINDI
P.O. Box 1693, Yellowknife, NWT X1A 2P3
Service between Snare Lake, Rae Lakes, Lutsel K'e, Wha Ti and Yellowknife.
Phone: 403-920-4177 (Yellowknife) Fax: 403-920-2836

AKLAK AIR
Service between Fort McPherson, Tuktoyaktuk, Sachs Harbour, Paulatuk and Inuvik.
Phone: 403-979-3777 (Inuvik) Fax: 403-979-3388

ARCTIC WINGS
Service between Aklavik, Tuktoyaktuk, Sachs Harbour and Inuvik.
Phone: 403-979-2220 (Inuvik) Fax: 403-979-3440

BUFFALO AIRWAYS
Service between Yellowknife and Hay River, Yellowknife and Fort Simpson.
Phone: 403-874-3333 (Hay River), 403-873-6112 (Yellowknife)
Fax: 403-874-3572 (Hay River), 403-873-8393 (Yellowknife)

CALM AIR INTERNATIONAL LTD.
Service to Rankin Inlet, Coral Harbour, Chesterfield Inlet, Whale Cove, Repulse Bay, Baker Lake and Arviat.
Phone: 204-778-6471 (Thompson, MB) Fax: 204-778-6954

CANADIAN NORTH
Service throughout the NWT.
Phone Toll Free: Eastern Arctic 1-800-665-1177; Keewatin 1-800-665-1430;
Western Arctic 1-800-661-1505; United States 1-800-426-7000
Phone: 403-873-5533 (Yellowknife) Fax: 403-873-8077

FIRST AIR
Service throughout the Central and Eastern Arctic and to Yellowknife.
Phone: 819-979-5810 (Iqaluit) or 403-873-6884 (Yellowknife)
Fax: 819-979-6760 (Iqaluit) or 403-920-7540 (Yellowknife)
Toll Free: 1-800-267-1247

GREAT BEAR AVIATION
Service between Wrigley, Fort Norman, Norman Wells, Fort Good Hope and Yellowknife.
Phone: 403-873-3626 (Yellowknife) Fax: 403-873-6195
Toll Free: 1-800-661-0719

NORTHWESTERN AIR LEASE
Service between Yellowknife, Fort Chipewyan, Fort McMurray, Lutsel K'e and Fort Smith.
Phone: 403-872-2216 (Fort Smith) Fax: 403-872-2214

NORTH-WRIGHT AIR LTD.
Bag Service 2200, Norman Wells, NWT X0E 0V0
Service between Yellowknife, Fort Good Hope, Fort Franklin, Fort Norman, Colville Lake, Inuvik and Norman Wells. Provides trips to the Keele, Mountain, Horton and Anderson rivers. Canoe and radio rentals available.
Phone: 403-587-2333 (Norman Wells) Fax: 403-587-2962
Toll Free: 1-800-661-0702

NWT AIR
Service throughout the NWT.
Phone: 403-920-2500 (Yellowknife), 403-979-2341 (Inuvik)
Toll Free: 1-800-661-0789

PTARMIGAN AIRWAYS
Service between Wah Ti, Rae Lakes, Lutsel K'e, Fort Resolution, Fort Simpson, Whitehorse, Coppermine, Holman, Baker Lake, Rankin Inlet, Hay River and Yellowknife.
Phone: 403-873-4461 (Yellowknife) Fax: 403-873-5209
Toll Free: 1-800-661-0808

SKYWARD AVIATION
Scheduled service between Baker Lake, Whale Cove, Arviat and Rankin Inlet. Charters also available.
Phone: 819-645-3200 (Rankin Inlet) Fax: 819-645-3208

WILLIAMS AERO/ARCTIC AIRLINES
Service between Fort Norman, Fort Good Hope, Deline, Colville Lake, Inuvik, Yellowknife and Norman Wells.
Phone: 403-587-2243 (Norman Wells) Fax: 403-587-2335

CHARTER AIR SERVICE (FIXED WING):

ADLAIR AVIATION, YELLOWKNIFE AND CAMBRIDGE BAY
Box 2946, Yellowknife, NWT X1A 2R3
Phone: 403-873-5161 Fax: 403-873-8475

AERO ARCTIC HELICOPTERS LTD., YELLOWKNIFE
Box 1496, Yellowknife, NWT X1A 2P1
Phone: 403-873-5230 Fax: 403-920-4488

AIR BAFFIN, IQALUIT
Box 1239, Iqaluit, NWT X0A 0H0
Phone: 819-979-4018 Fax 819-979-4318

AIR PROVIDENCE, FORT PROVIDENCE
Fort Providence, NWT X0E 0L0
Phone: 403-699-3551

AIR TINDI, YELLOWKNIFE
Box 1693, Yellowknife, NWT X1A 2P3
Phone: 403-920-4177 Fax: 403-920-7654

AKLAK AIR, INUVIK
Box 1190, Inuvik, NWT X0E 0T0
Phone: 403-979-3777 Fax: 403-979-3388

ARCTIC SUNWEST, YELLOWKNIFE
Box 1807, Yellowknife, NWT X1A 2P4
Phone: 403-873-4464 Fax: 403-920-2661

ARCTIC WINGS, INUVIK
Box 1159, Inuvik, NWT X0E 0T0
Phone: 403-979-2220 Fax: 403-979-3440

BEAUDEL AIR LTD., INUVIK
Box 2040, Inuvik, NWT X0E 0T0
Phone: 403-979-2333 Fax: 403-979-3758
Canoe and kayak rentals available. Aircraft on wheels, skis or floats.

BIG RIVER AIR LTD., FORT SMITH
Box 688, Fort Smith, NWT X0E 0P0
Phone: 403-872-3030 Fax: 403-872-5202

BLACKSTONE AVIATION, FORT SIMPSON
Box 30, Fort Simpson, NWT X0E 0N0
Phone: 403-695-2111 Fax: 403-695-2132

BUFFALO AIRWAYS, HAY RIVER AND YELLOWKNIFE
Box 1479, Hay River, NWT X0E 0R0
Box 2015, Yellowknife, NWT X1A 2R3
Phone: 403-874-3333 (Hay River) Fax: 403-874-3572
Phone: 403-873-6112 (Yellowknife) Fax: 403-873-8393

CARTER AIR SERVICES, HAY RIVER
Box 510, Hay River, NWT X0E 0R0
Phone/Fax: 403-874-2282

DEH CHO AIR LTD., FORT LIARD
R.C. Borrelli
Box 78, Fort Liard, NWT X0G 0A0
Phone: 403-770-4103 Fax: 403-770-4102

FIRST AIR
Head Office
3257 Carp Rd., Carp, ON K0A 1L0
Phone: 613-839-3131 Fax: 613-839-3280

IMPERIAL AVIATION, YELLOWKNIFE
#14, Yellowknife Airport, Yellowknife, NWT X1A 3T2
Phone: 403-920-2784 Fax: 403-873-5026

INUVIK AIR CHARTER, INUVIK
Box 2361, Inuvik, NWT X0E 0T0
Phone: 403-979-4242 Fax: 403-979-2037

KEEWATIN AIR LTD., RANKIN INLET
Box 38, Rankin Inlet, NWT X0C 0G0
Phone: 819-645-2992 Fax: 819-645-2330

KENN BOREK AIR, IQALUIT
Iqaluit, NWT X0A 0H0
Phone: 819-979-0040 Fax 819-979-0132

LANDA AVIATION, HAY RIVER
Box 420, Hay River, NWT X0E 0R0
Phone: 403-874-3500 Fax: 403-874-2927

NORTHERN AIRLINK, INUVIK
Box 1916, Inuvik, NWT X0E 0T0
Phone: 403-979-2800

NORTHWESTERN AIR LEASE, FORT SMITH
Box 249, Fort Smith, NWT X0E 0P0
Phone: 403-872-2216 Fax: 403-872-2214

NORTH-WRIGHT AIR LTD.
Bag Service 2200, Norman Wells, NWT X0E 0V0
Phone: 403-587-2333 Fax: 403-587-2962
North-wright Air provides trips to the Keele, Mountain, Horton and Anderson Rivers. Canoe and radio rentals are also available.

OLD TOWN FLOAT BASE, YELLOWKNIFE
Box 806, Yellowknife, NWT X1A 2N6
Phone: 403-873-5330 Fax: 403-873-5791

ORION AIRWAYS, YELLOWKNIFE
Box 2400, Yellowknife, NWT X1A 2P8
Phone: 403-873-8380 Fax: 403-873-6662

PTARMIGAN AIRWAYS, YELLOWKNIFE
Box 100, Yellowknife, NWT X1A 2N1
Phone: 403-873-4461 Fax: 403-873-5209
Toll Free: 1-800-661-0808

RELIANCE AIRWAYS, FORT SMITH
Box 1469, Fort Smith, NWT X0E 0P0
Phone: 403-872-2359

SOUTH NAHANNI AIRWAYS, FORT SIMPSON
Box 407, Fort Simpson, NWT X0E 0N0
Phone: 403-695-2007 Fax: 403-695-2943

SIMPSON AIR, FORT SIMPSON
Box 260, Fort Simpson, NWT X0E 0N0
Phone: 403-695-2505 Fax: 403-695-2925

SKYWARD AVIATION, RANKIN INLET
Box 562, Rankin Inlet, NWT X0C 0G0
Phone: 819-645-3200 Fax: 819-645-3208

SPUR AVIATION LTD., YELLOWKNIFE
Box 2635, Yellowknife, NWT X1A 2P9
Phone: 403-873-3626 Fax: 403-873-6195

URSUS AVIATION LTD., FORT NORMAN
General Delivery, Fort Norman, NWT X0E 0K0
Phone: 403-588-4141 Fax: 403-588-4131
Air bases located in: Wrigley, Fort Norman, Norman Wells, Fort Good Hope and Delinè.

WILLIAMS AERO/ARCTIC AIRLINES, NORMAN WELLS
Box 417, Norman Wells, NWT X0E 0V0
Phone: 403-587-2243 Fax: 403-587-2335

WOLVERINE AIR, FORT SIMPSON
Box 316, Fort Simpson, NWT X0E 0N0
Phone: 403-695-2263 Fax: 403-695-3400
Flying the north since 1973 including: the South Nahanni River, Mackenzie Mountains, Cirque of the Unclimbables and others. Flightseeing day trips to Virginia Falls and the Ram Plateau.

HIGHWAYS:

HIGHWAY CONDITIONS
Highways 1 to 7 – Toll Free: 1-800-661-0750
Highway 8 and Mackenzie Delta – Toll Free: 1-800-661-0752

FERRY SERVICE
Service is free. It may be intermittent or non-existent during break-up and freeze-up (May and November).
Highway 1 and 3 – Toll Free: 1-800-661-0751
Highway 8 (Dempster) – Toll Free: 1-800-661-0752

BARGE:

NORTHERN TRANSPORTATION COMPANY LTD. (NTCL)
Box 250, Hay River, NWT X0E 0R0
Phone: 403-874-2442 Fax: 403-874-5155
Cargo transport to the Mackenzie River and Arctic coast communities. An option for transporting canoes.

BUS SERVICES:

DEMPSTER HIGHWAY BUS SERVICE (Arctic Tour Co.)
Box 2021, Inuvik, NWT X0E 0T0
Phone: 403-979-4100 Fax: 403-979-2259
Toll Free: 1-800-661-0721
Summer bus service on the Dempster Highway between Dawson City and Inuvik.

FRONTIER COACHLINES
328 Old Airport Road, Yellowknife, NWT X1A 3T3
Phone: 403-873-4892 Fax: 403-873-6423
Year round bus service on the Mackenzie Highway to Yellowknife, Hay River and Fort Smith with connections to Greyhound Lines Canada-wide.

GREYHOUND LINES OF CANADA LTD.
10324 – 103 St., Edmonton, AB T5J 0Y9
Phone: 403-421-4211 Fax: 403-425-7829
Toll Free: 1-800-661-8747

PADDLING OUTFITTERS AND TOURS

ADVENTURE CANADA
Matthew Swan – Lochburn Landing, 14 Front St. South, Port Credit, ON L5H 2C4
Phone: (905) 271-4000 Fax: (905)271-5595
Toll Free: 1-800-363-7566
Nahanni River tours by raft and canoe. Adventure travel.

ARCTIC AND NAHANNI WILDERNESS ADVENTURES, NWA LTD.
Box 4, Site 6, RR #1, Didsbury, AB T0M 0W0
Phone/Fax: 403-637-3843
Specializing in first class/fully outfitted canoe and raft adventures on the NWT's classic mountain and Barrenland rivers. Scheduled departures, June – September on the South Nahanni, Coppermine, Burnside, Hood, Horton and Thelon Rivers. Canoe Schools, partially outfitted and rental services also available.

ARCTIC NATURE TOURS LTD.
Fred Carmichael, Miki O'Kane, Darielle Talarico – Box 1530, Inuvik, NWT X0E 0T0
Phone: 403-979-3300 Fax: 403-979-3400
Firth River rafting, wildlife viewing. One and multi-day tour packages in the western Arctic.

ARCTIC TOUR COMPANY
Kim Staples, Winnie or Roger Gruben – Box 2021, Inuvik, NWT X0E 0T0
Phone: 403-979-4100 Fax: 403-979-2259
Toll Free: 1-800-661-0721
Full service tour company. Horton River voyageur canoe expeditions.

ARCTIC WATERWAYS
RR 2, Stevensville, ON L0S 1S0
Phone: 905-382-3882
Wilderness rafting on the Horton, Coppermine and Anderson Rivers.

BATHURST ARCTIC SERVICES
Box 820, Yellowknife, NWT X1A 2N6
Phone: 403-873-2595 Fax: 403-920-4263
Canoe expediting, Burnside/Mara, Hood, Back, Thelon, etc. Air transport, canoes, accommodation, logistics: we do it all.

BLACK FEATHER WILDERNESS ADVENTURES
1960 Scott St., Ottawa, ON K1Z 8L8
Phone: 613-722-9717 Fax: 613-722-0245
OR RR#3 Parry Sound, ON P2A 2W9
Phone: 705-746-1372 Fax: 705-746-7048
Arctic canoeing specialists since 1971. Guided canoeing trips on the Nahanni, Mountain, Natla-Keele, Hood and Burnside rivers.

CANADA'S CANOE ADVENTURES
Canadian Recreational Canoeing Association
1029 Hyde Park Rd., Suite 5, Hyde Park, ON N0M 1Z0
Phone: 519-641-1261 Fax: 519-473-6560
Trips on the Coppermine, Mara/Burnside, Soper, Kazan, Thelon, South Nahanni, Mountain, Firth and Horton Rivers. Operated by the Canadian Recreational Canoeing Association with all proceeds being donated to the preservation and protection of Canada's waterways.

CANADIAN RIVER EXPEDITIONS LTD.
#47 – 3524 West 16th Ave., Vancouver, BC V6R 3C1
Phone: 604-938-6651 Fax: 604-938-6621
Toll Free: 1-800-898-7238
Firth River raft expedition. Emphasis on wilderness and wildlife rather than whitewater thrills.

CANADIAN WILDERNESS TRIPS
171 College St., Toronto, ON M5T 1P7
Phone: 416-977-5763 Fax: 416-977-7112
Guided canoe trips to the Nahanni.

CANOE ARCTIC INC.
Alex Hall – Box 130, Fort Smith, NWT X0E 0P0
Phone: 403-872-2308
Canoe trips on the Thelon, Back, Dubawnt and Coppermine river systems and more. Guided by Alex Hall, wildlife biologist. Operating since 1974.

ECOSUMMER EXPEDITIONS
1516 Duranleau St., Vancouver, B.C. V6H 3S4
Phone: 604-669-7741 Fax: 604-669-3244
Toll Free: 1-800-465-8884 (Canada) 1-800-688-8605 (USA)
Arctic sea kayak trips, rafting on the Firth and Tatshenshini, hiking or winter season dogsledding. Call for a colour catalogue.

GREAT CANADIAN ECOVENTURES
Tom Faess, Mgr. – P.O. Box 25181, Winnipeg, MB R2V 4C8
Phone: 604-730-0704 Fax: 604-733-8657
Toll Free: 1-800-667-WILD
Canoe and raft expeditions on the Thelon and Kazan. Canoe and equipment rentals and logistical support for the Kazan, Dubawnt, Thelon, Kunwok, Quoish, Back, Perry, Ellice and Armack.

MACKENZIE MOUNTAIN OUTFITTERS LTD.
Stan Stevens – Summer: Box 124, Norman Wells, NWT X0E 0V0
Phone: 403-587-2255
Winter: Box 235, Toms Lake, BC V0C 2L0
Phone/Fax: 604-786-5118
Rafting trips on rivers in the Mackenzie Mountains.

NAHANNI RIVER ADVENTURES
Neil Hartling – Box 4869, Whitehorse, YK Y1A 4N6
Phone: 403-668-3180 Fax: 403-668-3056
Guided canoe or raft trips on the Nahanni, Horton and Mountain rivers. Voyageur canoes available. Providing professional service for over ten years.

NARWAL NORTHERN ADVENTURES
Cathy Ayalik – #101 – 5103 51 Ave., Yellowknife, NWT X1A 1S8
Phone: 403-873-6443 Fax: (403) 873-0516
Guided trips. Canoeing and kayaking instructional programs. Lake, river and sea kayak applications. Canoe and kayak rentals.

NIGLASUK CO. LTD.
Box 39, Arctic Bay, NWT X0A 0A0
Phone: 819-439-9949 Fax: 819-439-8341
Kayaking in Admiralty Inlet.

NORTHCRAFT
Tom Hamilton – Box 1902, Yellowknife, NWT X1A 2P4
Phone: 403-873-3131 Fax: 403-873-3654
Day trips on the Cameron River. Booking through Northern Frontier Visitors Association.

NORTHWINDS ARCTIC ADVENTURE
Box 849, Iqaluit, NWT X0A 0H0
Phone/Fax: 819-979-0551
The Soper River to Lake Harbour.

RAVEN EYE OUTFITTERS
Box 698, Lynn Lake, MB R0B 0W0
Phone/Fax: 204-356-2243
Complete and partial outfitting. Fly out from Lynn Lake, 500 miles north of Winnipeg – the most convenient and cost effective method of reaching the Kazan, Dubawnt, Thelon and Thlewiaza rivers.

RENDEZVOUS LAKE OUTPOST CAMP
Billy Jacobson – Box 162, Tuktoyaktuk, NWT X0E 1C0
Phone: 403-977-2406
Guided river trips in the Anderson River area.

SUBARCTIC WILDERNESS ADVENTURES LTD.
Jacques Van Pelt – Box 685, Fort Smith, NWT X0E 0P0
Phone: 403-872-2467 Fax: 403-872-2126
We live here, three decades of outfitting/consulting for remote (fly-in) trips to the Taltson and Thelon river basins; guided swiftwater rafting/canoeing (drive-in) to Great Slave River rapids. Licensed outfitter.

WANAPITEI WILDERNESS CENTRE
393 Water Street, #14, Peterborough, ON K9H 3L7
Phone: 705-745-8314 Fax: 705-745-4971
Canada's Coppermine specialists since 1979. Other trips include: the Soper river (on Baffin Island) and the Mackenzie Valley's Mountain and Keele rivers. Join us for an exciting canoe adventure. Operating since 1931.

WHITEWOLF ADVENTURE EXPEDITIONS LTD.
Barry Beales – #41 – 1355 Citadel Dr., Suite 41, Port Coquitlam, BC V3C 5X6
Phone: 1-800-661-6659 or 604-944-5500 Fax: 604-944-3131
OR: Ron Globe – 634 Belvenia Rd., Burlington, ON L7L 4Z4
Phone: 905-681-6068 Fax: 905-637-2187
Guided natural history and photographic adventures by canoe or raft on the Nahanni, Burnside and Coppermine Rivers. Singles, novices, all ages and skill levels. Operating for over 17 years in the NWT.

WILDERNESS CANOE SCHOOLS
Steve Chambers, University of Calgary Outdoor Program Centre
2500 University Dr. NW, Calgary, AB T2N 1N4
Phone: 403-220-5038 Fax: 403-284-5867
Canoeing courses offered in the mountain and tundra regions of the NWT.

APPENDIX F

CANOE/EQUIPMENT RENTALS

EASTERN ARCTIC:

ECLIPSE SOUND OUTFITTING LTD., **POND INLET**
Box 60, Pond Inlet, NWT X0A 0S0
Phone: 819-899-8870 Fax: 819-899-8817
Kayaking supplies (folding and solid body).

NORTHWINDS ARCTIC ADVENTURES, **IQALUIT**
Box 849, Iqaluit, NWT X0A 0H0
Phone: 819-979-0551 Fax: 819-979-0573
Camping equipment, canoes, rafts, kayaks, life jackets, paddles, waterproof packs, trail food.

QAIRRULIK OUTFITTING LTD., **IQALUIT**
Box 863, Iqaluit, NWT X0A 0H0
Phone: 819-979-6280 Fax: 819-979-1950
Camping gear and accessories.

SUNRISE COUNTY CANOE EXPEDITIONS LTD.
Cathance Lake, Grove, ME 04638 USA
Phone: 207-454-7708 Fax: 207-454-3315
Canoe rentals in Iqaluit and Katannilik Park/Lake Harbour.

MACKENZIE VALLEY AND MOUNTAIN RIVERS:

AURORA SPORT FISHING AND TOURS, **FORT PROVIDENCE**
Fort Providence, NWT X0E 0L0
Phone: 403-699-3551
Canoes, paddles, fishing equipment.

MOUNTAIN RIVER OUTFITTERS, **NORMAN WELLS**
Box 449, Norman Wells, NWT X0E 0V0
Phone: 403-587-2324, -2285
Canoe rental.

WILLIAMS AERO SERVICES, **NORMAN WELLS**
Box 417, Norman Wells, NWT X0E 0V0
Phone: 403-587-2243 Fax: 403-587-2335
Canoe accessories.

WESTERN ARCTIC ADVENTURE & EQUIPMENT
Box 1554, Inuvik, NWT X0E 0T0
Phone/Fax: 403-979-4542
Canoe rentals and sales for the western NWT, Victoria Island and northern Yukon. Canoes available in Inuvik, Norman Wells and Cambridge Bay. Trip consulting and logistical planning service available.

NAHANNI AREA:

ARCTIC AND NAHANNI WILDERNESS ADVENTURES, NWA LTD.
Box 4, Site 6, RR #1, Didsbury, AB T0M 0W0
Phone/Fax: 403-637-3843
Canoe and equipment rentals for the South Nahanni, Coppermine, Burnside, Hood, Horton and Thelon Rivers.

BLACK FEATHER WILDERNESS ADVENTURES
1960 Scott St., Ottawa, ON K1Z 8L8
Phone: 613-722-9717 Fax: 613-722-0245
OR: RR#3 Parry Sound, ON P2A 2W9
Phone: 705-746-1372 Fax: 705-746-7048
Canoe, kayak and equipment rentals.

BLACKSTONE AVIATION, **FORT SIMPSON**
Box 30, Fort Simpson, NWT X0E 0N0
Phone: 403-695-2111 Fax: 403-695-2132
Canoes, rafts and accessories available for rent.

DEH CHO AIR LTD., **FORT LIARD**
R.C. Borrelli, Box 78, Fort Liard, NWT X0G 0A0
Phone: 403-770-4103 Fax: 403-770-4102
Self-guided rentals for groups from 2-18 people. Serving the South Nahanni River and the Natla-Keele rivers from Fort Liard, NWT. The most economical way of paddling the Nahanni; Old Town Canoes and lace-down skirts provided with every charter for free. Shuttle service provided. Colour brochure available.

NAHANNI MOUNTAIN LODGE, **FORT SIMPSON**
Box 260, Fort Simpson, NWT X0E 0N0
Phone: 403-695-2505 Fax: 403-695-2925
Canoes, canoeing and camping equipment.

NAHANNI RIVER ADVENTURES
Neil Hartling – Box 4869, Whitehorse, YK Y1A 4N6
Phone: 403-668-3180 Fax: 403-668-3056
Canoe and raft rentals.

YELLOWKNIFE AREA:

NARWAL NORTHERN ADVENTURES, **YELLOWKNIFE**
Box 1175, Yellowknife, NWT X1A 2N9
Phone: 403-873-6443 Fax: 403-873-4079
Canoe rentals. Canoe and kayak instruction.

OVERLANDER SPORTS, **YELLOWKNIFE**
Box 964, Yellowknife, NWT X1A 2N8
Phone: 403-873-2474 Fax: 403-920-4079
Canoe and kayak rentals. A complete line of outdoor equipment and camping supplies. Maps available.

THE SPORTSMAN, **YELLOWKNIFE**
5118 – 50th St., Box 162, Yellowknife, NWT X1A 2N2
Phone: 403-873-2911, 3424 Fax: 403-920-2932
Canoe and camping equipment rental. Maps on NWT available.

APPENDIX G
BIBLIOGRAPHY
HISTORY

Adney, Edwin T. and Howard I. Chapelle
The Bark Canoes and Skin Boats of North America. Washington: Smithsonian Institution, 1964.
Back, George Captain, R.N.
Narrative of the Arctic Land Expedition. Edmonton: M.G. Hurtig Ltd., 1970.
The Nunavut Atlas
Franklin, John
Narrative of a Journey to the Polar Sea in the Years 1819-20, 21 and 22. New York: Greenwood Press, 1969.
Franklin, John
Narrative of a Journey to the Shores of the Polar Sea in the Years 1825, 26 and 1827. John Murray London, 1828 (reprint by Greenwood Press).
Glover, Richard, ed.
A Journey from Prince of Wales Fort in Hudson Bay to the Northern Oceans in 1769, 1770, 1772, and 1773 by Samuel Hearne. Toronto: The Macmillan Company of Canada, Ltd., 1958.
Hanbury, David T.
Sport and Travel in the Northland of Canada. London: Edward Arnold, 1904.
Harper, Francis
Caribou Eskimos of the Upper Kazan, Keewatin. Kansas: University of Kansas, 1964.
Houston, C. Stuart, ed.
To the Arctic by Canoe, 1819-21, the Journal and Paintings of Robert Hood, Midshipman with Franklin. Montreal: Queen's University Press, 1974.
Mackenzie, Alexander
Voyages from Montreal to the Frozen and Pacific Oceans in the Years 1789 and 1793. C.E. Tuttle Pub.
Morse, Eric W.
Fur Trade Canoe Routes of Canada/Then and Now. Ottawa: Information Canada, 1968.
Pelly, David F.
Expedition. An Arctic Journey Through History on George Back's River. Toronto: Betelguese Books, 1981.
Pelly, David F. and Christopher C. Hanks, editors
The Kazan: Journey into an Emerging Land. Yellowknife: Outcrop Publishing, 1991.
Perkins, Robert
Into the Great Solitude: An Arctic Journey. New York: Henry Holt and Company, 1991.
Seton, Ernest Thompson
The Arctic Prairies, A Canoe Journey. New York: International University Press.
Simpson, Thomas
A Narrative of Discoveries on the North Coast of America. London: Richard Bentley, 1843.
Tyrell, J.W.
Across the Sub-Arctics of Canada. Toronto: facsimile ed. Coles Publishing Company, 1973.
Tyrell, Joseph Burr
Report on the Doobaunt, Kazan and Ferguson Rivers and the Northwest Coast of Hudson Bay. The Geological Survey of Canada Annual Report NS, Vol. 9, 1896, Report F.

Whalley, George
The Legend of John Hornby. 1st Laurentian Library Edition 1977. Toronto: The Macmillan Company of Canada Ltd., 1962.
Waldron, Malcolm
The Snow Man, John Hornby in the Barrenlands. Boston and New York: Houghton Mifflin Company, The Riverside Press, Cambridge, 1931.

NATURAL HISTORY

Canada's North (The Reference Manual). Indian and Northern Affairs Canada, 1983.
Clark, C.H.D.
A Biological Investigation of the Thelon Game Sanctuary. Canada Department of Mines and Resources, Mines and Geology Branch, National Museum of Canada. Bulletin # 96.
Walker, Marilyn
Harvesting the Northern Wild. Yellowknife: Outcrop Ltd., 1984.
NWT Data Book
Yellowknife: Outcrop Ltd., May 1984.

CANOEING/KAYAKING

The American National Red Cross
Canoeing. Garden City: Doubleday and Company Inc., 1977.
Bechdel, Les and Slim Ray
River Rescue. Boston: Appalachian Mountain Club, 1985.
Canadian Recreational Canoeing Association
Standard Tests of Achievement in Canoeing Manual. Hyde Park: Canadian Recreational Canoeing Association, 1984.
Canadian Recreational Canoeing Association
Canoe Travel Handbook. Hyde Park: Canadian Recreational Canoeing Association, 1988.
Davidson, James West and John Rugge
The Complete Wilderness Paddler. New York: Random House, 1975.
Environment Canada Publication
Historical Streamflow Summary Yukon and Northwest Territories to 1982. Inland Waters Directorate Water Resources Branch, Water Survey of Canada, 1983.
Forgey, Wm.W.M.D.
Hypothermia Death by Exposure. Merrillville: ICS Books, Inc., 1985.
Jacobson, Cliff
Canoeing Wild Rivers. Merrillville: ICS Books Inc., 1984.
McKay, John W.
A Kazan River Journal. Toronto: Betelguese Books, 1983.
Parks Canada
Wild Rivers Surveys: Wild Rivers of the Barrenlands and the Wild Rivers of the Northwest Mountains. Ottawa, 1973.
Reid Crowther and Partners Ltd.
Canadian Heritage Rivers System, Background Report in Support of Nomination of Thelon River, Northwest Territories. December, 1984.
Travel Arctic (GNWT)
Rivers North: Canoeing and Boating in the Northwest Territories. Yellowknife: Dept. of Economic Development and Tourism, GNWT,1981.
Wilkerson, James A., M.D.
Medicine for Mountaineering (3rd. edition). Seattle: The Mountaineers, 1985.

Supplementary Reading

Cody, W.J. and A.E. Porsild
Vascular Plants of Continental NWT. Canadian National Museum of Natural Sciences, National Museum of Canada.

Doan, Marlyn
Starting Small in the Wilderness. San Francisco: Sierra Club Books, 1979.

Dowd, John
Sea Kayaking: A Manual for Long-distance Touring. Vancouver: Douglas and McIntyre Ltd., 1981.

Forgey, William W., M.D.
Wilderness Medicine. Indiana: Indiana Camp Supply Books, 1979.

Franks, C.E.S.
The Canoe and White Water. Toronto: University of Toronto Press, 1977.

Hartling, Neil
Nahanni...River of Gold, River of Dreams. Hyde Park: Canadian Recreational Canoeing Association, 1993.

Hancock, Lyn
The Mighty Mackenzie, Highway to the Arctic Ocean. Saanichton: Hancock House Publishers, 1974.

Herfindahl, O.C.
Across the Barrens by Canoe. North, Sept./Oct. 1965.

Mason, Bill
Path of the Paddle. Toronto: Van Nostrand Reinhold Ltd., 1980.

Moore, Joanne Ronan
Nahanni Trailhead. Ottawa: Deneau and Greenberg Publishers Ltd., 1980.

Morse, Eric W.
Fresh Water Northwest Passage. The Royal Canadian Geographical Society, Ottawa, Canada.

Morse, Eric W.
Summer Travel in the Canadian Barrens. The Royal Canadian Geographical Society, Ottawa, Canada.

Nickels, Nick
Canoe Canada. Toronto: Van Nostrand Reinhold Ltd., 1980.

Patterson, R.M.
The Dangerous River. Toronto: Gray's Publishing, 1966.

Raffan, James
Summer North of 60. Toronto: Key Porter Books, 1990

Riviere, Bill
Pole, Paddle and Portage. New York: Van Nostrand Reinhold, 1969.

Sanders, William
Kayak Touring. Harrisburg: Stackpole Books, 1984.

Sandreuter, William O.
Whitewater Canoeing. South Hackensack: Stoeger Publishing Company, 1976.

Watters, Ron
The White-Water River Book. Vancouver: Douglas and McIntyre Ltd., 1982.

Wiebe, Judy
A Discovery of Strangers, 1994.

APPENDIX H

About the editor

Mary McCreadie lives in Yellowknife, and over the past 12 years, has paddled and portaged several of the canoe routes in this book. Mary coordinated the efforts of the people who edited the original manuscript of this book for publishing. In addition to having a passion for the canoe, Mary is an avid gardener and a recreational dog musher. Her working life is mostly dedicated to community development, research and facilitation.

The NWT Canoeing Association was founded in 1983 to promote canoeing throughout the NWT. It is a volunteer organization with representation from local paddling clubs across the Territories. The NWTCA provides information on paddling and paddling routes, and each summer canoe courses are offered in a number of NWT communities. The Association assists with Territorial canoeing events and races. The NWTCA initiated the work that resulted in this book.

About the publisher

Founded in 1971 as a result of an individual paddler who was unable to obtain information on a canoe trip being planned to La Ronge in northern Saskatchewan, the Canadian Recreational Canoeing Association (CRCA) has dramatically increased the availability of information to paddlers worldwide on how to experience Canada's waterways. From its early, meagre beginnings, the CRCA has become known across Canada for the many services provided to canoeists, kayakers and sea kayakers.

The Association publishes *KANAWA* Magazine, the voice of paddling in Canada, which is available on a quarterly basis for $20 per year plus 7% GST. (U.S.A. and international orders $20 U.S. per year plus 7% GST.) Other programs and services include liability insurance for instructors, canoe courses offered through provincial/territorial affiliates and canoe clubs, the Bill Mason Memorial Scholarship Fund, National Let's Go Paddling Week, Canadian Canoe Route Environmental Clean Up Project and the Nikon Canadian Canoe Photography Contest, as well as guided canoe and sea kayaking trips through its adventure travel arm, Canada's Canoe Adventures.

The CRCA not only publishes guide books and maps on paddling Canada, but also keeps in inventory – the largest collection of material available on paddling Canada. Call or write for a *Paddling Catalogue*, available free of charge upon request. Before your next paddling adventure, be sure to contact us:

*"Canada's
Paddling
Information
Specialists"*

Canadian Recreational Canoeing Association
1029 Hyde Park Rd., Suite 5
Hyde Park (London), Ontario, Canada N0M 1Z0
Phone (519) 473-2109/641-1261 Fax (519) 473-6560
(Please note that the Association will be moving to its Outdoor Education Centre in Merrickville, Ontario as of December 1996.)